The Harvard Business School Guide to Careers in Finance 2001 Edition

Edited by
Helen Lee
and
Ying Liu

IN ASSOCIATION WITH THE HARVARD BUSINESS SCHOOL FINANCE CLUB

ISBN 1-57851-324-3
ISSN 0899-7098

Contents

Preface

Welcome to the ninth edition of the *Harvard Business School Finance Club Career Guide!* If you are new to this book, our hope is that you find it a comprehensive finance career research source. If you have used prior editions, you will find a more updated version here that includes profiles of new companies and locations of their Web pages related to finance. This book's most unique and most helpful feature for business school students and alumni heading into the job search is the company profile section. The profiles include investment and commercial banks, Fortune 500 companies, and other international and regional firms. They have been compiled in a standardized format so that information on each company is readily accessible and may be easily compared to that on its peers.

You will also find articles written specifically for this guide by distinguished Harvard Business School professors as well as interviews with HBS alumni concerning their careers in finance. Drs. James Waldroop and Timothy Butler, directors of career development programs at Harvard Business School, offer insights on career self-assessment for those considering a career in finance. A glossary of finance terms and, thanks to Carol Elsen at Baker Library, listings of additional finance career sources also await you.

In an effort to leverage the vast intellectual resources of the Harvard Business School, the guide provides insights from Professor Joshua Lerner. His introduction reflects the latest thinking on careers in finance. To Professor Lerner we offer many thanks. Additionally, HBS alumni Vikram Gandhi, Girish Nadkarni, and Joel Peterson devoted time to the guide in documenting each of their unique experiences in the field of finance. To them we are also grateful.

A debt of gratitude is also owed to Claudia Bruce of HBS Publishing for her continuing support and assistance to the Finance Club and to the publication of the eighth edition. Finally, we thank the many profiled firms for their time and energy in helping prepare this guide.

We hope that you will find this guide a useful tool while conducting your research of the world of finance. Best of luck in your job search!

Helen Lee and
Ying Liu

Is a Career in Finance (and Which One?) Right for You?

Drs. James Waldroop and Timothy Butler

Drs. Waldroop and Butler are directors of career development programs at the Harvard Business School and principals and co-founders of Waldroop Butler Associates, a consulting firm in Brookline, Massachusetts that specializes in career development assessment and counseling and executive coaching. They are the developers of CareerLeader™, *an Internet-based, interactive career assessment program (www.careerdiscovery.com/hbsp), and the authors of* Discovering Your Career in Business *(Addison-Wesley, 1997),* "The Executive as Coach" *(the* Harvard Business Review, November–December, 1996) *and* "Finding the Job You Should Want" *(Fortune, March 2, 1998).*

If you're considering a career in finance, you're probably just starting out: you're either about to graduate from college or business school, or are within a year or two of either milestone. This is an ideal time to take a step back to look at yourself before heading down one career path or another. Everyone agrees thoughtful career self-assessment is a terrific idea—and then 90% don't carry through with it. Some people then "drift" into a good career, but that's a *very* high-risk approach to life. Careful self-assessment and strategic career planning can save you a lot of grief down the road.

Good self-assessment can be carried out in a number of ways; at a minimum it should include a careful and subtle assessment of your "deep personality structure" interests, your work reward values, your business career-relevant abilities, and other aspects of your personality. Our approach includes conducting an in-depth interview and examination of a client's life history, employing sophisticated, objective, psychological assessment instruments, and soliciting letters from six to ten people who know the client well. You could do much of this on your own. What is important is not *how* you do it but *that* you do it. Taking the time now will put you way ahead.

We've worked extensively with business professionals working in all areas of finance, and have had the opportunity to collect data on many of these areas. The career assessment model utilized in *CareerLeader,* our business career self-assessment program, is the product of this research and experience; it's what we'll be using to describe careers in finance. *CareerLeader* is based on a

twelve-year research study examining the match between people's personality structures and the work they find meaningful and in which they are successful. It comprises three career self-assessment inventories—the *Business Career Interest Inventory*™, the *Management and Professional Reward Profile*™, and the *Management and Professional Abilities Profile*™ (see page 5)—that measure people's interests, reward values, and abilities. The structures on which each of these instruments is based serve as a guide for this discussion.

As Professor Lerner's Introduction makes clear, there is a tremendous variety of careers in finance, each of which allows for the expression of different patterns of your interests, for the gratification of your reward values, and for your strengths to be utilized to different degrees. In the next three sections we'll talk about careers in finance in terms of these three categories: interests, rewards, and abilities.

Interest Patterns in Finance Careers

Our research into the interests and core activities of business professionals revealed eight sets of activities that comprise, in varying mixtures, almost all work done in business settings. The *Business Career Interest Inventory* was then designed to measure people's interests in those "business core functions." One core function common to all finance careers is that of *Quantitative Analysis.* Whether you are working inside an operating company, in an accounting firm, or commercial bank, on Wall Street (the "sell side" of the investment business), or as an investor (the "buy side"), *Quantitative Analysis*—more specifically, financial analysis—is such a large part of the work that if you are not strongly interested in it, you will be both unhappy and, ultimately, unsuccessful. That said, some areas of work in finance require *very* high interest in *Quantitative Analysis*—working as a computer modeler in the bond group of an investment management firm, for example—while for others, e.g., retail brokers, a more moderate level of interest and skill will suffice. But it is an unusual finance professional who does not have a substantial interest in the work of *Quantitative Analysis.*

Many, though not all, finance professionals share an interest in *Enterprise Control:* the running of an operation or a "transaction." The Chief Financial Officer of a company is more likely to be interested in the operational side of *Enterprise Control,* while a mergers-and-acquisitions specialist will be interested in the "deal-making"/ transactional aspect. Some finance professionals, e.g., investment analysts, may have a much lower interest in *Enterprise Control.* But if you have a strong interest in *Quantitative Analysis* and *Enterprise Control,* there are plenty of opportunities for you under the career umbrella of finance.

A distinguishing characteristic of finance professionals who work in operating companies as opposed to transaction-oriented financial services firms, is that of their interest in *Managing People.* Our sample of satisfied, successful investment bankers has two major interest elevations— *Quantitative Analysis* and *Enterprise Control*—while our sample of finance professionals working in corporate settings shares these interests but *adds* a high level of interest in *Managing People.* Financial services, with its transactional nature, frequently draws people who are largely uninterested in the work of managing other people. (In the words of one highly successful hedge fund manager we worked with, "I just can't understand why anyone would want to do a thing like that!") Working in an operating company, by contrast, will inevitably involve managing others. If you have a strong interest in *Managing People,* you are more likely to find your finance career within an operating company—regardless of size—or to find that you are more satisfied with a management role within a financial services firm than you were with your early career role of executing transactions.

The work of *Influence Through Language and Ideas,* while very useful in most business careers, is critically important in such finance careers as financial planning, stock brokerage, commercial lending, investment banking, and institutional securities sales. All of these careers call for establishing and maintaining relationships with clients, whether they be individuals or institutions. Although a very strong interest in *Influence Through Language and Ideas* is not absolutely necessary for success in these finance careers, to the extent that your interest in this function is *low,* your general satisfaction is also likely to be lower.

The last key core function interest is *Creative Production.* In the world of finance, it is expressed both through working in a finance capacity for companies whose product or service has a distinctly creative element—entertainment and media, for example—and in "creative finance," venture capital being the best example. This is not to say that venture capital or other areas of private equity investing require a high interest in *Creative Production;* however, if your interest *is* high *and* you are strongly interested in finance, these may be good careers to consider. Alternately, some finance professionals with a strong interest in *Creative Production* gravitate toward launching their own entrepreneurial ventures as opposed to working in a venture capital firm.

Rewards in Finance Careers

CareerLeader's value assessment instrument, the *Management and Professional Reward Profile,* measures the value you place on thirteen different rewards most commonly available in business settings (such as *Financial Gain, Autonomy,* and *Variety*). People who go into certain finance careers do so for a wide variety of reasons, and their work reward value patterns are numerous. Certain finance careers may provide a given reward in abundance, while others may not provide that reward at all. Taken as a whole, careers in finance offer the opportunity for a high level of *Financial Gain* ("exceptional financial reward"). It seems that the more closely one works with capital, the more of that capital accrues to the individual! *Prestige* is, of course, in the eye of the beholder, but most people consider working in the financial services industry (Wall Street, investment management, banking, working as a CPA, etc.) to be prestigious at some level. Working in the finance area of an operating company is also generally seen as holding some prestige.

Depending again on one's definition, *Power and Influence* ("being an influential decision maker") is a reward that many people associate with working in the financial field. To the extent that capital is one important form of power, working in financial careers, i.e., working with capital, provides the reward of *Power and Influence* to a level that most people find satisfying. This may be more true at top levels in some financially related careers (e.g., CFO, managing director of a top-level investment bank, investment portfolio manager) than in such others as retail stock brokerage or institutional sales. But in general, finance careers offer sufficient *Power and Influence* reward value to satisfy most people's desires.

One reward that varies greatly in its availability within finance careers is *Lifestyle.* Some finance careers are famously bad in terms of their *Lifestyle* aspects—investment banking heads the list, with private equity investing not far behind. If you don't know already, investment banking involves long and *unpredictable* hours: it's one thing to decide that you want to stay late or work over the weekend, and quite another to have someone tell you at 6:00 P.M. on Friday that your weekend plans to meet your fiancee's parents have to be scrubbed. In investment banking, you don't know if you're going to have the weekend free until it's all over, so both *Lifestyle* and *Autonomy* are rewards that are not found in abundance—or at least for the first several years. Both institutional securities sales and investment management for individuals ("private client services," "private banking," or simply retail brokerage) involve frequent entertaining of clients as part of the work, which can cut into free evening time with the family. So if being home most nights is part of your idea of a good *Lifestyle*, this could be a problem. (On the other hand, having free tickets to sporting and cultural events may sound like a fine life; here again, each reward is defined to some degree by the individual.) Working on the "buy side"—investment management—gives you some control over your life, although the hours are typically long. And working on the trading floor provides both predictability—you know when the market is going to open and when it's going to close—and sheer hour control: you can't make trades when the market is closed. As a trader, though, you have to be there when the opening bell rings and you're tied to the desk until the close, so the *Autonomy* factor may work against this career, depending on your personal definition of autonomy.

Although many finance professionals will tell you that the work is not, as they say, rocket science, most find their work to have sufficient *Intellectual Challenge* to satisfy their desires. By contrast, few say that they find that their work meets their needs for helping others (*Altruism*), and so they look to nonwork activities for this reward. Finally, there seems to be ample *Affiliation* in most areas of finance. Of course, in some financial arenas it is possible to spend much of your time alone, if *Affiliation* is not a high priority for you; but in careers such as trading, investment banking, and institutional sales, you'll be spending almost all of your time with your coworkers or customers, whether you like it or not.

So if your scores on *Financial Gain, Power and Influence, Prestige, Intellectual Challenge,* and *Affiliation* are high, and they are on the low side on *Lifestyle, Altruism,* and *Autonomy,* it's likely that you can find a career in finance that will match your "reward value wish list" closely enough to make it a satisfying path to pursue. But because this is a *very* brief overview, keep in mind that certain individual situations do *not* have much by way of the rewards listed above (*Financial Gain, Power and Influence,* etc.), while others supply *Lifestyle, Altruism,* and *Autonomy* in abundance.

Abilities

CareerLeader's abilities assessment instrument, the *Management and Professional Abilities Profile* measures people's business-related abilities in three different areas—*Problem Solving, Taking Initiative,* and *Interpersonal Effectiveness*—with different specific abilities measured in each of these groups. Not surprisingly, different finance

careers require different abilities for success; moreover, at different stages in the careers some abilities become more or less important. Competence in *Quantitative Analysis,* for example, is critical for success at the early stage of every finance career, but becomes less so at the highest levels of investment banking, when the *Sociability* needed for business development becomes more essential. However, just as you have to be an excellent consultant to get the chance to become a successful firm partner, you also have to have the analytical capabilities to work at junior levels in an investment bank to make it to the senior level.

Quick Thinking is an asset in any finance career, but in securities trading it is, along with *Dominance,* crucial. Unless they are simply processing trade orders, traders must be able to respond quickly to changing situations and feel comfortable taking risks. Traders frequently say that what makes them successful is the ability to size up a situation, evaluate the risks, make the call—and sleep well that night, regardless of whether they won or lost. Like an athlete taking the winning or losing shot in the final seconds of a game, traders make the call—and enjoy looking at the score at the end of the trading day.

Skill in *Communication* is also important in a trading role: one head trader described the work as "playing high stakes poker with words instead of cards." But, combined with *Sociability,* it is even more important in commercial lending, brokerage, and institutional securities sales careers. These are finance careers in which both listening skills and persuasive oral communication skills are critical for success. The other key ingredient is forming and maintaining relationships with other finance professionals or with individual investors.

Action-orientation, Critical Thinking, Leveraging, and the ability to *Multi-focus* are critical for success in financial careers in corporate settings and in management roles in investment and commercial banks and investment management firms. These are really general management jobs, so it is not surprising that, along with the ever present need for skill in *Quantitative Analysis,* such abilities come to the fore in thinking about these finance careers.

Unlike interests, which are deep-structure aspects of who we all are, abilities can be developed—*if* you have the raw intellectual "horsepower" and the motivation to do so. Think about the necessary levels of ability for the skills required for each finance career in terms of a threshold: you have to be *good enough* to get above that threshold, not necessarily able to clear it by miles. That threshold may be very high, as it is for quantitative analysts in a bond group, all of whom have Ph.D.s in applied mathematics or physics. Often, however, it is not. So if you are very interested in the work of, say, equities trading or investment banking but do not have a strong quantitative analytical background, chances are that you can master those abilities and *become* "good enough." Conversely, if you are an extreme introvert and have always had weak social skills and confidence, it may be more difficult to build those skills to the level necessary for success in sales or trading.

In sum, there is a multitude of careers under the general umbrella of finance. We have described the highlights of the career self-assessment profiles likely to lead to success and satisfaction in some—by necessity leaving out others, such as hedge fund management and leveraged buy-out work altogether. The trick is to look at yourself as objectively as possible—doing your "career due diligence," so to speak—to find the right career match. This can be especially difficult given the "herd effect" felt on many campuses, which dictates that the very best careers are X or Y. It is this very fact that makes it all the more crucial to find what is right *for you*—don't be stampeded into taking the right career path for someone else!

Business Career Interest Inventory Scales and Descriptions

Application of Technology: Taking an engineering-like approach to business problems, and using technology to solve them (e.g., production and operations process analysis; business process redesign; production planning)

Quantitative Analysis: Problem solving that relies on mathematical and financial analysis (e.g., determining the most advantageous debt/equity structure for a business; analyzing market research)

Theory Development and Conceptual Thinking: Taking a broadly conceptual, quasi-academic approach to business problems (e.g., developing a new general economic theory or model of market behavior)

Creative Production: Highly creative activities (e.g., the generation of new business ideas; the development of new marketing concepts)

Counseling and Mentoring: Developing personal relationships in the work setting and helping others in their careers (e.g., coaching, training, and mentoring)

Managing People and Relationships: Accomplishing business goals through working directly with people (e.g., as a manager, team leader, director, or supervisor)

Enterprise Control: Having ultimate strategy-setting and decision-making authority, and resource control for an operation (e.g., as a division manager, president, CEO, partner in a professional services firm, or entrepreneur)

Influence Through Language and Ideas: Exercising influence through the skillful use of persuasion (e.g., negotiating, deal-making, sales, and relationship development)

Management and Professional Abilities Profile Scales and Descriptions

Problem Solving

Critical Thinking: Able to think critically (define a problem and determine the information needed to solve it; understand unspoken assumptions; form and test hypotheses; and judge the validity of conclusions).

Quantitative Analysis: Skillful in using quantitative analysis to understand business issues.

Creativity: Able to think creatively, generating new ideas and approaches to issues, and recognizing new opportunities.

Quick Thinking: Have a quick intellect—I pick up new information and ideas easily and can "think on my feet."

Taking Initiative

Dominance: Ambitious, forceful, competitive, comfortable with using power and taking risks.

Action-orientation: Action-oriented—I am someone who makes decisions and then makes sure they are implemented.

Multi-focus: Able to juggle many ideas, responsibilities, and projects at once.

Leveraging: Able to leverage my time well (e.g., set priorities and keep to them, delegate when appropriate).

Interpersonal Effectiveness

Confidence: Able to feel and project self-confidence—I can be persuasive even in uncertain and difficult situations.

Leading/Managing: Able to lead, motivate, and directly manage other people effectively.

Sociability: Socially venturesome and self-assured—I form and maintain relationships easily.

Teamwork: A team player, cooperative, work well as part of a group.

Communication: Able to listen well—Write and speak to individuals and groups in a clear and effective manner.

Management and Professional Reward Profile Scales and Descriptions

Financial Gain: The position provides excellent opportunity for exceptional financial reward.

Power and Influence: The position offers the opportunity to exercise power and influence (to be an influential decision maker).

Variety: The position offers a great deal of variety in the nature of the work performed.

Lifestyle: The position allows ample time to pursue other important aspects of my lifestyle (family, leisure activities, etc.).

Autonomy: The position offers considerable autonomy and independence.

Intellectual Challenge: The position offers consistent intellectual challenge.

Altruism: The position offers the satisfaction of regularly helping others with their individual or business concerns.

Security: The position offers a great deal of security in terms of predictable salary, benefits, and future employment.

Prestige: The position is with an organization that commands a great deal of prestige in its field.

Affiliation: The position offers a setting with enjoyable colleagues with whom I feel a sense of belonging.

Positioning: The position offers experience and access to people and opportunities that will position me well for my next career move.

Managing People: The position offers the opportunity to manage and direct other people.

Recognition: The position is in an environment where individual accomplishments are recognized with praise from peers and superiors.

Introduction

Joshua Lerner
Professor of Business Administration
Harvard Business School

Business school faculty have many occasions to counsel students gearing up for the post-MBA job market. It is, to be sure, a time of high expectations. At the same time, the post-MBA job search can be daunting, even for those who have been through a search before.

Identifying and landing a job in the field of finance presents many of the same challenges of other functional areas: identifying promising potential employers, evaluating and discriminating among various job possibilities, assessing the long-term potential of a particular entry-level job, and so forth. At the same time, a finance job search raises some special considerations. This book will give you a head start in the investigatory "due diligence" effort we all go through in the course of a job campaign.

The word *financial* in a job description usually reveals very little about the work content. One business school student took a summer job between the first and second years of his MBA program that seemed to promise opportunities for financial analysis within a large corporation. He had in mind the sort of strategic decision-making process that had dominated his first-year finance course. The actual job content turned out to be bread-and-butter accounting. Thankfully, the job was only temporary; he gamely did the work as competently as possible and then gracefully withdrew at the end of the summer.

Although it is difficult to categorize financial jobs, they can be broken down into those that take place within a corporate organization and those whose setting is a particular financial institution, whether large or small. The structure of finance functions within a corporation is easier to articulate. Typically, there is a chief financial officer (CFO) under whom internal financial (controllership) and external financial (treasurer) activities are grouped. In many companies, strategic and long-range planning have considerable finance content and may also report to the CFO, if only on a dotted-line basis.

Jobs concerned with the collection, measurement, and evaluation of financial data generated from internal operations are typically placed under the controller's supervision. In these jobs, training in accounting (and possibly auditing) is very useful. An organization's relations with financial markets and institutions are often grouped under the supervision of the treasurer. These include management of bank lines and other credit facilities to ensure that the company can pay its bills in a timely fashion, communication with shareholders, and oversight of offshore financing arrangements. (The increasing frequency of foreign activities reflects the growing integration of national economies into a large, interdependent global market.) Evaluation of external acquisitions, or the sale of parts of the company's own operations, are often grouped under the treasurer's umbrella or within a separate office often referred to as the business development group.

Most ambitious MBA graduates are eager to be at the heart of the real action in a company. In many ways this is what you have been trained for. If you are of this disposition, it is important to determine the center of financial action within a prospective company.

Many graduating MBAs are immediately attracted to the treasury function and to strategic financial planning. These seem glamorous and represent activities that are closely related to the newly minted MBAs' training. In some companies, primarily those serving essentially as holding companies for a number of decentralized operating units, the financial focus may be on the company's relations with external capital markets. But despite the glitz associated with strategic planning and the treasurer's contacts with Wall Street and other external organizations, the real guts of the financial function for most firms—the site of the real action—is internal control.

Turning to financial vendors—commercial banks, investment banks, insurance companies, private equity groups, and money management firms—the array of job possibilities is extremely broad:

Corporate finance
Investment analysis
Portfolio management
Trading
Venture capital and private equity investing
Institutional and retail sales

"Financial engineering," or the application of quantitative methods to the construction of financial products

General management

Corporate finance in the context of a financial vendor typically involves the basket of products, services, and counsel marketed to nonfinancial companies. This is an elastic definition. For investment banks, it encompasses the structuring and issuance of new securities to the public. For finance companies, such as GE Credit, corporate finance has a different meaning. GE Credit does not itself underwrite securities but does offer a broad variety of services to corporate customers, including secured financing and consulting on corporate financial strategy.

Investment analysis is usually associated with the role of the analyst of publicly traded securities. Typically focusing on only one category of securities (e.g., the auto industry, "junk" bonds), analysts are employed by many different vendors. These may be on either the buy side (investment management firms or other institutional investors such as insurance companies and pension managers) or the sell side (securities firms and commercial banks). Sell-side analysts typically focus on products that they and their institutional sales colleagues think can be sold to portfolio managers responsible for the investment of large pools of savings. Buy-side analysts generally play the role of thoughtful skeptics in evaluating ideas generated by vendor firms.

Portfolio managers are often veteran security analysts, although some vendors hire young people for direct assignment as assistants to portfolio managers. Some portfolio managers describe their field as the place "where the buck stops." While the analyst recommends actions on certain securities, the portfolio manager makes the ultimate decisions and is evaluated on the consequences.

If portfolio managers are under the gun to demonstrate quarter-by-quarter performance, traders of particular categories of stocks, bonds, and derivatives live minute-by-minute. The consequences of their judgments are usually priced out each day for everyone to see. In many cases, the traders work alongside individuals trained in mathematics or physics—the "quants"—who develop and refine models to value particular securities. Whether working in an investment bank or an independent "hedge fund," this is an exciting but stressful life. It is a "white-knuckle" business that attracts certain types of personalities.

At the opposite extreme are private equity investors. Their investments in venture capital and leveraged buyout deals can take years to mature to the point of being har-

vested, typically through the sale of stock to the public. Private equity investments are made by investment banks and other large financial institutions. But the bulk of the action takes place in small, independent organizations, typically organized as limited partnerships. Each group tends to focus on a specific style of investments (e.g., late-stage venture investments in profitable firms, consolidations of small firms in mature industries). The partners in these funds raise and invest capital from institutional and individual investors, and receive a substantial share (20% to 30%) of any capital gains that they produce.

Many MBAs are attracted to such private equity investing, which combines the satisfaction of building companies during their formative years with the potential for impressive capital gains. Unfortunately, the number of job openings each year in this area is modest, typically a few hundred nationwide. Those interested in a career in private equity investing should bear in mind the stern odds against them and remember that many of the most successful investors first had experience as operating managers or in other financial sectors. In looking for a venture capital or private equity position, it is important to focus on the type of firms—indeed, even the individual partners at those firms—who are most likely to find one's background attractive.

Institutional sales people work closely with traders and security analysts and create a bridge between them and the big institutions whose investment activities dominate modern public markets. They sell products that their firms have either developed or acquired for resale, and they must be conversant with the details of these products and how they serve the objectives of their institutional customers. The days of the "gentleman bond salesman" immortalized by F. Scott Fitzgerald are long gone. This is a demanding business—and the rewards for success are extraordinary.

Retail securities sales involves the marketing of stocks, bonds, and other financial products to individual investors. These investors are, on the average, likely to be less sophisticated than institutional investors and therefore are dependent on their brokers for more comprehensive counsel. Building a retail customer base takes time, but these customers tend to be loyal to their individual brokers and often follow them if they move from one brokerage house to another in search of a more lucrative deal or better support. Retail brokerage is one of the last bastions of relationship-based financial business,

Today, however, retail brokers are coming under severe pressure with the proliferation of on-line trading and other financial services. Many of these upstarts promise to deliver the same services much more cost efficiently,

7

by taking advantage of the revolution in information technology and exploiting their greater flexibility. While still in the very early stages of growth, the numerous on-line entities focusing on the delivery of financial services to consumers present numerous opportunities for the adventurous. Before joining one of these groups, however, it is best to determine that the firm has sufficient financial resources and a plausible business model.

Derivative securities—the disaggregation and reconstruction of securities with features specifically tailored to particular types of investors or issues—have become big business for many financial vendors and their clients. For vendors possessing the proprietary quantitative techniques used to construct and price out these hybrid securities, derivatives have been very profitable, although fraught with risk.

Jobs focusing on the *management* of financial service firms have gotten much more attention in recent years. More than a decade of acquisitions, mergers, and internally generated growth has made these firms larger and more complex; they no longer lend themselves to the informal managerial oversight long characteristic of business. Back-office jobs are a case in point. After a variety of securities vendors became overloaded by trading volume in the late 1960s and 1970s, the firms' leadership realized that the fate of their organizations was tied to their ability to get their internal paperwork and controls better organized. This change has raised the stature of professionals opting for internal management careers. Similarly, commercial banks discovered that a secret to successful expansion and profitability in the contemporary marketplace lies in the management of their own information systems. John Reed, Co-Chairman of Citigroup, owes his leadership post, at least in part, to his successful mastery of this area.

It should be cautioned, however, that many general managers of financial service organizations have come up through the ranks as specialists in a product or service, rather than through an initial career entry into the vendor's internal management structure. Many of these organizations still hold the highest places of honor for top business getters and revenue producers. However, an appreciation for professional management skills is gradually developing.

Students seeking to enter the finance profession must grapple with several challenging decisions. A crucial issue is whether finance is the right occupation. A finance career almost invariably involves long hours, stress, and often great uncertainty. If the field itself does not genuinely excite you or stimulate your curiosity, it is unlikely to be a happy choice, no matter how generous the compensation.

The next question is the appropriate subfields of finance on which to focus the job search. The demands of various subfields vary considerably. Some areas, such as trading and selling complex derivative securities, place a premium on quantitative abilities. In others, such as retail brokerage, the ability to communicate clearly and persuasively is paramount. The time demands of these positions also vary considerably. For instance, while corporate finance demands a considerable amount of time—to the point of serious conflicts between family and work—trading positions have traditionally been less demanding from an hours-per-week perspective.

A third decision relates to the institutions on which to focus job-searching efforts. Each organization has a distinctive personality. Finding a good match between an employer's personality and your own is an important prerequisite to long-run success. The descriptions contained in this book and the promotional material you will receive during the interview process should provide some indication of these firm-by-firm differences. Important insights can also be gathered through conversations with peers who have worked or are currently working for these organizations. But ultimately it is very difficult for others to point you toward the best match; it is a personal choice and an issue to which you should be particularly sensitive during the interview process.

Concerning the job search itself, several thoughts may be helpful. One frequent source of students' concern relates to the résumé. What résumé features, students wonder, will pique the interest of a financial services vendor? How do you avoid either overselling or underselling your credentials? How should the "job objective" section be handled? Although there is no single answer to these questions, among the key things potential employers look for is evidence of your purpose and direction. Do you appreciate the demands of the position that you are seeking? Do you understand the characteristics of the firm that you are pursuing? Are you serious about a finance career, or is this just one more option along with consulting, marketing, and other industries? The importance of thorough preparation for the job search process cannot be overestimated. This same concern applies to the interview process, only more so.

The successful completion of a job search is just a beginning. To translate the promise of a new job into long-term success requires the same careful thought and planning that won the job. A sure prerequisite is unmistakable enthusiasm for the work, which manifests itself as energy and personal innovation.

As you take your first position, be aware of several pitfalls that have derailed promising careers. The first relates to work load. As already mentioned, finance jobs tend to be high pressure and demand long hours. Giving the job the best you have is essential. But it is also necessary to pace yourself and ensure that the office does not entirely dominate your life. Without outside interests and time to enjoy them, it will be only a question of when, not if, you will burn out.

A second mistake can be to move too quickly toward specialization. One objective of your initial position should be to illuminate the variety of potential career opportunities. Limiting your early career experience to a narrow focus on a particular product or a single industry, for instance, may limit your ability to move on to other opportunities as they present themselves.

A final point concerns the very nature of "opportunities." Our natural tendency, when faced with an uncertain future, is to plan our way out of it. But developing too precise a plan, and sticking rigidly to it, is likely to be a mistake. Career opportunities have a way of surfacing when one least expects them. Be alert for new and unanticipated opportunities that will almost surely come along. As Disraeli warned, "What we anticipate seldom comes; what we least expected generally happens."

Good luck!

Jobs in Investment Banking

Seth A. Rosenblatt
Harvard Business School, Class of 1993

What Is Investment Banking?

Investment banking denotes and connotes a number of different ideas. For those who have not worked in the industry before and are considering a summer or full-time position in investment banking, the job search can bring confusion and frustration.

In a very general sense, the term *investment bank* is broadly used to describe any financial institution that provides services in the areas of security issuing and brokering, financial advisory, or asset management. From the smallest boutiques to the large full-service firms, the term *investment bank* is far too often used. Large investment banks such as the "bulge-bracket" firms engage in many arenas outside traditional commercial banking or insurance underwriting. However, the function of investment banking requires a narrower industry definition. Investment banking generally encompasses four functions, all interrelated. Some firms may engage in all of these functions, while some may specialize in one or more of these areas:

1. Corporate finance.
2. Mergers and acquisitions.
3. Merchant banking.
4. Advisory/financial consulting.

In addition, many firms may specialize in one or two industry groups. The largest firms tend to have many functional and/or industry groups to serve their client base fully. Although many of the terms used here are fairly universal, the terminology in different countries does vary. If you are looking for an investment banking job outside the United States, become familiar with specific terminology used there (exact translations do not necessarily apply).

Corporate Finance

Corporate finance is the process of raising money for corporate clients (or public institutions) in the form of equity, debt, convertible, or other derivative security. This process involves two steps: (1) determining the funding needs of the client (type, amount, and structure) and (2) finding investors to supply those funds. This second step

can generally be accomplished through either of two methods: a public issue or a private placement. A public issuance of a security involves the investment bank's acting as an underwriter of the securities, purchasing the securities from the issuer and then reselling them on the public market. For larger investment banks, this process will involve other areas of the firm, such as sales and trading, research, and a syndicate function (sharing the underwriting responsibilities with other investment banks). A private placement, on the other hand, calls for the investment bank to act solely as an agent, matching the issuer of the security with one or a handful of potential investors in an offering not made available to the public.

Mergers and Acquisitions

For investment bankers the much publicized "M&A" business has the banker acting as an advisor to a company in transactions involving the sale of a whole company, a division, or just certain assets. The investment banker acts as an advisor to the client (on either the buy side or sell side), determines an appropriate valuation range, and negotiates terms most favorable to the client. The investment bank may also take a more active role by participating as a principal in the transaction. From an auction to a negotiated sale, from a stock swap to an LBO, the form and structure of an M&A transaction vary widely.

Merchant Banking

Merchant banking is the process whereby an investment bank acts as a principal in a transaction, either by purchasing newly issued securities of a firm or by purchasing (or selling) a stake in an M&A transaction. Some firms specialize only in merchant banking, while the largest investment banks tend to have a separate group to perform this function. Merchant banking is closely tied to the functions of corporate finance and M&A, and bankers from different industry or functional groups normally work on a merchant banking transaction together.

Advisory

Advisory work is linked to corporate finance, M&A, and merchant banking. It is generally performed as part of the overall service given to clients, or it may be tied to a specific transaction. Advisory or consulting work can take an infinite number of forms, including capital structure analysis, comparable analysis, and industry research. Much of the specific work is dependent on the particular client's industry. In addition, the past few years have seen a dramatic growth in advisory work related to corporate restructurings and reorganizations.

Looking for a Job in Investment Banking

For those who have not previously worked in the industry, a lot of anxiety arises in the investment banking job search. For first-year students who are seriously considering making a career switch into investment banking, I strongly recommend that you work in the field for the summer. Not only will this make it easier to find a job with an investment bank after your second year, but you will learn what the industry is all about. Investment banking is such a unique field that it is difficult to understand the work, the environment, and the culture without experiencing it.

When beginning your self-assessment and your job search, first speak to as many people as you can who are or have been in the industry. In your class, you will probably find at least a dozen people who worked in an investment bank for at least two years. Your peers will be your greatest resource. Ask a lot of questions; you will get a good cross-section of various experiences, good and bad.

Many of your business school classmates have been former "analysts." *Analyst* is the usual entry-level title for undergraduates. Understand, that if hired, you will probably enter at the associate level (or equivalent). Although the long hours may be similar, the responsibilities may be very different. Try to understand the general career path in investment banking and the specific one in each firm.

Your next stops should be at the placement center and the library. Try to research each firm in which you may be interested. Understand which firms are full-service broker-dealers and investment bankers, which are middle-market firms, and which are boutiques. What appears to be the corporate culture and reputation of each firm? Does a firm specialize in a particular industry, function, or geographic region? Does it match your interests? Try to discover, through speaking with peers and research, which firms are the leaders in each of the areas (industries or functions) in which you are interested. There are a number of specific places where you can look for information on each firm that you are researching. Your career resource center will have the following information:

- Annual reports, 10-Ks, 10-Qs, prospectuses (if it is a public company)

- Recruiting brochures

- Company files

- Industry file/packet

- Summer job reports

- Current and previous job descriptions

- Lotus One Source/Other on-line services

- Alumni career advisor list

- Book of job search and salary statistics

Additionally, check these sources:

- Company recruiting briefings and dinners

- *Wall Street Journal*

- Business magazines (*BusinessWeek, Forbes, Fortune, Economist*)

- LEXIS/NEXIS news searches (available on-line)

- Job Search Guide (available from your career center)

- Career fairs

- Friends, relatives, classmates, professors

- This book

Most of the larger investment banking firms, although they may have offices throughout the country and the rest of the world, tend to be based in New York City and do all recruiting from there. Regardless of which office you may be interested in, you may have to go through a general interviewing process based in New York. Be sure to understand each firm's policies and procedures for hiring outside the main office, particularly internationally. Many firms have a bias toward hiring nationals of a particular country to work in an office located there. If you are unsure, ask. During the correspondence and interviewing process, make your geographic preferences clear. If you can work only in city X, you will find it very frustrating to go through the entire process and be offered a job, only to find that the firm is not hiring this year in city X. Try to understand office placement policies before the interview.

Attend as many recruiting briefings as you can to get an idea of each firm's strategy, focus, and culture. Compare the people who have been successful in each firm to your own track record and where (or who) you would like to be in 5, 10, or 20 years. Finally, make it a practice to read the newspaper (the *Wall Street Journal* in particular) to get a good sense of what is going on in the industry and with specific firms.

If you have done sufficient researching and querying, the interview should be the easiest part of the process. These interviews are generally not like "stress" consulting interviews. You will probably not be asked the implications of an inverted yield curve or queried as to the number of restaurants in New York City. This, of course, varies by firm (and there are stories of difficult interviews), but in general, investment banks are looking to see if you

- Are a hard worker and detail oriented

- Have leadership skills and enjoy working in groups

- Have a genuine interest in the industry and are excited about it

- Show good judgment and demonstrate responsibility

- Are analytically inclined and comfortable with numbers and computers

- Understand the lifestyle and are willing to make the sacrifices required

- Are a fun person to be around ("Would I like to go to dinner with you?")

Conclusion

You must determine what methods of research work best for you. Speak to people whose advice you value, and then draw your own conclusions. Two issues that need to be addressed are the money and the hours. Much time has been spent talking about both of these subjects.

All in all, I found investment banking to be a great experience. It was stimulating and challenging, and I got to work with some fascinating people. If you decide to make a career of it, do it for reasons like this. If you find, through talking to peers or through a summer job, that you do not expect to get the same kind of fun, challenge, or excitement that I did, do not go into the industry. You will be miserable. Investment banking is not for everybody. Where I worked, there were a few of my peers who thought that it was the greatest experience of their lives, while others, doing the exact same job, were miserable. In other words, the money should *not* be the deciding factor. There is little doubt that investment banking is one of the best-paying positions (in the short run) that you can take, and money is certainly not unimportant. Although compensation is always a consideration in any job decision, the people I knew who regretted the job the most were the ones who took it solely for the cash.

As for the hours, this is something also that has sparked quite a legend on Wall Street—and throughout the rest of the business world. Stories of all-nighters and ruined weekends plague the minds of former analysts. While it is true that investment bankers work very long hours, the variance within and among firms is so large that it defies most generalizations. Nevertheless, there usually is some lifestyle sacrifice that particularly a junior banker will have to make in investment banking. The only way to get an accurate sense of the hours is for you to talk to friends or classmates who worked for a particular firm. Even then, their information may not be accurate because different departments in the same firm may require much different hours. Additionally, changes in the business cycle and season can dramatically affect the work load in any firm.

Only through asking a lot of questions and through a little soul-searching can you determine if the investment banking lifestyle is indeed right for you.

Finance Careers in Manufacturing Companies

Brian M. Webber
Harvard Business School, Class of 1993

A variety of career opportunities are available to students interested in finance other than well-known financial services jobs. Manufacturing companies have positions in strategic planning, product development, and division controllers' offices. I worked as a financial analyst in product development at Ford Motor Company prior to attending HBS.

In the controller's office of product development, I worked on various product development teams associated with the development of new models of Taurus and Sable. Product development teams consist of engineers, marketing people, planning people, and a finance person. My main responsibility was to perform the financial analysis required by the team when making product decisions, but I was also exposed to a wide array of team decisions and problems and to the team strategies and solutions employed throughout the development process. I met daily with team members to review, update, and discuss the progress of the new product. The requirements of this assignment were to visit the plants of small suppliers, assist with cost control and financial projections, and work closely with development engineers and designers to report the financial status of the program to senior management. Since each team member is encouraged to contribute and to assume responsibility where feasible, I quickly gained a reasonable knowledge of the entire development process. Interaction with engineering, marketing, planning, and outside suppliers was extremely interesting and helped me to understand the engineering and marketing functions. Often the various functional areas are faced with conflicting goals, and compromises among team members are required. Frequently team meetings are held at supplier locations, where the team analyzes specific product proposals, or meetings are held in the prototype plant next to a prototype vehicle so that decisions can be implemented in real time. Finance positions in product development allow a finance person to work closely with the manufacturing process. Every member of the product development team provides input for decisions that affect the outcome of the product.

The environment in product development finance is intense, and the hours are demanding. The hours do not compare to investment banking hours but are considerably longer than other positions within the company.

A great deal of responsibility is heaped on finance representatives with respect to reporting to senior management the financial status of the new product, preparing financial models to analyze the impact of various proposals, and assuming team leadership at times when financial analysis has a major impact on a product decision. Analysts may also evaluate future marketing programs and compare competitors' products from a financial perspective. Analysts perform business analyses for new programs that include profitability, return on capital, evaluation of alternatives, and presentations to senior management.

Product development is only one aspect of finance within a manufacturing company. Other areas requiring financial expertise are sales and marketing, capital markets, and manufacturing.

Sales and marketing finance positions require analysts to evaluate and develop appropriate strategies for retail pricing and various incentive programs. With recent developments in automobile pricing, such as cash back and low interest financing, a great deal of analysis is required to recommend appropriate pricing levels. Analysts also evaluate competitors' pricing strategies and form arguments for an appropriate counterresponse.

Capital markets finance positions exist both within credit areas, such as Ford Motor Credit, and in various treasury areas. Analysts provide financial support for issuance of commercial paper, long-term debt, common and preferred stock, and sale leaseback transactions. Analysts act as buyers of various investment banking services. Analysts recommend strategies for capital structure and dividend policies, manage daily cash flow, and perform analyses for acquisitions and divestitures.

Manufacturing finance positions involve developing capital budgets and analyzing specific capital spending projects. Analysts are involved with site analysis and evaluate new plant proposals. They also analyze financial and operating results of manufacturing plants.

A finance background can often open doors for international assignments depending on the size and needs of the company. Many of my colleagues planned to work internationally, and I saw doors open up for them to do so.

There are many things to consider when choosing a summer job or a career, including location and corporate environment. The best source of information is often individuals who have worked in the industry or have worked for the specific company you are considering. Do not hesitate to contact someone who has worked for a company or in an area you are considering.

Interviews: Three Harvard Business School Alumni Reflect on Careers in Finance

Vikram Gandhi
Harvard Business School, Class of 1989
Managing Director
Morgan Stanley Dean Witter

Describe the stages of your career path and changes in responsibility.

During the first couple of years, my career developed along a diversified set of experiences. I worked in Capital Markets, the Natural Resource Area, and the Merger and Acquisitions/Restructuring Area. These two years served as a time to build a network of relationships and access pockets of knowledge throughout the firm. In addition to being exposed to new functional and industry arenas, this stage enabled me to develop and refine my teamwork skills further. My role was primarily to complete modules of a large project and to contribute to the team's efforts in executing transactions.

The opportunity to move around in the first two years was a valuable experience for two reasons. First, given the nature of the investment banking industry and flux of the business, you should not expect to have a "home" for good, and so it is worthwhile to share in multiple experiences in case you need to shift specialties in the future. Second, given the importance of working with a variety of people, the more people you meet, the better you will be positioned later in your career.

My first two years emphasized agenda execution; my current career stage emphasizes agenda setting as a team manager in the M&A group. I now work more directly with the principals and managing directors, am responsible for ensuring the quality of the team's work, and manage analysts and new associates. A critical junction in my role as team manager is to manage upward and across specialty areas to ensure that the necessary expertise is brought to bear to solve client problems.

What have been the obstacles and challenges of your career progression?

Three challenges in my career have been managing up, coordinating resources, and motivating down. First, since I am now responsible for ensuring the quality of work yet lack many years of experience, it is imperative that I seek the perspective of senior people, and getting their time is not easy. Therefore, it is critical to get them to focus, and one must manage and communicate effectively to accomplish this feat.

Second, a key success factor in investment banking is bringing various resources of the firm to bear on a project. This requires a healthy dose of coordination, especially since I work on six to seven projects at a time. Achieving cooperation in a firm with many egos is a challenge. One must massage egos when coordinating to ensure that what colleagues and senior people say is intelligently articulated to the client.

A third challenge is motivating down. We work hard at Morgan Stanley Dean Witter, and it is vital to maintain a good experience for the analysts and new associates. I must position the work as a valuable and fun experience so that junior people do not mind being at work until 1 A.M. I need to motivate them so they feel involved and they have a high degree of job satisfaction.

Can you describe an experience that has significantly influenced your career?

While working in M&A in the investment banking area in New York, the senior management of Morgan Stanley Dean Witter asked me to come to India where we already had an operation, to help beef it up, identify the right strategy for us in India, and implement it. It was a much broader role than I held previously—involving not just investment banking, but managing an office and determining the firm's strategy in a country very different from the United States. I became country head of Morgan Stanley Dean Witter in India with much wider responsibilities. Our office grew from one hundred to three hundred people, and today we are one of the leaders in India in both investment banking equities and asset management. We have formed a joint venture with a large domestic investment bank called JM Financial, and the company is called JM Morgan Stanley Dean Witter.

This opportunity was completely unanticipated. I was happy doing what I was doing but this seemed to be a very challenging professional opportunity, and I have had no regrets at all. A lot of the initial phase of my career after business school was very deal-driven and project-driven, and my work here is much more general management and strategy-driven. What I learned in business school is a great help out here, because now I am dealing with people issues—the organizational behavior issues, which everyone normally doesn't like to deal with—in addition to how to work with clients and help them solve their problems.

Some might wonder why a banker would want to go from New York to an underdeveloped capital market in India. I had spent seven years in New York and I had seen all that. Here I am doing general management work and that's very different from what I would do in Morgan Stanley Dean Witter in New York. As you grow in your career, you have to show leadership. Ultimately leadership is what will drive your career and this kind of opportunity has allowed me to demonstrate that. Ultimately someone within every organization has to go out in the field—and when developing a global business, going out and actually being part of that development and growth can be very exciting.

At this stage in my career, I don't do as much analytics any more. My work requires leadership skills, people management skills, and providing leadership and vision. Some of my favorite courses at HBS focused on those issues.

What strengths have helped you excel in your career?

A strength that has helped me in my career is being analytically oriented. This should come as no big surprise, but it is especially relevant to M&A given the abundance of valuation and creative structuring required. Another strength is being involved in many extracurricular activities while at school. This involvement was valuable for enabling me to obtain a better understanding of how people think and work. The key to success at Morgan Stanley Dean Witter is teamwork, and my extracurricular activities enhanced my ability to manage my time, to motivate, and to keep people interested in what they are doing while getting the most out of them.

Where do you see your career going over the next ten years? How will you prepare for such changes?

I'm happy in investment banking. I enjoy what I do because it builds on my strengths, and there is a fair degree of variety in the projects I work on. Yes, investment banking is tiring and difficult, but it's also fun. Hence, I'd like to continue for at least the next few years as I transition from a team manager to a team leader. Yet over the long haul, I can see myself getting involved on the principal side of the business.

To prepare for the future, I focus on my interactions with senior firm officials and senior client officials. Eventually,

it will be important for me to secure clients if I hope to transition to a team leader. Therefore, I make sure I know current clients well and build those relationships while establishing others. Preparing for the future means that when a client has a problem, he or she will call on me.

To what extent did your HBS degree prepare you for the day-to-day life of Morgan Stanley?

HBS definitely prepares you for investment banking. One works on six to seven projects at a time in different industries, and the work requires creative problem solving. At Morgan Stanley Dean Witter, I might be considering a joint venture for a natural resource client, a buying opportunity for an auto client, and a selling opportunity for a telecommunications client. This might be only half of the projects on my plate at any given time. And like HBS, even though I had less time to think about the business situation, I would have to grasp key issues of three business situations each evening. So, similar to the requirements for being an exceptional investment banker, HBS prepares one to handle a lot of stuff in a short amount of time and effectively deal with the intensity of work.

The second way HBS prepared me was in the exercise of analytics. Every day I have to go through thick documents or consider complicated situations and come up with three key issues. The client describes a problem, and it's my job to figure out some options and decide which makes the most sense for the client. This type of work is not too different from discussions that occurred every day in Aldrich Hall.

Finally, a third way that HBS prepared me was with regard to people. The people at HBS are the same type that I work with at Morgan Stanley Dean Witter; they're smart and hard working, but they often have large egos. HBS prepared me well for those types of people.

Is there anything else you would recommend to future HBS graduates entering the finance industry?

First, teamwork is critical to success and should not be underestimated. HBS makes some people think they can be a solo star, but it just doesn't work that way.

Second, don't try to run before you can walk. Coming out of HBS, you may think there's not much more to learn. Nothing could be further from the truth. A place like Morgan Stanley Dean Witter can humble you. Consider your first couple of years as an opportunity where you are being paid to learn. I strongly recommend that you demonstrate an eagerness to learn.

Third, recognize that investment banking is a cyclical industry. You must anticipate that while today the equity product might be hot while M&A is slow, the situation could reverse itself very quickly. Given this industry nature, you should be flexible to change as it may become necessary to shift to different industry or function groups during your career. But the good thing to remember is that the HBS education enables you to be flexible because of the exposure to many industries, functions, people, and business situations.

Girish V. Nadkarni
Harvard Business School, Class of 1988
Vice President, Strategic Transactions
The Prudential Insurance Company of America

Describe the stages of your career path and changes in responsibility.

Before attending HBS, I practiced law on Wall Street: three years with Coudert Brothers and three years with Shearman & Sterling. Hence, my first job after HBS is not typical for MBAs straight out of school. After graduating from HBS, I was hired as Vice President and Assistant to the Vice Chairman of The Prudential Insurance Co. of America, responsible for handling a variety of special projects for the Vice Chairman. I also was "on loan" to the heads of several business units throughout The Prudential. The work I was assigned often pertained to strategic initiatives and gave me wide exposure to Prudential's businesses. For instance, one of the special projects required me to work on a task force to assess the sensitivity of Prudential's leveraged buyout (LBO) portfolio to recession.

Fourteen months later, I was promoted to Corporate Vice President in the Central Financial Services Group of Prudential Capital Corporation, responsible for new product development. One of the products I created was Pru-Shelf, a proprietary medium-term note program. Our first Pru-Shelf transaction was a $200 million financing with Toys R Us. To date, The Prudential has executed approximately 24 Pru-Shelf transactions totaling $1.6 billion. The product was featured in articles in *Corporate Finance, Investment Dealer's Digest,* and *Investors Daily* and was also included in a *Business Week* cover story on innovative financial instruments. I also led a team that helped Prudential Capital's 14 regional offices manage complex transactions, such as LBOs and cashouts.

In 1990, I transferred to the work-out area of Prudential Capital and assumed a portfolio of 16 troubled companies. No other job has stretched me so much physically, emotionally, and intellectually. Every day was a crisis. Extensive negotiating and posturing skills were critical in this job, and when I was reassigned to my current position 18 months later, I knew my strengths and weaknesses.

For a number of reasons that range from Hurricane Andrew to the new risk-based capital requirements imposed on insurance companies, The Prudential has embarked on a reassessment of its main lines of business. Consequently, in my current position as Vice President, Strategic Transactions with the Prudential Investment Corporation, I help with the strategic assessment of different businesses and carry out the decisions to eliminate or expand a business unit. If we decide to expand a business or acquire companies, then I might lead an effort to raise external capital. If, on the other hand, we decide to exit a business, then I will execute a sale of our operations in that business.

What have been the obstacles and challenges of your career progression?

I have faced three challenges: diversity, politics, and a line versus staff trade-off. I was born and raised in India and therefore am different from most of the other people at The Prudential. I have independent opinions, and I tend to state them. There is the natural challenge of being different from the status quo and the challenge of peers resisting someone like me who does not always agree with their decisions, analyses, and opinions.

Entering an organization at a high level has its own challenges. People often resent you for not having paid your dues. It therefore takes a lot of effort and time to establish your credibility.

I also have been challenged by my lack of roots to a home unit within The Prudential. This has come about because of my constant transfers from one area of the company to another—wherever the action is hot. I'm not really complaining, though, because putting out fires has been exciting. But movements between line and staff positions can be difficult. It's especially hard to move back into a line assignment after having been in a staff position. But, unfortunately, I am not considered part of the family by any group or senior person and there is no one other than myself who looks after my career.

Can you describe an experience that has significantly influenced your career?

Our business is fraught with legal issues; if we take the wrong step, we'll be sued. And though I am not trained in bankruptcy law, my legal background provides me with the ability to understand most of the intricacies of the work-out business. I also know how to make the most of our own lawyers. In fact, because of my legal experience, the synergy between our legal counsel and me is fantastic. Between us, we make one and one equal six.

A second significant experience is my assignment in the work-out area, where I honed my negotiating skills and learned and practiced the art of diplomacy, often facing people with diverging interests and constantly shifting alliances. I developed a better understanding of finance and strengthened my structuring skills. And I achieved better credit analysis as I saw what can and does go wrong in companies. I also learned that you cannot underestimate the critical need and value for good management and should not analyze a company without considering the probable significant changes imminent within the industry.

What strengths have helped you excel in your career?

My legal background has been a remarkable strength. Another strength is my generalist experience at The Prudential. Although it sometimes hurts not to have a home, transferring throughout the organization has given me wide exposure and a holistic view of Prudential's business. It also taught me to get up to speed quickly. The problems with diversity are synthesizing experiences that will make me an excellent senior manager in the long run. Other strengths include creative problem solving, structuring, and negotiating skills.

Where do you see your career going over the next ten years? How will you prepare for such changes?

I honestly have no clue where my career will be in ten years. The Prudential is experiencing a major transition. Its business is already very different than it was just five years ago. Uncertainty is a big problem. Like most other Harvard Business School alumni, I wouldn't mind being on my own one day, maybe with my own fund. And perhaps unlike most other HBS alumni, I have a strong interest in politics and am likely to run for some type of office one day. The future is definitely uncertain but exciting.

Preparing for uncertainty is a challenge. Often it's not what you know that is important but who you know. It is very important to know the right people—those who make the decisions and not those who make the most noise. It is valuable to adopt a mentor and build credibility.

To what extent did your HBS degree prepare you for the day-to-day life of The Prudential?

I loved my two years at HBS. They gave me tremendous analytical and problem-solving capabilities, as well as frameworks and paradigms to guide my thinking. The education forced me to understand the economics of a business. I graduated appreciating that there are times when the process of making decisions is more important than the substance; that achieving commitment, involvement, and organizational buy-in is not easy; that getting the rank and file to adopt and implement plans is about applying the right process; and that treating customers and employees well is critical to survival.

Nevertheless, HBS failed to prepare me for many of the soft issues that one deals with every day. Perhaps I wasn't listening, but it didn't teach me how to manage my career in a political organization. HBS taught me how to manage others but not how to be managed. It's like expecting one to be a parent before he or she has finished being a child. Furthermore, HBS fell short of enabling me to handle entering an organization at a high-profile level and to fight the stereotypes of an "HBS Baker Scholar type."

Is there anything else you would recommend to future HBS graduates entering the finance industry?

First, make sure you know why you want to be in finance. Too many people think it's a stepping-stone to bigger and better things. For instance, many people think investment banking or mergers and acquisitions is a stepping-stone to running your own business one day. Nothing in investment banking prepares you for running your own business. If you want to operate a business, then consider marketing. Investment banking teaches one only how to process transactions. Make sure you know what working life will be like on a day-to-day basis. Don't choose money management because you want your photograph in the newspaper as the next Peter Lynch. Make sure you understand what Peter Lynch did at Fidelity on a daily basis.

Know your strengths and play to them, and don't forget soft issues both inside and outside your company. Remember that judgment is more important than technical skills. It's critical to reach a judgment based on what the numbers say and not just crunch them. Don't hesitate to push the envelope. Too many people think they are pushing the envelope, but often they don't know where the envelope really is, or they define it too narrowly. Finally, to succeed at the top, it's helpful to be a generalist. Yet there's a trade-off, because to get to the top you need to be a specialist and the risk is obsolescence of your specialty; so be careful to follow industry dynamics constantly, and if they change, manage your career accordingly.

Joel W. Peterson
Harvard Business School, Class of 1983
Managing Director, Utilities
CIBC, a subsidiary of Canadian Imperial Bank of Commerce

Describe the stages of your career path and changes in responsibility.

I would describe my career in five stages: the Learning Stage, "Just Another Banker" Stage, "Not Just Another Banker" Stage, People Manager Stage, and "Not Just Another Manager" Stage.

> *The Learning Stage* (about one year): This is the period right after business school, when I tried to absorb as much information as possible, figure out who's who, and simply do my best even though I was not sure what specific career benefit would accrue from a particular work matter.

> *"Just Another Banker" Stage* (about two years): In this stage I sought valuable personal contacts and team-building opportunities. I knew enough to be dangerous yet not enough to be noticed or have too much impact.

> *"Not Just Another Banker" Stage* (about three years): At this point in my career, I had real impact. This was manifested in specific transactions in which I could differentiate myself through personal excellence and organizational team-building skills.

> *People Manager Stage* (about two years): Although I have always managed projects and people to some extent in my career (you have to manage people up, down, and sideways throughout a successful career), it was during this stage about three years ago that I had responsibility for ten direct reports.

> *"Not Just Another Manager" Stage:* Finally, in the fifth stage, I now differentiate myself by fostering a culture of productivity and compatibility, hiring sincere and motivated people, and setting high standards that are consistently met.

It's important to note that throughout the five stages it has been personal knowledge and abilities that enabled me to be successful. At the beginning of my career, technical, industry, and job knowledge were important, but my progression is rewarded and will continue to be rewarded due to personal knowledge and organizational abilities, which are competencies honed at HBS.

What have been the obstacles and challenges of your career progression?

The biggest challenge has been managing up. I didn't realize the critical importance of managing up, especially with respect to making sure my manager understands what I'm doing. I'm not promoting brown-nosing but rather the notion of effective communication of one's ideas. What good is the world's best idea if you can't effectively communicate it? Upward management through effective communication yields believability, credibility, and promotability. It is especially important and challenging to manage up when personal rapport with the manager is not ideal. I think that talking to unbiased parties and bouncing ideas off them—mentors or peers—is a great way to assess whether you're seeing the big picture and test how such should be communicated to your superiors.

Another challenge to keep in mind is that there are advantages and disadvantages to being in your company's corporate headquarters. In fact, I think there are better reasons for *not* being at headquarters, which is contrary to what many people usually believe. People often want to be located at headquarters because they feel they will reap benefits of greater visibility to the chairman. However, so much time at headquarters is spent gossiping and not enough on business. A satellite office operates as if it were running its own business. Being in a satellite office is liberating.

The other two challenges involve people. First, don't be surprised when the seemingly most neutral colleague backstabs you. The people who openly disagree are at least willing to talk about it; however, it's the people who are quiet who are plotting their actions against you and preparing for guerrilla warfare. Never expect to win every battle. Take the long-term view. Second, career advancement requires successful people management. It requires a lot of time and attention. Don't patronize and don't ignore your people because it may come back to haunt you. People management is more time intensive and critical than technical problems. Take care of people problems first.

Can you describe an experience that has significantly influenced your career?

The experience that significantly influenced my career is when I left First Chicago to pursue a long-term management opportunity at CIBC, where I would be more than just a banker. I took a long-term perspective regarding my career and took a risk in pursuit of this long-term opportunity because I was confident in my abilities to make another move if the CIBC opportunity did not materialize. As the saying goes, "No risk, no return."

What strengths have helped you excel in your career?

Three strengths that have enabled me to excel in my career are communicating persuasively, having a long-term perspective, and completing tasks I set out to perform. With regard to the first strength, anyone can run a computer or regression analysis, but those who excel can also communicate the analysis into a coherent strategy to follow. And to the strength of always completing tasks I set out to perform, I call this "consistent integrity"—doing what I promised. I will not make commitments I cannot keep; everyone is watching everything I do.

Where do you see your career going over the next ten years? How will you prepare for such changes?

Right now I'm at a juncture. I could continue my career per the status quo, but the limiting factor is the trend of flattening organizations, and hence increasing responsibility becoming limited. I like what I do, especially with respect to managing people, and I would not mind moving into more senior management levels, which suggests that I strongly consider broadening my horizons and perspective. But doing my own thing could be fun as well. I also think about working for a client.

Preparing for the future means continuing to develop and refine my skills, talking to a lot of people, and building a network of contacts and a broad knowledge base. It would be great to have a guardian angel, but it just doesn't work that way. In fact, mentor time is limited, and career development is usually nonexistent except for the first couple of years. Advice can be expected but is often unorganized and from many sources. In short, preparing for the future is difficult.

To what extent did your HBS degree prepare you for the day-to-day life of CIBC?

HBS attracts leaders and hones those skills. Personal values, knowledge, and abilities are extremely important, and I think HBS excels at developing and refining these personal attributes. Any smart person can learn technical, industry, and job knowledge, but it's the general, broad knowledge base and personal values that enable excellence, and HBS is distinguished at developing them. Because of my HBS education, I am well organized and see the big picture. These attributes are important in the day-to-day life at CIBC. Also, HBS made me sensitive to other cultures and international differences. This is especially important in the increasingly global world and has made a significant difference in my career.

Is there anything else you would recommend to future HBS graduates entering the finance industry?

I recommend that you set short-term, mid-term, and long-term goals. Evaluate these goals for yourself and your company. Ask yourself questions and ponder answers. Are you compatible with your job and the people around you at work? Do you enjoy your job? If not, then leave, because life is too short. But to a certain extent, you also have to put up with some things you don't like.

A helpful analogy is to think of your career as an investment. You would not put money in a stock and let it sit for 50 years. You would probably look at that investment every six months. Do the same for your career; HBS is an investment in yourself. Don't keep doing something you don't like. If you're unhappy, it will be obvious in your work and in your life.

About This Project

During the spring of 2000, a variety of firms that typically hire MBAs for positions in finance were contacted and asked to respond to the following questionnaire:

Company Description

Describe your firm's business and the types of clients served by your finance group(s).

Describe your ownership structure.

How does your approach to finance differ from that of other firms, and what do you consider to be your strengths and distinctive capabilities?

Discuss changes in your firm's revenues (both domestic and international) and professional staff over the past year; over the past five years.

The Finance MBA's Job Description

Describe the career path and corresponding responsibilities for an MBA at your firm.

Describe the opportunities for professional mobility between the various departments in your firm.

Discuss the lifestyle aspects of a career with your firm (i.e., average hours per week, amount of travel, flexibility to change offices, corporate culture, etc.).

The Recruiting Process

Describe your recruiting process and the criteria by which you select candidates. Is prior experience necessary?

How many permanent associates and analysts do you hire in a typical year? How many summer interns do you expect to hire? If you have a formal summer program, please describe it. Please be sure to indicate whether the summer program is in place for all offices or just some.

What international opportunities does your firm offer for U.S. citizens? For foreign nationals?

The firms contacted include investment banking firms, commercial banks, Fortune 500 firms, and regional companies. Responses from firms in this section are printed, for the most part, as received.

A.G. Edwards & Sons, Inc.

One North Jefferson
St. Louis, MO 63103
(314) 955-3000
Web site: www.agedwards.com

MBA Recruiting Contact(s):
Barbara H. Boyle
Managing Director—Investment Banking
E-mail: boylebh@agedwards.com

Company Description

Describe your firm's business and the types of clients served by your finance group(s).

Founded in 1887, A.G. Edwards is the largest securities firm headquartered off Wall Street; it is one of the few firms described as a "national full-line" firm by the Securities and Exchange Commission and the Securities Industry Association. For more than 100 years, the firm has played a major role in providing financial services to a variety of clients nationwide. From its headquarters in St. Louis, the firm and its subsidiaries provide securities and commodities brokerage, asset management, insurance, real estate, and investment banking services. Our department provides investment banking services in the areas of Corporate Finance, Mergers and Acquisitions, and Valuations.

Public and Structured Finance, a department that is separate and distinct from that discussed below, is also part of A.G. Edwards's investment banking services. While the Public and Structured Finance department does not currently recruit on college campuses, inquiries can be made to Charlie Forrest, (314) 955-5838, at the address listed above.

Describe your ownership structure.

A.G. Edwards, a publicly owned corporation for more than 20 years, is traded on the New York Stock Exchange under the symbol AGE.

How does your approach to finance differ from that of other firms, and what do you consider to be your strengths and distinctive capabilities?

Our success has been built in large part on our orientation toward relationship banking. Rather than emphasizing individual transactions, we provide a variety of services that meet our clients' needs and further our long-term relationships with them. Although our clients range from Fortune 500 corporations to small private companies, we consider our niche to be middle-market companies. We serve clients coast to coast and compete with other national, as well as regional, investment banks.

The close attention we provide our clients gives A.G. Edwards the distinction of being the nation's only retail brokerage firm to be included in both editions of *The Service Edge95: 101 Companies That Profit from Customer Care* and both editions of *The 100 Best Companies to Work for in America*. We attribute the firm's success to our emphasis on consistently maintaining the customers' success as a primary focus, creating value with the services we deliver, and treating our employees "like members of the family."

According to The Securities Industry Association, as of January 1, 1999, A.G. Edwards was the third largest securities firm in the United States based on the number of offices (more than 630 in 48 states), and the sixth largest based on the number of registered representatives (more than 6,400). Well known within the industry for our national distribution network, our distribution of securities in small amounts to a large number of investors results in a large, geographically dispersed shareholder/bondholder base for the issuer.

Discuss changes in your firm's revenues (both domestic and international) and professional staff over the past year; over the past five years.

Although most of A.G. Edwards's revenues are derived from commissions generated by selling securities to individual investors, our department's revenues are derived from a diversified base of business that includes underwritings of equity and debt, mergers and acquisitions, valuations, and financial advisory projects. Our department has significantly expanded both the breadth and depth of our capability over the past decade. The rapid growth of our department affords a motivated individual the opportunity to make a meaningful contribution to A.G. Edwards. The number of professionals in the Corporate Finance, Mergers and Acquisitions, and Valuations departments has grown from 7 professionals in 1983 to more than 100 professionals in 1999. Associates are hired for our St. Louis headquarters, where over 4,300 of our more than 14,000 employees work.

The Finance MBA's Job Description

Describe the career path and corresponding responsibilities for an MBA at your firm.

A.G. Edwards's Corporate Finance and Mergers and Acquisitions department is a rapidly developing area of the company that affords talented, hard-working individuals recognition and responsibility early in their career development. A generalist program for an associate's development is strongly emphasized, and new associates in investment banking are given a wide variety of projects in corporate finance, mergers and acquisitions, and valuations.

A.G. Edwards emphasizes teamwork. Teams are small, and new associates can expect to work directly on client assignments with senior investment banking professionals, ensuring the associates' visibility and responsibility on projects. In addition, we have developed a system of semiannual and annual reviews, as well as specific project reviews, to provide individuals with feedback on their development.

Describe the opportunities for professional mobility between the various departments in your firm.

We assign associates to either industry or product groups in the early stage of their careers. Because there are no rigid boundaries separating these areas, new associates will be involved in projects in all of these areas. Associates are allowed to develop areas of expertise and specialization as they gain experience in investment banking.

Discuss the lifestyle aspects of a career with your firm (i.e., average hours per week, amount of travel, flexibility to change offices, corporate culture, etc.).

Demands and expectations at A.G. Edwards are very high. The firm, however, tries to maintain a reasonable balance between work and personal interests, which is reflected by a low turnover rate for our employees. St. Louis offers a very affordable and pleasant quality of life. The city consistently rates in the top ten of U.S. metropolitan areas in terms of quality of life. St. Louis provides an array of dance, theater, music, art, leisure activities, and sports and includes many nationally recognized landmarks. The city is also home to a significant number of Fortune 500 companies.

The Recruiting Process

Describe your recruiting process and the criteria by which you select candidates. Is prior experience necessary?

Our strategy for selecting new investment banking associates is to employ those whom we feel have the skills and compatibility to build long-term careers at A.G. Edwards. We have avoided the cutbacks common in our industry because we do not initially overhire. Instead, the number of new positions is commensurate with the firm's steady growth. Each new associate is carefully chosen to assume a role in which long-term dedication and a commitment to manage increasing responsibility are expected.

Leadership, personal integrity, academic success, and demonstrated success in other areas are some of the criteria we use to judge individual candidates. A commitment to investment banking, shown by summer internships or relevant experience prior to graduate school, is also an important criterion.

How many permanent associates and analysts do you hire in a typical year? How many summer interns do you expect to hire? If you have a formal summer program, please describe it. Please be sure to indicate whether the summer program is in place for all offices or just some.

We add new associates and analysts according to the quality of individual candidates and the compatibility of those candidates with A.G. Edwards. Therefore, we do not set yearly quotas for hiring. We offer summer associate positions in our St. Louis headquarters location. Recruiting for summer associates begins in February each year.

What international opportunities does your firm offer for U.S. citizens? For foreign nationals?

While A.G. Edwards does participate in the international marketing of underwritings to a limited extent, all of our investment banking operations, are located in the United States.

AMVESCAP, PLC

1315 Peachtree Street, N.E.
Atlanta, GA 30309
(404) 892-0896
Fax: (404) 898-1884

MBA Recruiting Contact:
Mariclare Scott
(404) 724-4254

Company Description

Describe your firm's business and the types of clients served by your finance groups.

One of the largest independent investment management organizations in the world, AMVESCAP—through its AIM and INVESCO subsidiaries—is a major force in global investment management, with $280 billion in assets managed on behalf of clients from over 100 countries. We manage a full range of domestic, foreign, and global investment products including equity, balanced, fixed income, money market, and real estate investment categories.

Describe your ownership structure.

We are a publicly traded holding company, quoted on the London, New York, and Paris stock exchanges under the AVZ ticker symbol.

How does your approach to finance differ from that of other firms, and what do you consider to be your strengths and distinctive capabilities?

AMVESCAP has a significant presence in the institutional and retail segments of the investment management industry in North America and Europe, and a growing presence in Asia. Unlike many of our competitors, our business is focused entirely on investment management. We are one of the few independent investment managers with the ability to offer a broad range of investment products in a variety of investment styles. Through our diverse distribution channels, these products are offered to institutional and individual clients in each of the world's major capital markets. With a team of over 500 investment professionals and approximately 5,000 support staff located around the world, we believe our approach consisting of local investment managers with global resources, provides us with a competitive advantage. In addition, within each investment product category we utilize multiple investment styles, which allows us to offer our worldwide clients a diverse range of product alternatives.

Within each geographic market, AMVESCAP offers a wide array of distribution alternatives appropriate for that region. In the United States, we offer products and services to retail and institutional clients including both load and no-load mutual funds, private account management, institutional funds, and "wrap" accounts. Retail distribution in the United States includes products sold primarily through financial intermediaries under the AIM brand name and directly to investors under the INVESCO brand name. Outside of the United States, we offer our investment products through unit trusts and other European and Asian mutual funds as well as separate accounts for private and institutional investors.

At all times, AMVESCAP seeks to maximize the benefits of having a local presence while exploiting the synergies of a global organization.

Discuss changes in your firm's revenues (both domestic and international) and professional staff over the past year; over the past five years.

AMVESCAP has experienced significant and rapid change over the past five years resulting in its status as one of the world's premier independent fund management companies. Our financial results for 1998 reached record levels of revenue and income, extending our record performance to six consecutive years.

The Finance MBA's Job Description

Describe the career path and corresponding responsibilities for an MBA at your firm.

AMVESCAP's Corporate Development Program provides opportunities to outstanding individuals to enhance the success of both the organization and the individuals who comprise the team. The goal of the associate is to be eligible, at the appropriate time, for nomination to our Global Partners Group—a team of highly motivated, conservatively aggressive professionals who take the calculated risks necessary to continue the phenomenal growth and acumen of AMVESCAP and share meaningfully in its success.

New associates will be involved in a two-year program that includes personalized, custom-tailored path training and involvement in real-time decisions, contributing responsibly to AMVESCAP's global investment services. A global partner will serve as a mentor throughout the associate's two-year development program, providing invaluable insights, experience, training, and sponsorship. Depending on the chosen career path, those involved in the Corporate Development Program will complete several medium-term assignments culminating in a longer-term assignment working closely with a Global Partner in a fund management or general management related capacity.

Describe the opportunities for professional mobility between the various departments in your firm.

Associates will have the opportunity to actively participate in and become familiar with our operations in the United States as well as in our offices throughout the world. Upon completion of the Corporate Development Program the associates will have a strong knowledge base of the entire AMVESCAP organization, providing a solid base upon which to build a successful career with AMVESCAP and better serve AMVESCAP's clients.

Discuss the lifestyle aspects of a career with your firm (i.e., average hours per week, amount of travel, flexibility to change offices, corporate culture, etc.).

One philosophy binds the organization: *Clients First.* It is important to us to provide our clients with excellent service and performance. Occasional overtime may be required to complete special projects; however, staffing throughout the organization is maintained at a level which allows conformance to the average workweek. Because AMVESCAP's strategy is one of local service with global resources, and due to the fact that we have a presence in over 100 countries, an associate may be required to travel regularly throughout the country. The company is committed to providing a positive work environment that will attract and retain good people by encouraging entrepreneurial behavior and productivity, welcoming creativity, valuing open and honest communications, and providing opportunity, training, and superior compensation.

Describe your recruiting process and the criteria by which you select candidates. Is prior experience necessary?

The global partners of AMVESCAP will consider each candidate based on technical competence, entrepreneurial attitude, high ethical standards, work experience, relationship skills, commitment, and global perspective. Additional consideration will be given to the candidate's career interests and goals, undergraduate degree(s), foreign language skills, and location preferences. While prior experience is not mandatory, we look for individuals with two to four years of meaningful work experience.

How many permanent associates and analysts do you hire in a typical year? How many summer interns do you expect to hire? If you have a formal summer program, please describe it. Please be sure to indicate whether the summer program is in place for all offices or just some.

AMVESCAP expects to hire ten corporate associates and six summer interns this year.

The Corporate Development Summer Intern Program is designed for a twelve-week or more (minimum ten-week) rotation, with consideration for the intern's schedule and AMVESCAP's needs. Positions exist within the Investment Management as well as the General Business Management areas, primarily in our Atlanta, New York, Dallas, and Houston offices. These summer intern positions are often stepping-stones to career positions within the Corporate Development Program.

What international opportunities does your firm offer for U.S. citizens? For foreign nationals?

As part of the two-year Corporate Associate Program, at least one international rotation is required. Permanent international opportunities within the company depend on availability and the qualifications of the candidate. The program has hired foreign nationals in the past and will continue to do so in the future.

Banco Pactual S.A.

Av. Rep. do Chile, 230/29° andar
Rio de Janeiro-RJ, 20.031-170
Brazil
55 21 272-1300
Fax: 55 21 533-1661

MBA Recruiting Contact(s):
Rachel Goldgrob

Company Description

Describe your firm's business and the types of clients served by your finance group(s).

Banco Pactual S.A. is an investment banking firm based in Rio de Janeiro, Brazil, that specializes in proprietary trading, of Brazilian and other Latin American securities, portfolio management, and corporate finance activities.

The firm has an office in São Paulo, a broker-dealer in New York, subsidiary companies in Uruguay and the Cayman Islands, as well as affiliates in England, Chile, and Argentina.

Pactual has consistently produced high returns on investment, both for its own account and for its clients. The firm is managed in an entrepreneurial spirit, with a lean and flat organizational structure focusing on opportunities that will offer potentially significant margins while seeking to reduce downside risk.

Describe your ownership structure.

Pactual is a limited partnership, currently with twenty-one partners. Furthermore, it is a requirement that all partners must be active executives of the bank. All professionals at Pactual work in a highly entrepreneurial environment and everyone is encouraged to become a partner of the firm.

How does your approach to finance differ from that of other firms, and what do you consider to be your strengths and distinctive capabilities?

If there is one key factor for Pactual's success over the past fourteen years it is the firm's ability to remain flexible and adapted to Brazil's volatile financial market and increasing competitiveness. Pactual believes Brazil is undergoing a transformation toward a more open, competitive, and internationally integrated economy, although many political obstacles still remain to be overcome. A truly international perspective and understanding of events not only in Brazil but in other countries and markets is imperative. Pactual is firmly committed to ensuring that both our professionals and the structure of the firm enable it to stay at the forefront of these changes.

Discuss changes in your firm's revenues (both domestic and international) and professional staff over the past year; over the past five years.

Pactual was founded in 1983 as a securities dealer with US$600,000 of capital, focusing principally on proprietary trading and financial intermediation. Since then, Pactual has grown at an impressive rate to become one of the most successful investment banks in Brazil. Over the last five-year period, the number of employees has increased 186% and, more specifically, from 305 in 1995 to 350 in 1996.

The Finance MBA's job description

Describe the career path and corresponding responsibilities for an MBA at your firm.

Hired candidates start at the associate level. Candidates may start at any of the bank's main business divisions (Proprietary Trading, Sales & Trading, Corporate Finance, Research, Portfolio Management and Risk Management) and will work under the supervision of one of the firm's partners. We tend to emphasize performance in determining compensation. The semiannual bonus is usually a substantial part of overall compensation.

Discuss the lifestyle aspects of a career with your firm (i.e., average hours per week, amount of travel, flexibility to change offices, corporate culture, etc.).

Lifestyle varies from one business division to another, being in line with typical investment banking conditions. Pactual's corporate culture—also comparable with that of other successful investment banks—is entrepreneurial, aggressive, intense, fast changing, and demand driven.

The Recruiting Process

Describe your recruiting process and the criteria by which you select candidates. Is prior experience necessary?

We have a strong commitment to recruiting the best people, with emphasis given to individuals with independent thinking, drive, aptitude for numbers, and initiative to work without constant supervision. No prior banking experience is needed. We are strongly committed to promoting a working environment that places a premium on internal cooperation.

Selected candidates will be interviewed in New York, Miami, or Brazil. Interviews are expected to start in late November (Miami) and December (Brazil and New York).

How many permanent associates and analysts do you hire in a typical year? How many summer interns do you expect to hire? If you have a formal summer program, please describe it. Please be sure to indicate whether the summer program is in place for all offices or just some.

Pactual actively recruits students graduating from prestigious foreign institutions. In 1995 and 1996, Pactual hired, on average, thirteen graduates from top American and European Schools. Typically, two summer interns are hired per year and are normally taken on by the Rio de Janeiro and São Paulo offices.

What international opportunities does your firm offer for U.S. citizens? For foreign students?

We offer full time and summer positions in Rio de Janeiro, São Paulo, and eventually in London and New York.

Barclays Capital

5 North Colonnade
Canary Wharf
London, E14 4BB
United Kingdom
Web site: www.barcap.com

222 Broadway
New York, NY 10038
USA

MBA Recruiting Contact(s):
Lisa Tomlin-Houston
Manager, Recruitment—Americas
Tazmin Walker
Manager, Recruitment—Europe/Asia
To apply, visit www.barcap.com/graduatecareers

Company Description

Describe your firm's business and the types of clients served by your finance group(s).

Barclays Capital is the global investment banking division of Barclays PLC, one of the world's largest multinational financial services groups. We have international locations in all the major financial centers and recruit for our headquarters in London, New York, Hong Kong, Singapore, and Tokyo.

We provide our clients with a broad range of integrated financing and risk management products, distinguishing ourselves from other investment banks through our excellence in debt capital markets origination and advisory services. Our operational strength is enhanced through the backing of Barclays' $393 bn balance sheet and AA credit rating

Barclays Capital businesses are grouped around two principal asset classes: credit and rates. Credit includes the origination, sales, trading, and research related to loans, securitized assets, bonds, commodities and their related derivative instruments, equity derivatives, and private equity investments.

Rates include sales, trading, and research relating to government bonds, money markets, foreign exchange, and their related derivative instruments. For more details, visit our Web site www.barcap.com/graduatecareers.

The Recruiting Process

How many permanent associates and analysts do you hire in a typical year? How many summer interns do you expect to hire? If you have a formal summer program, please describe it. Please be sure to indicate whether the summer program is in place for all offices or just some.

We are looking to hire approximately 40 associates and 40 summer associates globally for our sales, trading, and investment banking divisions. Associates will start making a contribution to our business from day one of their placement. Barclays Capital offers a meritocratic working environment where individual talents are recognized and rewarded. We are looking for associates with an entrepreneurial spirit, who enjoy being visible and are willing to take on responsibility and make an immediate contribution.

Our On-line Induction Program

Barclays Capital will offer you the opportunity to participate in our unique On-line Induction Program as you finish your final year of study. Each candidate is required to complete 12 training modules based on aspects of Barclays Capital's products and services. Thus, you arrive equipped with all the relevant knowledge necessary to put your skills into action. As an added incentive, we will pay you a monthly salary and a lump sum for each training module completed. In addition to the On-line Induction Program during your final year of study, a four-week training program in London will be provided once you come on board.

Visit our Web site at www.barcap.com/graduatecareers to start the application process and register for our on-campus competition. On-line you can learn more about what we have to offer and our application criteria. We are looking for academic excellence in candidates, high GMAT scores, and a career focus in business. We seek talented and team oriented individuals with leadership qualities. If you are interested in this career opportunity, you can apply on-line in the fall for full-time and summer positions.

Bear, Stearns & Co. Inc.

245 Park Avenue
New York, NY 10167
(212) 272-2000

MBA Recruiting Contact(s):
Melissa Salerno
MBA Recruiting Manager
Investment Banking
(212) 272-9203
Fax: (212) 272-3052

Amy Williams
MBA Recruiting Manager
Debt and Equity Markets
(212) 272-3586

Company Description

Describe your firm's business and the types of clients served by your finance group(s).

The Bear, Stearns Companies Inc. is the parent company of Bear, Stearns & Co. Inc., a leading worldwide investment banking and securities trading firm.

With approximately $18.9 billion in capital, Bear Stearns serves corporations, governments, institutions, and individuals worldwide. The firm's business includes corporate finance, mergers and acquisitions, public finance, institutional equities and fixed income sales and trading, private client services, foreign exchange, futures sales and trading, equity and fixed income research, derivatives, and asset management. Through its wholly owned subsidiary, Bear, Stearns Securities Corp., it provides professional and correspondent clearing services, including securities lending. Custodial Trust Company, a wholly owned subsidiary of the Bear, Stearns Companies Inc., provides master trust, custody, and government and securities clearing services.

In its seventy-six-year history, Bear Stearns has never had an unprofitable year. The firm has grown rapidly in size and capital since becoming a publicly held company in 1985. Bear Stearns has built a reputation as an aggressive and innovative investment banking and trading firm by carefully managing its capital and underwriting commitments in order to achieve disciplined and sustained growth.

Headquartered in New York City, Bear Stearns employs over 9,500 people worldwide with domestic offices in Atlanta, Boston, Chicago, Dallas, Los Angeles, and San Francisco and an international presence in Beijing, Buenos Aires, Dublin, Hong Kong, London, Lugano, São Paulo, Shanghai, Singapore, and Tokyo.

Investment Banking Division

Bear Stearns is a leading worldwide investment bank, having built its franchise across a wide spectrum of capabilities, industries, and product lines while developing long-term client relationships. Professionals in the Investment Banking Division specialize in capital markets (equities, investment grade debt, and high-yield securities), corporate finance, financial restructuring, mergers and acquisitions, and public finance. By integrating a unique breadth and depth of industry expertise with product disciplines, Bear Stearns's client-coverage teams act as advisers and capital raisers within the most dynamic industries.

The firm's investment banking expertise was recognized in 1998 for its role in eight diverse transactions that received "Deal of the Year" acclaim. *Industrial Investor* cited McKesson Corp.'s $14.1 billion acquisition of HBO & Co., and Seagram Co.'s $10.4 billion acquisition of Polygram, in the mergers and acquisitions sector; the Federal National Mortgage Association's $42 billion benchmark note offering in the corporate finance sector; and Long Island Power Authority's $6.73 billion bond offerings in the public finance sector. *Corporate Finance* selected Ford Motor Credit Company's $3.25 billion global debt offering and General Motors Corporation's $1.6 billion global debt offering as joint winners in the international bond category. *Euroweek* noted Associates Corporation of North America's $4.8 billion global debt offering in both the corporate borrower and U.S. dollars-fixed rate segments, as well as Yanzhou Coal Mining Company's U.S. $267 million IPO as the "Best Chinese Equity Issue" for 1998.

In 1998 Bear Stearns raised more than $424 billion in capital for clients worldwide. Notable equity offerings included an $800 million secondary offering for Federal-Mogul Corporation, the largest equity offering lead managed by the firm to date; an $815 million follow-on offering for Carnival Corporation; and a $32.4 million IPO for theglobe.com, Inc. In the investment-grade sector Bear Stearns joint-lead managed a $2 billion global note offering for General Motors Acceptance Corporation and an $800 million note offering for Comcast Cable Communications, Inc. In January 1999 Bear Stearns joint-lead managed a $2.8 billion global note offering for Ford

Motor Company. In the high yield sector, highlights for the year included lead managing a $300 million two-tranche global offering for Dolphin Telecom PLC and a $575 million offering for MetroNet Escrow Corp.

In 1998 Bear Stearns provided M&A advice on ninety-two deals with total value in excess of $161 billion. Clients include Bell Atlantic Corp., the Blackstone Group, Culligan Water Technologies Inc., Depuy Inc., McKesson Corp., Seagram Co., and Six Flags Theme Parks Inc.

In the municipal sector, Bear Stearns lead managed 115 bond underwritings in 1998—totaling $17.24 billion—giving Bear Stearns the largest average deal size in the industry. Major milestones for the department included senior managing Long Island Power Authority's $3.45 billion initial bond offering, the largest municipal financing ever, and lead managing a $1.4 billion bond offering for the California's Veterans Home Loan Program, the largest housing deal ever completed in the municipal market.

Fixed Income Division

Bear Stearns is a leader in every sector of the primary and secondary fixed income markets, providing liquidity for clients, market and product information for investors, and distribution power for issuers. Clients benefit from one of the industry's largest and most experienced sales, trading, and research organizations and a proprietary state-of-the-art analytical system, both of which underpin the firm's success in the fixed income markets. The firm has leveraged all of its fixed income capabilities to build a larger, more integrated global business while at the same time providing the clients with the tools they need to execute their strategies most effectively and efficiently.

The Fixed Income Department provides in-depth coverage of every sector of the fixed income universe. In *Institutional Investor*'s 1998 All-America Fixed-Income Research Team survey, Bear Stearns had an overall rating of number two on a weighted basis with more first-team rankings than any other Wall Street firm; specifically, Bear Stearns ranked number two and number three for high yield research and high grade research, respectively. The primary analytical tools for research, trading, and sales in fixed income are provided through the advanced technology of the Financial Analytics & Structured Transactions Group (F.A.S.T.)—an innovator in the design and development of securitized fixed income products. Bear Stearns has one of the largest sales and trading staffs in the industry—enabling clients to buy, sell, and hedge securities across the entire fixed income spectrum. Sales and trading desks are located in Atlanta, Boston, Chicago, Dallas, Hong Kong, London, Los Angeles, New York, San Francisco, Singapore, and Tokyo. The Fixed Income Division's product and market expertise encompasses the asset-backed, corporate, derivatives, emerging markets, foreign exchange, futures, government, high yield, mortgages, and municipal sectors.

Institutional Equities Division

Bear Stearns is widely acknowledged as a premier equities trading firm, providing clients with superior trading and execution capabilities as well as comprehensive market coverage. Through the combined efforts of its sales, trading, and equity research professionals, the Institutional Equities Division offers a high quality, client-focused equity product. In addition to our position in the U.S. markets, the division has grown its international capabilities in order to meet the global demand of its clients.

The Equity Research Department drives our institutional equities effort, providing coverage of 1,100 companies in over 100 industries. Through in-depth analysis, the department provides a steady stream of insight and ideas to the salesforce and Bear Stearns's clients. The Research Department works with sales, trading, and banking and is a resource to both our buyside and corporate clients. The department also has a dedicated emerging markets research team that follows companies in Latin America and Asia. All of Bear Stearns's research is available to clients on the firm's Internet Web site.

Bear Stearns is dedicated to broadening equity investment opportunities for clients. Equity Capital Markets coordinates the efforts of research, trading, investment banking, and sales throughout the capital-raising process. Bear Stearns consistently represents about 10 percent of the volume on the NYSE—more than any other firm on Wall Street. The firm is among the largest market-makers on the NASDAQ over-the-counter market and consistently ranks among the top full-service firms in OTC trading volume. Our Convertible Securities Department is one of the largest integrated research, sales, and trading efforts on Wall Street. The Risk Arbitrage Department has the only salesforce dedicated to risk arbitrageurs on the Street and offers the most comprehensive research covering mergers, acquisitions, and tender offers. Our Portfolio Trading Group, a market leader in systematic portfolio trading in the U.S., recently executed nondollar equity portfolios in fifty markets worldwide.

The Finance MBA's Job Description

Describe the career path and corresponding responsibilities for an MBA at your firm.

Investment Banking

Associates work on a wide variety of corporate finance and merger and acquisition transactions in a variety of different industries. Often an associate will be working on three to five different transactions in project teams that typically consist of three to four people.

Job responsibilities include detailed financial analysis and modeling; due diligence with respect to a client's business, industry, financial results, and projects; creation of new business proposals/presentations; and preparation of internal memoranda for the various committees that review and approve transactions.

Associates are typically eligible for promotion to vice president after three years. The timing of future promotions is based entirely on performance.

Sales and Trading

Sales & Trading associates are hired by either the Fixed Income or Equity divisions. The associates will participate in a classroom training program for a period of eight weeks and then they will rotate among the various product areas within the division in which they have been hired. After a period of three months of rotations the associates will be placed on a desk based on the preference of the associates and the needs of the firm. The timing and frequency of promotions are based entirely on an individual's performance.

The Recruiting Process

Describe your recruiting process and the criteria by which you select candidates. Is prior experience necessary?

Bear Stearns endeavors to hire individuals who have demonstrated outstanding academic achievement and have a proven track record of performance excellence. In addition, a candidate should possess strong oral and written communication skills, attention to detail and concern for accuracy, the ability to work well with others under pressure, and a willingness to work long hours. No specific academic major is a prerequisite; however, a strong finance and accounting background is desired and candidates must be proficient with financial and mathematical concepts.

How many permanent associates and analysts do you hire in a typical year? How many summer interns do you expect to hire? If you have a formal summer program, please describe it. Please be sure to indicate whether the summer program is in place for all offices or just some.

Bear Stearns has a summer associate program in which MBA candidates are hired as generalists in Investment Banking and Debt and Equity Markets. Over the course of the summer, Investment Banking Summer Associates will have the opportunity to work on a variety of projects in the mergers and acquisitions, capital markets, and corporate finance areas. Debt and Equity Markets Summer Associates have the opportunity to work with the firm's sales and trading professionals in a variety of different product areas. Bear Stearns views the summer associate program as an important part of its overall hiring process and recruits summer associates to obtain the best possible assessment of an individual's long-term potential.

BMO Nesbitt Burns Inc.

1 First Canadian Place
4th Floor, P.O. Box 150
Toronto, Ontario M5X 1H3
Canada
(416) 359-4000

MBA Recruiting Contact(s):
Jeff Watchorn
Emma Loewen
(416) 359-4001

Company Description

Describe your firm's business and the types of clients served by your finance group(s).

BMO Nesbitt Burns is a bulge-bracket investment bank in Canada, which provides a comprehensive suite of services to all business sectors. In Canada, BMO Nesbitt Burns has a strong reputational franchise as a leader in serving the needs of individual, corporation, government, and institutional clients. In the United States, BMO Nesbitt Burns is building on its historical strength in the energy sector and its expertise in the emerging media and telecom area.

BMO Nesbitt Burns is committed to excellence in each and every area of its businesses. We are determined to build, in partnership with the Bank of Montreal, a prominent North American investment bank with strong global capabilities.

BMO Nesbitt Burns aspires to be recognized for the highest standards of excellence, integrity, and professionalism. As an organization committed to learning, we will continue to foster a culture that is challenging, rewarding, and entrepreneurial.

With the power of knowledge, teamwork, creativity, and innovation, we create value and wealth for our clients. We contribute meaningfully to the economy and the well-being of the communities in which we work.

- BMO Nesbitt Burns employs approximately 4,000 individuals who are located in over 144 offices across Canada and in 13 international locations. The firm is one of the largest Canadian investment firms in terms of capital employed.

- 1,364 investment advisors serve the needs of individual investors by providing them with top-ranked research information, timely advice, the highest quality service, and the broadest selection of products. The firm is recognized for having the most comprehensive investment advisor training program in the industry.

- BMO Nesbitt Burns is a leading underwriter of Canadian corporate issues with the number one marketshare in 1999 of 19.4%.

- BMO Nesbitt Burns' Institutional Equity Sales and Trading is the top trader and distributor of Canadian equity securities throughout the world.

- BMO Nesbitt Burns' Fixed Income team is one of Canada's largest and offers the greatest depth of any Canadian firm. The group provides bond sales and trading, money market, fixed income research, derivative products, and securitization services to its domestic and international clients.

- BMO Nesbitt Burns is Canada's leader in advisory services including mergers, acquisitions and divestitures, valuations and fairness opinions, and restructuring and recapitalization.

- BMO Nesbitt Burns is a manager for nine out of the ten provinces, which represents nearly all of provincial borrowing and is a leading advisor to governments, government agencies, and Crown Corporations in Canada.

- Jones Heward, the firm's wholly owned investment management company, founded in 1925, provides investment counselling services to individuals, estates, foundations, and corporations resident in Canada and abroad. Jones Heward has displayed strong asset growth and performance in each of its three distinct businesses: private wealth management, mutual funds, and pension fund management.

Describe your ownership structure.

BMO Nesbitt Burns is part of the Bank of Montreal financial group and operates autonomously to offer securities-related services on its behalf. Our partnership with the bank reinforces our capital base, increases our distribution capabilities, and greatly enhances our ability to compete effectively in the global capital markets.

How does your approach to finance differ from that of other firms, and what do you consider to be your strengths and distinctive capabilities?

Our focus on uncompromising quality and integrity is incorporated in all aspects of the way we do business. It underpins the success we have had in identifying financing opportunities and designing new products, the preeminence we have achieved as a major market maker in Canadian corporate and government securities, and the stature we have attained as a world-ranked mergers and acquisitions financial advisor. Our work throughout has been supported by our top-ranked economics and investment research team.

BMO Nesbitt Burns' Investment & Corporate Banking Group consists of approximately 232 professionals in Canada, the U.S., the U.K., and Mexico. Our Canadian-based professionals are located in Toronto, Montreal, Calgary, and Vancouver, while 69 investment & corporate bankers are based in New York, Chicago, and Houston. Our London, U.K. Investment & Corporate Banking Group has five professionals and we have also recently opened an office in Mexico City. The Investment & Corporate Banking Department provides a broad range of services, including corporate finance, loans, mergers, acquisitions and divestitures, restructuring, and consulting and advisory services to corporation, governments, and other organizations. We achieve success for our clients by having a thorough understanding of client needs combined with a sensitivity and swift response to market opportunities. For BMO Nesbitt Burns, a corporate client relationship is a long-term partnership. Conscious of our continuing obligation to provide financial services, a team of highly skilled individuals is assembled to ensure full client coverage. Our team approach to assignments serves as a catalyst to combine experience and knowledge with innovation and creativity.

Investment & Corporate Banking includes industry specialists who focus on the real estate, mining, financial services, forest products, media, telecom and technology, utilities, oil and gas, and consumer products industries. Industry specialists work closely with product specialists. The approach of our Investment & Corporate Banking Group is to combine an in-depth knowledge of our clients' needs and goals with creative thought, a thorough understanding of the capital markets, and integrity.

The Finance MBA's Job Description

Describe the career path and corresponding responsibilities for an MBA at your firm.

Career opportunities are available in all areas of the firm, including Investment & Corporate Banking, and Fixed Income, and Equity Sales and Trading.

BMO Nesbitt Burns encourages investment banking associates to generalize during their first two years in order to develop a broad range of investment banking skills. Associates work with senior members of the department on a variety of corporate financing and M&A related projects, including drafting prospectuses or offering memorandums, analyzing a corporation's financing needs, creating corporate presentations, assisting on valuations and fairness opinions, managing solicitations, and assisting in the marketing of new issues, both public and private. As an associate gains more experience and product knowledge, he or she may decide to specialize in a particular industry or product group.

A career in Fixed Income or Institutional Equity begins directly on the sales and trading floor. Working alongside an experienced professional, the trainee will master an understanding of market behaviour and will develop marketing skills and strategies for arbitrage, market making, and taking positions as both principal and agent.

BMO Nesbitt Burns offers a dynamic, challenging work environment with tremendous career opportunities. BMO Nesbitt Burns stresses a team-oriented approach to assignments and encourages an environment open to providing innovative solutions for clients.

Discuss the lifestyle aspects of a career with your firm (i.e. average hours per week, amount of travel, flexibility to change offices, corporate culture, etc.).

To provide the quality of work necessary in the competitive investment banking environment, the time commitment required is considerable, particularly of new recruits.

The Recruiting Process

Describe your recruiting process and the criteria by which you select candidates. Is prior experience necessary?

We look for highly motivated individuals with strong analytical skills, sound judgement, and a high level of integrity. Academic achievement is important. Prior related work experience is an asset.

How many permanent associates and analysts do you hire in a typical year? How many summer interns do you expect to hire?

In a typical year, BMO Nesbitt Burns hires three or four associates, four or five analysts, and others as required. In the past, we have also hired summer associates and summer analysts.

For MBA candidates from U.S. schools, eligibility to work in Canada is a prerequisite.

Broadview Int'l. LLC

One Bridge Plaza
Fort Lee, NJ 07024
(201) 346-9000
Fax: (201) 346-9191
Web site: www.broadview.com

MBA Recruiting Contact(s):
Russel Klein, Associate and
Harvard Team Captain
Justin Kulo, Recruiting Manager

Company Description

Describe your firm's business and the types of clients served by your finance group(s).

Broadview is a leading global investment bank focused on the IT, communications, and media industries worldwide. The firm assists clients with mergers and acquisitions, restructurings, and private financings. It is also a private equity investor in these industries in the U.S. and Europe. Over the last 25 years, Broadview has grown to become the world's largest M&A investment bank of its kind, operating across the United States, Europe, and Asia. Combining a powerful mix of transaction expertise, industry knowledge, and strategic insight, Broadview helps clients to capitalize on the forces of change and realize opportunities for maximizing shareholder value. Founded in 1973, Broadview last year completed 82 transactions with a total value of more than $5.5 billion. Broadview provides private equity investment services through Broadview Capital Partners, a late-stage private equity fund, as well as through an alliance with Kennet Capital. The firm also maintains a strategic partnership with AxcessNet, a financial services firm specializing in Israel's rapidly growing IT industry.

Broadview represents both buyer and seller clients ranging from large firms to smaller, specialized companies in the IT, communications, and media marketplaces. In many cases, companies seek a sustainable competitive advantage and look to boost shareholder value by adding technologies, products, operations, and access to markets. Frequently, their objectives can be satisfied by acquiring part or all of a smaller, niche player. Alternatively, seller clients that want to manage the passage between early growth stages and sustainable, superior equity value seek to leverage the resources of a larger, more established enterprise. Typically, companies wishing to sell have developed new technologies and products, gained unique market positions, or marshaled unique human resource capabilities that they cannot fully exploit alone. An appropriate partner for a seller client can telescope market-product development cycles, provide required capital, shrink the associated risks, and gain an innovative and focused management team.

The interaction of these corporate supply and demand forces has made the IT, communications, and media industries the most M&A-intensive in the world. Given the complexity and rapid change in these industries, finding the right strategic fit can be a difficult task. Broadview has more than 225 employees located in offices in New York (Fort Lee, NJ), Silicon Valley (Foster City, CA), Boston, London, and Tokyo. Opportunities for career growth and development exist throughout the firm.

Describe your ownership structure.

Broadview Int'l. LLC is structured as a limited liability corporation. The firm's nineteen managing directors are recognized as experts in the industries they serve and are leading spokespeople on matters related to strategic M&A.

How does your approach to finance differ from that of other firms, and what do you consider to be your strengths and distinctive capabilities?

Developed and honed through twenty-five years of service to the IT, communications, and media industries, Broadview's distinctive capabilities include

- *Transaction expertise.* Broadview brings formidable experience to the practice of strategic M&A in the IT, communications, and media industries. Among the ranks of senior management are founders of privately held IT companies as well as corporate officers of public companies. Most of our professional staff bring hands-on executive, operational, or engineer-level experience. Broadview staff integrate a clear understanding of the strategic business case, a firm grip on the technology issues, penetrating financial analysis, and highly effective negotiating skills into every transaction.

- People. Broadview actively fosters an environment in which its professionals can think and act *multidimensionally,* recognizing hidden interdependencies between industries and relationships between technologies. It is precisely this breadth and depth of industry insight and perspective, combined with vertical knowledge, that distinguishes Broadview's professionals as experts.

- *Industry knowledge.* The same comprehensive focus Broadview brings to every transaction is brought to gathering and interpreting information. Broadview's proprietary, in-depth stores of operational, financial, transaction, and valuation data on companies worldwide constitute an unparalleled information backbone. Tracking more than 10,000 mergers and acquisitions throughout North America, Europe, and Asia is one of the ways Broadview retains authoritative knowledge of trends and momentum within its core industries.

- *Relationships.* Broadview employs relationships with world-class IT, communications, and media companies, as well as access to leading sources of capital, to help its clients realize strategic growth opportunities in an increasingly competitive global market. Much of its success in providing superior strategic advisory services stems from the longevity and integrity of its relationships spanning three industries and the global investment community.

The Finance MBA's Job Description

Describe the career path and corresponding responsibilities for an MBA at your firm.

Associates are quickly given client management responsibility. The associate assists in the development of acquisition and divestiture strategies, identifies companies in relevant IT segments that represent potential partners, handles approaches to target companies, and ultimately helps to structure and negotiate deals between client and target companies. In managing the client relationship, the associate usually serves as part of a three-person team, joined by a managing director and an analyst. Each team member has unique responsibilities and interacts with other team members daily. The associate manages daily client contact and coordinates activities among team members.

Discuss the lifestyle aspects of a career with your firm (i.e., average hours per week, amount of travel, flexibility to change offices, corporate culture, etc.).

Broadview attracts and seeks dedicated, self-motivated professionals who can generate a superior quality of work without sacrificing their lifestyles. Travel is required, though the extent varies by specific assignment.

The Recruiting Process

Describe your recruiting process and the criteria by which you select candidates. Is prior experience necessary?

Broadview seeks individuals with excellent written and oral communication skills, transaction experience, and demonstrated interest or experience in the IT industry. The ideal candidate must also be a highly motivated self-starter and possess strong interpersonal skills.

If you have a formal summer program, please describe it.

A summer associate at Broadview will work with the firm's senior management team on one of a number of projects to advance Broadview's position in the market. Projects are likely to include

1. Analysis of opportunities in Asia for IT M&A
2. Research of emerging niche markets and companies in software, hardware, digital media, and/or wireless telecommunications services
3. Assessment of new management practices that can advance Broadview's franchise

What international opportunities does your firm offer for U.S. citizens? For foreign nationals?

Broadview's London office is staffed by U.S. citizens and foreign nationals from France, Germany, the United Kingdom, and other European countries. Candidates for the London office typically have foreign language fluency. Broadview's Tokyo office plays a key role in business development and affords new growth opportunities for the firm.

Chase H&Q

One Bush Street
San Francisco CA 94104
(800) 227-3958
Fax: (415) 439-3016
Web site: www.chasehq.com

Recruiting Contact(s):
Brandi Tamo, Recruiting Administrator

Location of Offices:
San Francisco, New York, Boston, Atlanta, and London

Total Number of Professionals (U.S. and worldwide):
1,083

Company Description

Describe your firm's business and the types of clients served by your finance group(s).

In September 1999, Chase Manhattan Corporation acquired Hambrecht & Quist Group. Hambrecht & Quist, whose revenue and income had increased fivefold in the previous five years, chose Chase as a partner to offer the right financial relationships for companies in the "New Economy"—from Venture Capital to IPO to mature company. H&Q's clients benefit from the availability of Chase's market-leading products. Chase's clients benefit from H&Q's award-winning equity research and its high-quality equity platform.

How does your approach to finance differ from that of other firms, and what do you consider to be your strengths and distinctive capabilities?

"Financing the New Economy" is a good way to describe what we do at Chase H&Q. The New Economy represents the largest and fastest-growing segments of the economy as a whole, and includes the following industry sector focus areas at Chase H&Q: eBusiness, eConsumer, Internet Media, Applied Technologies, Communications Technologies, Systems & Semiconductors, and Healthcare. These sectors account for approximately half of all economic growth and Chase H&Q plays a vital role in their development. We function as the intermediary between growth companies and growth investors, raising capital for and offering advice to entrepreneurs and the companies they create. To us, the "New Economy" isn't

new at all. We've been focused on growth companies and growth investors since the firm was founded in 1968.

Chase H&Q realizes that one of the most important assets in the financial services industry is the people. We believe opportunities for personal growth and the realization of professional and financial goals are maximized when the style and direction of a firm closely matches those of the individual. We invite you to get to know us and decide whether Chase H&Q offers the right career opportunity for you.

The Finance MBA's Job Description

Describe the career path and corresponding responsibilities for an MBA at your firm.

Investment Banking Associate. The professionals on our Corporate Finance teams are extremely well versed in the dynamics of the technology and healthcare industries and the sectors on which they focus. They're experts on the business of raising capital and will work on equity offerings for companies that need additional capital in addition to funding acquisitions in order to finance new strategies, or to give companies the funds they need for the next evolution of their growth. Associates will also underwrite convertible debt offerings when that particular structure makes sense in light of a company's position and current market conditions.

Research Associate. The research associate position allows an individual to work directly with a senior equity analyst in the analysis of a particular industry sector in one of the primary focus areas of Chase H&Q Research. The research associate will aid in the analyst's effort to bring timely, well-founded investment recommendations to our investor clients. Primary day-to-day tasks will involve financial modeling, writing company reports, data compilation and analysis, and client interaction. The Chase H&Q research associate will have access to company management teams, consultants, and other industry resources in their sectors.

The Recruiting Process

Describe your recruiting process and the criteria by which you select candidates. Is prior experience necessary?

Chase H&Q is committed to hiring individuals who combine a drive to excel with demonstrated integrity, intelligence, and strong leadership and interpersonal skills. The ideal candidate prefers to work in a fast-paced environment with a team-oriented approach.

In addition, we look for individuals with:

- Interest in emerging growth companies

- Prior investment banking experience or in-depth industry knowledge

- Demonstrated capabilities in financial and strategic business analysis

- Ability to manage multiple projects, priorities, and reporting relationships

We encourage you to evaluate your personal fit with each of the firms where you interview.

We are confident that Chase H&Q's exciting entrepreneurial environment is an exceptional setting in which to continue your business career.

How many permanent associates and analysts do you hire in a typical year? How many summer interns do you expect to hire? If you have a formal summer program, please describe it. Please be sure to indicate whether the summer program is in place for all offices or just some.

Chase H&Q expects to hire approximately twenty to twenty-five associates in Corporate Finance; six to eight associates in Research; and one or two associates in Sales & Trading.

Chase H&Q plans to have a limited summer associate program.

Chevron Corporation

575 Market Street
Suite 3438
San Francisco, CA 94105
(415) 894-2752
Web site: www.chevron.com

MBA Recruiting Contact(s):
Suzy Taherian, Manager
Finance MBA Development Program

Company Description

Describe your firm's business and the types of clients served by your finance group(s).

Chevron Corporation is an international, integrated petroleum company consistently ranked among the leaders of the Fortune 500. Approximately 34,000 employees generate $30 billion in annual revenues and are responsible for $36 billion in assets.

Headquartered in San Francisco, we are one of the largest producers of petroleum products and natural gas in the United States. Chevron has operations in over 90 countries and is pursuing worldwide ventures in petroleum exploration, production, refining, and marketing. Chevron is an industry leader that is positioned for international growth, building on a rich history of innovation and making the investments needed to provide the world with clean, safe, and economical energy.

In an age of accelerating globalization of the world's national economies, the petroleum industry was one of the first and remains one of the largest, truly global enterprises. The products of this industry drive the engine of our global economy, providing the energy to run our factories, fuel our transportation networks, and heat our homes. This industry vividly defines the risk/reward trade-off: not all multimillion-dollar wells drilled will result in commercially viable finds, and capital-intensive developments often require investments of billions of dollars over time horizons of 10–50 years.

The Finance MBA's Job Description

Describe the career path and corresponding responsibilities for an MBA at your firm.

We are always seeking highly motivated individuals to help us achieve our goals. Chevron recruits MBAs to bring bright, highly talented, and ambitious individuals with leadership and management potential into the finance function. Our goal is to develop senior financial management both at the corporate level and at any of our worldwide operating companies (predominantly headquartered in the Bay Area). Chevron purposefully provides top performers experience in many financial arenas in preparation for senior management positions.

In order to launch MBAs into this environment, Chevron maintains the Finance MBA Development Program, designed to give MBAs rapid exposure to the company and the finance function. This is a select, management track program that has been successfully developing financial and general managers for over 50 years. The program provides its members with four six-month assignments over a two-year period and is designed to give them broad exposure to financial and operating activities throughout the corporation. In addition, it provides MBAs with opportunities to apply the financial skills they acquired in business school to activities that contribute directly to the achievement of Chevron's business goals. These assignments are generally greater in responsibility than entry-level positions offered to graduating MBAs by other companies.

The assignments available to program members are located typically in organizations where financial skills are at a premium—corporate units such as the Comptroller's and Treasury Departments, plus finance, planning, and other functional positions at major operating companies such as Chevron Production, Chevron Products, Chevron Chemical, Chevron Shipping, and Chevron Overseas Petroleum. There is no preestablished sequence of assignments. Instead, a balanced program is tailored to fit each individual's evolving needs and preferences while meeting the company's changing business requirements.

Having rapidly acquired expertise in many of Chevron's business areas and an outstanding range of company contacts, program members are placed in challenging positions at the program's conclusion. Many MBAs return to a group in which they had program assignments, while others undertake positions in areas new to them. An individual's personal preferences are considered in conjunction with company needs. By virtue of the high caliber of the participants and the broad experience they have gained in the program, MBAs are in great demand and are well positioned to pursue careers leading to senior financial and, often, general managerial positions. For example, Chevron's CFO, Comptroller, and Treasurer as well as President-Chevron overseas, Vice President-Strategic Planning, and Vice President-Public Affairs are all program alumni.

The Recruiting Process

Describe your recruiting process and the criteria by which you select candidates. Is prior experience necessary?

Applicants must have permanent United States work authorization (does not include practical training authorization). Although Chevron does not restrict candidates to specific majors or levels of work experience, the Finance MBA Development Program is considered to be most attractive to MBAs with a strong interest in finance who welcome the opportunity to gain rapid exposure to a wide variety of financial activities at Chevron. On average, program members have three to five years of work experience before obtaining their MBA.

How many permanent associates and analysts do you hire in a typical year? How many summer interns do you expect to hire? If you have a formal summer program, please describe it. Please be sure to indicate whether the summer program is in place for all offices or just some.

We hire four to six MBAs into the Finance MBA Development Program each year.

The Finance MBA Development Program sponsors an ongoing summer internship program. Similar to full-time Development Program members, summer interns are challenged by hands-on, meaningful work that provides an opportunity to experience the issues and actions of one of the world's leading corporations. Interns are placed within corporate groups (e.g., Treasury, Comptroller's, or Planning) and operating companies (e.g., Chevron Products, Shipping, or Chemical).

Internships are typically project oriented, utilizing strong analytical, organizational, and communication skills. Application of financial theory to actual business problem solving is encouraged. All positions are in the San Francisco Bay Area. Exposure to the company and managers outside each intern's particular work group is enhanced by a series of communications meetings, organizational presentations, and other activities. Interns usually have the opportunity to present their accomplishments and conclusions to finance managers at the end of the summer.

In recruiting summer interns, we look for individuals with strong interpersonal and analytical skills, leadership potential, and knowledge of a broad range of financial theory, from financial accounting to capital markets. Prospective interns should have long-term interests in careers in financial management. Again, applicants must have permanent United States work authorization (does not include practical training authorization).

What international opportunities does your firm offer for U.S. citizens? For foreign nationals?

Although the domestic petroleum industry is often characterized as mature, Chevron continues to pursue growth opportunities around the globe. We are aggressively expanding our activities in Kazakhstan, Australia, West Africa, and Indonesia.

MBAs can almost immediately gain exposure to our international operations with Bay Area assignments working in the worldwide headquarters of our international subsidiaries. Some opportunities to work overseas are also available to program members. We historically have not hired foreign national MBAs into our Development Program.

Credit Suisse First Boston

Eleven Madison Avenue
New York, NY 10010
(212) 325-4444
Web Site: www.csfb.com

MBA Recruiting Contact(s):
Office of Global Recruiting:
Lori Todd, Assistant Vice President
Kelly Davis, Assistant Vice President

Investment Banking/Private Equity:
Jennifer Bruch, Vice President

Equity:
Sheila Cull, Vice President

Fixed Income:
Joanne Giardinelli, Assistant Vice President

Europe:
Sophie Walker, Assistant Vice President,
Investment Banking
Michelle DeSena, Equity/Fixed Income

Company Description

Describe your firm's business and the types of clients served by your finance groups.

Credit Suisse First Boston (CSFB) is one of the world's leading global investment banks, providing comprehensive financial advisory, capital raising, sales and trading, and financial products for wholesale users and suppliers of capital around the world. Headquartered in New York, with home markets in London, Hong Kong, and Sao Paulo, we operate over 60 offices across more than 30 countries and 6 continents with more than 14,500 employees. In 1999, CSFB's total revenues were approximately $6.7 billion and $7.7 billion in equity and $275 billion in assets.

Credit Suisse First Boston is organized around four major operating divisions:

• Investment Banking

• Fixed Income and Derivatives

• Equity

• Private Equity

Describe your ownership structure.

Credit Suisse First Boston is one of five business units of the Credit Suisse Group, one of the world's leading financial services groups. Credit Suisse Group also includes Swiss domestic banking, private banking, institutional asset management, and the Winterthur insurance businesses.

How does your approach to finance differ from that of other firms, and what do you consider to be your strengths and distinctive capabilities?

CSFB is positioned at the forefront of our industry, having successfully executed an aggressive strategic plan. Our recent accomplishments include: selective acquisitions of BZW in Europe and Asia, which solidified our franchise in those regions; the acquistion of Garantia, Brazil's leading investment bank, which has made us the preeminent firm in Latin America; the acquisition of First New Zealand and First Pacific which consolidated our efforts in Australia; the hiring of Frank Quattrone and his technology group, which has given us the number one technology franchise on Wall Street; the hiring of 33 healthcare professionals, which has created one of the largest healthcare practices in the industry; and the addition of 14 professionals in Germany—one of the world's largest economies.

In 1999, we reaped the benefits of these efforts. We were named the "Best Bank of the Last 25 Years" in July by the *International Financing Review,* in addition to our recognition as "The Best Bond House of the Last 25 Years". In describing CSFB, IFR called us, "arguably the original, multi-cultural, global investment bank. Focused on pure, wholesale investment banking, it existed only to solve the problems of, and raise capital for, corporations, governments and supranationals. Over the years, it has preserved a tremendous franchise through constantly reevaluating and rebuilding." IRF also said, "CSFB has the most balanced business mix (between the U.S. and Europe) of the bulge-bracket firms, employs roughly the same number of people on both sides of the Atlantic, and derives roughly the same amount of profit from each location." Moreover, we were ranked number four across the board in Global Mergers & Acquisitions, Global Equity, and Global Debt.

CSFB consistently manages large, complex global transactions that often reshape the competitive environments in which our clients operate. A prime example of this was the transformation of AT&T from its traditional base as a long-distance provider into a dynamic telecommunications company offering the full gamut of services through voice, data, wireless, and cable-television transmission. Credit Suisse First Boston has been advising AT&T since the company first embarked on this strategy. It began in 1998 with the $11.3 billion acquisition of Teleport Communications Group in which AT&T acquired direct connections to the biggest corporate customers in the Baby Bells' territories. Later that year, AT&T acquired Tele-Communications Inc. in a $70 billion transaction that boldly signaled a new direction: to transform the telecommunications industry through the convergence of telephony, video, and data transmission. The combination gave AT&T direct access to consumers' homes with the potential of reaching nearly one-third of all U.S. households. Then in 1999, in an authoritative follow-up, AT&T moved to acquire MediaOne, another leading cable provider, for $65.4 billion in a transaction that ranks as the largest successful unsolicited offer, with AT&T topping an offer for MediaOne from Comcast. In a separate but related transaction, AT&T and Microsoft have agreed to a partnership in which Microsoft will make a $5 billion equity investment in AT&T. *Investment Dealers' Digest* named the transaction as its M&A Deal of the Year, noting that it "signified the foresight, financial innovation, and complexity required in order to bring about industry transformation these days."

Other noteworthy transactions and accomplishments in 1999 were:

- DaimlerChrysler North America Holding Corporation's $4.5 billion inaugural global bond offering. This was the second largest corporate bond deal in the market and represented the largest lead-managed corporate bond deal in CSFB's history.

- Conoco's $4.0 billion global bond offering. The transaction was the largest energy bond ever executed, and became the benchmark for the energy sector and the market in general.

- Commerce One's IPO in June 1999, the best performing IPO worldwide.

- Freeserve PLC's IPO, which established Freeserve as the U.K.'s largest Internet service provider and a leading Internet portal. The offering was oversubscribed by a factor of over 30 times, as almost 1,000 institutional investors worldwide and 50,000 individuals in the U.K. applied for stock. The IPO of Freeserve achieved several milestones for the European equity market and for

CSFB: the largest ever IPO of an Internet portal; Euope's largest-ever Internet IPO; the first time the London Stock Exchange agreed to list a company without a three-year track record; and the first time that online registration has been used for retail applicants in a U.K. IPO. The Freeserve IPO is now regarded as the founding father of Internet issuance in Europe.

- Express Scripts' multiple transactions, evidencing the breadth of CSFB's resources, enabled the company to become the largest independent pharmacy benefit management company. We first assisted Express Scripts on a number of significant transactions related to its acquisition of Diversified Pharmaceutical Services. CSFB initiated the acquisition of Diversified Pharmaceutical Services from SmithKline Beecham for $700 million in cash and served as Express Scripts' financial advisor. To accomplish the acquisition, CSFB acted as lead arranger on a $1.05 billion senior secured credit facility and a $150 million senior subordinated bridge credit facility. CSFB also acted as Lead Manager for additional capital raising in the form of a $316 million common stock offering—one of the largest issues completed in the health-care services sector in 1999. CSFB also lead managed $250 million in senior notes, the demand for which enabled the offering to be increased from $200 million to $250 million. Finally, CSFB was advisor to the company on its sale of YourPharmacy.com and its strategic alliance with PlanetRX.com.

1999 also witnessed the continued rapid expansion of CSFB Private Equity. At year-end, Private Equity had combined committed capital of over $3.6 billion in its U.S. and International Funds, compared with $2.5 billion in 1998. Several significant transactions were closed, and nine investments in Private Equity's portfolios were sold at overall attractive rates of return.

No other firm offers the range of investment banking and lending products that CSFB offers with the same global reach. Added to this is CSFB's flair for innovative solutions, our focus on product quality, and our emphasis on the highest standards of client service.

The Finance MBA's Job Description

Describe the career path and corresponding responsibilities for an MBA at your firm.

At CSFB, there are no hard and fast rules for moving up; highly talented individuals can ascend to significant levels of responsibility at a rapid pace. In general, MBAs begin their careers as associates and assist in the execution of complex transactions early in their careers. Within approximately 3–4 years, an associate will typically demonstrate the analytical proficiency and leadership ability necessary to become a vice president. The path to director usually follows within two years. In order to be considered for the managing director level, an employee must demonstrate the following four key strengths:

1. A proven ability to manage a significant business area, contributing to the generation or development of revenues and/or helping to improve the running of our business
2. Being a role model of ethical and professional conduct; playing a meaningful role in improving the firm's governance and in the recruitment and development of strong talent
3. A recognized facility to develop and encourage others to high standards of achievement, consistently demonstrating strong leadership, team building efforts, and momentum toward a clear, common goal
4. Being a relationship leader—developing new clients or customers for the firm as well as providing a high level of customer service

Describe the opportunities for professional mobility between the various department in your firm.

CSFB is highly flexible environment that seeks to accommodate the needs of talented and capable employees. Internal mobility is supported within departments and where skill bases are applicable, movement across business areas occurs as well.

CSFB employees are highly creative, hardworking, and intelligent people who often seem to perform best in a competitive but collegial atmosphere. The culture at the firm is flexible and encourages motivated individuals to take on increasing responsibility and leadership roles. Hours depend on the type of business in which you are involved. Sales and Trading positions usually require approximately 60 hours per week; investment banking requires significantly more time. Travel is highly dependent on client base.

The Recruiting Process

Describe your recruiting process and the criteria by which you select candidates. Is prior experience necessary?

Credit Suisse First Boston actively recruits at various U.S. and international graduate schools for both full-time and summer employment. Please see your career services office to see if we recruit at your school. All students should mail/e-mail their résumé and cover letter to the appropriate recruiting manger (see above), indicating the program they are interested in. Typically, associates participate in three rounds of interviews (on-campus, and two in-office rounds) before an offer is made. Candidates should be highly motivated individuals who have demonstrated academic achievement and are particularly adept quantitatively. They should possess a proven record of leadership and a willingness to participate in team and goal oriented tasks. Prior experience is not mandatory, but often distinguishes a candidate.

How many permanent associates and analysts do you hire in a typical year? How many summer interns do you expect to hire? If you have a formal summer program, please describe it. Please be sure to indicate whether the summer program is in place for all offices or just some.

In 2000, CSFB will hire approximately 200 undergraduates world-wide, approximately 70 associates world-wide and 85 summer associates world-wide.

Summer Associates

Students entering their final year of business or law school may join our ten-to-twelve week Summer Associate Program. The program is structured to allow students to get a very real picture of life as a full-time associate at CSFB. We see this program as a primary source of hiring for full-time associate positions. Summer associates are exposed to all aspects of our business through weekly seminars delivered by senior management.

In the Investment Banking Division (IBD), summer associates are members of various client and transaction teams and their responsibilities include preparing and analyzing financial models of various companies; examining the impact of a transaction on both a client's capital structure and financial results; initiating acquisition ideas for a client; and participating in due diligence sessions and client presentations. Most of the IBD summer associate positions are located in our New York and London offices, but there are opportunities in other U.S. offices as well.

The Sales and Trading Summer Associate Program is ten weeks in duration. Summer associates may choose to rotate within both Equities and Fixed Income or to rotate solely within one division. This program takes place in our New York and London offices. In Sales and Trading, the summer associate gains direct exposure to a wide variety of products and markets, delivers presentations to senior management, and completes product-specific projects. Most importantly, she or he gains knowledge unparalleled to that of the classroom while developing marketing and communication skills. The Sales and Trading summer associate leaves the program with a comprehensive understanding of both CSFB and our Sales and Trading team.

The Equity Research Summer Associate Program is twelve weeks in duration. The summer associate is assigned to work directly with one analyst on a particular project that is global in nature and that is designed to enhance the integration of the individual analysts of a sector team. This program takes place in the New York office. The summer associates will acquire financial analysis skills and gain direct exposure to CSFB valuation techniques, including EVA. The Equity Research summer associate will leave the program with a solid understanding of the culture of CSFB and of the responsibilities of an equity research analyst.

What international opportunities does your firm offer for U.S. citizens? For foreign nationals?

Employment opportunities are available to U.S. citizens abroad, and foreign nationals here in the United States, provided that the candidate is able to obtain the proper employment visa.

Credit Suisse First Boston has a wide variety of career opportunities for MBAs. During the 1999–2000 recruiting season, CSFB interviewed MBA students for positions in the following areas: Investment Banking, Private Equity, Equity Research, Equity Sales and Trading, Fixed Income Sales and Trading, Asset Finance, and High Yield Research. Listed below are job descriptions for two major areas in our recruiting efforts:

Associate: Sales and Trading
Analyst: Equity Research

The Positions

The firm is seeking to hire new Sales and Trading associates to work in the Americas and Europe. New associates are hired into specific product groups in either Fixed Income or Equity Sales and Trading.

The firm's Equity Research Analyst position is a tremendous opportunity to join a respected team of research analysts covering U.S., European, Latin American, and Asian stocks. Our research is noted for its creative and value-added focus, and we are industry leaders in our valuation techniques.

What We Look For

Credit Suisse First Boston is noted for the diversity of its employees, but seeks candidates with a common set of abilities—highly motivated individuals who have demonstrated academic achievement, including finance and accounting courses, and strength in verbal and written communication.

The dynamic, information-intensive environment of the trading floor requires candidates who are able to create and master new concepts quickly, who possess a high degree of creativity and strong interpersonal skills, can lead and work on a team, and are geographically mobile. Foreign language fluency is required for European offices, and computer literacy is essential to all that we do.

The Equity Research Analyst position requires candidates who are self-directed and entrepreneurial; independent, creative thinkers who can identify patterns and trends within complex data; and the ability to operate under time pressure. Foreign language fluency is required for European offices.

What You Can Expect

As a first-year sales and trading associate, you will participate in twelve weeks of intensive classroom training in New York. The training program includes: an orientation to the firm; an overview of global debt and equity markets and instruments; an introduction to the sales and trading groups; trading simulations; and training in computer systems and applications.

Working in a fast-moving, team-oriented environment, you will be expected to react to changing market conditions, elicit Credit Suisse First Boston research opinions, formulate a trade strategy, communicate with accounts, and execute trades. As your career progresses, you will be encouraged to continue developing your professional and technical skills to meet the challenges of evolving global financial markets.

Incoming graduates joining Equity Research can expect a stimulating work environment that allows for rapid individual development and professional growth. You will be introduced to the equity research arena and will be assigned to a team within a specific industry sector. You will become familiar with earnings modeling and forecasting, sector trends and issues, and investigate research and business writing. You will interact with senior management from top companies, partner with the industry's top research analysts, and service the top institutional investors. Within two years, associates can expect to assume research coverage of several companies within their assigned sector team.

Associate: Investment Banking

The Position

Associates work as important members of various client and transaction teams. Career opportunities for Investment Banking associates may include product specialization in mergers and acquisitions, leveraged finance, private finance, or project finance. Alternatively, associates may specialize in industry sectors such as media, telecommunications, natural resources, retail, consumer products, health care, technology, or financial institutions. Associates may work in New York, one of our U.S. regional offices, London, or one of our European offices.

What We Look For

Associate candidates typically have earned graduate degrees in business or law, or have significant relevant prior experience. Credit Suisse First Boston is noted for the diversity of its employees, but the firm does look for certain characteristics in all of its candidates—highly motivated individuals who have demonstrated academic achievement, quantitative skills, and strength in verbal and written communication. Computer literacy is essential to all that we do. In addition, we seek individuals with a proven record of leadership, strong interpersonal skills, a willingness to participate in team—and goal—oriented tasks, and a fundamental grasp of the principles of finance.

What You Can Expect

All associates go through a month-long formal training program, which provides them with overviews of CSFB's businesses, as well as the tools they need to succeed. Once they start in their groups, associates immediately become active bankers while working on all aspects of advising and transacting business for clients. Associate responsibilities broadly includes preparing and analyzing financial models of various companies; examining the impact of a transaction on a client's capital structure and financial results; initiating acquisition ideas for a client; and participating in due diligence sessions and client presentations.

Successful associates possess strong interpersonal skills and a keen ability to solve problems. They are able to balance a multitude of tasks and they demonstrate a high level of dedication.

Dain Rauscher Wessels

A Division of Dain Rauscher Corporation

60 South Sixth Street
Minneapolis, MN 55402
(612) 371-2711
Fax: (612) 371-2763
Web site: www.dainrauscher.com

MBA Recruiting Contact(s):
Lisa Brezonik, Human Resources Manager
E-mail: jobs@dainrauscher.com

Company Description

Describe your firm's business and the types of clients served by your finance group(s).

Dain Rauscher Wessels is the equity capital markets division of Dain Rauscher Corporation, a full-service investment banking firm founded in 1909 and headquartered in Minneapolis, Minnesota. Dain Rauscher Wessels was created through the combination of Dain Rauscher and Wessels, Arnold & Henderson in March 1998. The two firms led or co-managed a combined total of 316 corporate finance transactions valued at over $21.5 billion from 1995 through 1997.

Dain Rauscher Wessels is comprised of Corporate Finance, Equity Research, Equity Trading, and Institutional Sales. Each of these departments maintains a presence throughout the country. Corporate Finance, comprised of bankers located in Minneapolis, Palo Alto, Seattle, Dallas, and Houston, provides a full range of investment banking services including public offerings, merger and acquisition advisory, and private capital and principal transactions in the industries we serve. The firm's equity analysts and research associates, located in Minneapolis, Palo Alto, Seattle, Dallas, and Houston, follow more than 200 high-growth public companies. Equity traders in Minneapolis, New York, Seattle, Dallas, and Boston make a market in the stocks followed by the firm's research analysts. The institutional sales staff is comprised of equity investment executives in Minneapolis, Dallas, and Boston and maintains and develops long-term established relationships with mutual funds, pension funds, insurance companies, and other institutional investment groups in the United States and Europe. In addition, Dain

Rauscher Wessels has a highly respected retail division known as the Private Client Group, which is comprised of over 1,270 investment executives and provides retail distribution and brokerage services throughout the United States.

Describe your ownership structure.

Dain Rauscher Wessels is a division of Dain Rauscher Corporation (NYSE ticker "DRC"). DRC is the 10th-largest securities firm in the United States. Approximately one-third of DRC's 12 million outstanding shares are held by its employees, assuring a commitment to superior client service and shareholder value.

How does your approach to finance differ from that of other firms, and what do you consider to be your strengths and distinctive capabilities?

The firm's mission is to attract high-quality, motivated people committed to excellence, apply our expertise to enhance our customers' success, and align our interests with the interests of our clients. Dain Rauscher Wessels is committed to growth companies in select industry sectors: consumer, energy, financial services, healthcare, and technology. Dain Rauscher Wessels adds value to its clients through industry expertise, beginning with research and encompassing sales, trading, and corporate finance. Our clients include the vast majority of institutional buyers of growth stocks in the United States and Europe. The firm's investment banking corporate finance efforts emphasize relationships with leading growth companies and their financial backers, including many prominent venture capitalists. Lastly, we manage our business for the long term. Each of our departments is an equal contributor to our success, reinforced by a single compensation plan that keeps all professionals focused on the same objectives. We believe that this integrated structure keeps the interests of our customers and ourselves in concert.

Discuss changes in your firm's revenues (both domestic and international) and professional staff over the past year; over the past five years.

For the year ended December 31, 1997, Dain Rauscher Corporation's revenues were $750 million, up 10% from 1996. Revenues from equity capital markets for 1997 were $97 million. These amounts do not include revenues from Wessels, Arnold & Henderson. Over the past five years, Dain Rauscher has shown strong positive trends in revenues, with a compounded growth rate of 12%.

The Finance MBA's Job Description

Describe the career path and corresponding responsibilities for an MBA at your firm.

Associates can expect to be involved in a variety of transactions, including public offerings, merger and acquisition advisory, and private and principal transactions in the industries we serve. Since project teams at Dain Rauscher Wessels are typically quite small, associates are given significant responsibilities, often working directly with the senior management of our clients. With this foundation of experience, associates eventually join industry-specific or functional groups and take on incremental client management responsibilities.

Discuss lifestyle aspects of a career with your firm (i.e., average hours per week, amount of travel, flexibility to change offices, corporate culture, etc.).

Dain Rauscher Wessels' employees are an entrepreneurial group of experienced Wall Street professionals who promote excellence, reward high performance, and share a common vision to be the premier investment bank for the industries served. The firm provides a true meritocracy where reward is based on performance with no predetermined time requirements for advancement. An immediate opportunity to learn is provided through lean deal teams, while the chance to work with senior bankers is the norm rather than the exception.

A career with Dain Rauscher Wessels provides for many exciting opportunities that require dedication and a strong commitment. Travel is typically frequent and the number of work hours per week varies depending on the individual and the work load encountered. A quality life outside the firm is highly encouraged and is influenced by the tremendous cultural and outdoor recreational activities available in the Twin Cities and other cities where the firm is located.

The Recruiting Process

Describe your recruiting process and the criteria by which you select candidates. Is prior experience necessary?

Dain Rauscher Wessels recruits MBAs from the top business schools in the nation for positions within its Corporate Finance, Research, Institutional Equity Sales, Equity Trading, and Public Finance business segments. Dain Rauscher Wessels participates in on-campus recruiting and attends finance club fairs and other recruiting functions at select schools. Final hiring decisions are made after a series of interviews with persons representing a variety of our industry and functional groups. Dain Rauscher Wessels seeks candidates with a proven record of success, both work-related and academic, and a strong desire to be a part of our continuing effort to be the premier investment bank in the industries that we serve. The firm's entrepreneurial environment requires individuals who are self-motivated and demonstrate the ability to take initiative and proceed independently. In addition, personal integrity, leadership qualities, strong verbal and written communication skills, and the ability to be a team player in a fast-paced and challenging environment are also essential. Although prior investment banking experience may be considered favorably, it is not a requirement for potential hires.

How many permanent associates and analysts do you hire in a typical year? How many summer interns do you expect to hire? If you have a formal summer program, please describe it. Please be sure to indicate whether the summer program is in place for all offices or just some.

Dain Rauscher Wessels typically hires recruits based on the needs of each department. Accordingly, the number of new hires in any given year may fluctuate. The firm does maintain a formal summer associate program and qualified MBA students who have completed their first year may be considered for a summer internship. Summer internships are designed to mirror the experience of a full-time associate.

What international opportunities does your firm offer for U.S. citizens? For foreign nationals?

All of Dain Rauscher Wessels' offices are located in the United States. While there are opportunities to work with international clients, these opportunities are limited. Foreign nationals having proper authority to work in the United States are encouraged to apply.

D.H. Blair Investment Banking Corp.

44 Wall Street
New York, NY 10005
(212) 495-4000
Web site: www.dhblair.com

MBA Recruiting Contact(s):
J. Morton Davis, Chairman
(212) 495-5000

Company Description

Describe your firm's business and the types of clients served by your finance group(s).

D.H. Blair is an independent investment bank based in New York City. The firm has a capital base of over $150 million. Blair specializes in financings of small- and medium-size growth companies, as well as early-stage venture financings. Established in 1904, D.H. Blair has a strong and growing track record of providing financing for these types of companies. Equity financings include initial public offerings, private placements, venture capital, merchant banking, and mergers and acquisitions. Leveraged buyout (LBO) debt financings are growing in number and size at Blair. As a result of our long-standing relationships built up over many years with these companies, Blair has the opportunity to provide many investment banking services to its clients.

Describe your ownership structure.

D.H. Blair is an independent, privately held investment bank.

How does your approach to finance differ from that of other firms, and what do you consider to be your strengths and distinctive capabilities?

D.H. Blair is a focused, well-capitalized investment bank. It does not attempt to provide services outside its specific niche. The firm provides private and public equity and debt financing for small- and medium-size emerging-growth and high-technology companies. D.H. Blair has purposely remained an agile, niche organization with a strong capital base and retail client base. This gives us the flexibility and strength to act very quickly on finding and funding significant investment opportunities. Due to the numerous client and portfolio companies served over many years, D.H. Blair has developed relationships with several of the largest industrial and service companies in the United States as well as overseas. These relationships have led to many acquisitions, joint ventures, and other forms of investment in these D.H. Blair companies.

Discuss changes in your firm's revenues (both domestic and international) and professional staff over the past year; over the past five years.

D.H. Blair is located in New York City. The Investment Banking Group includes approximately 25 individuals. The firm has grown rapidly over the past decade and is committed to maintaining this growth. Because D.H. Blair is an entrepreneurial firm serving this nation's entrepreneurs, the current national trend toward increased levels of this activity provides even greater demands for our services.

The Finance MBA's Job Description

Describe the career path and corresponding responsibilities for an MBA at your firm.

The Corporate Finance Department of D.H. Blair considers highly motivated and aggressive MBAs who have a great deal of initiative and desire to work in various areas of investment banking. Public and private placements of equity and debt securities, as well as merchant banking, venture capital, and LBOs, are areas of opportunity at D.H. Blair. Due to the firm's entrepreneurial flair and structure, there is a great deal of opportunity for the aggressive individual to assume primary responsibility at an early stage. Thinly staffed teams allow us to recruit people looking to take on responsibility quickly. The investment banker should be able to handle all aspects of a deal, as opposed to being a transaction specialist. The banker should be able to understand all areas of a client's business, including knowledge of product, market, financial, and other nonfinancial analyses. The banker should be able to assist in management presentation, negotiation, and sales. Also, the investment banker will be responsible for solicitation of new business opportunities. The speed at which the banker will grow in importance at the firm will depend on the banker's ability to assume responsibility and develop business opportunities.

Describe the opportunities for professional mobility between the various departments in your firm.

Career paths vary greatly depending on an individual's abilities and goals. There is not the rigid structure found in larger investment banks. D.H. Blair encourages individuals to experiment in new areas in order to seek out the best opportunities and further their career goals. Due to the thin staffing structure, there is plenty of opportunity for the banker to be observed by and interact with the staff in order to determine which areas are the most appropriate for career growth.

Discuss the lifestyle aspects of a career with your firm (i.e., average hours per week, amount of travel, flexibility to change offices, corporate culture, etc.).

A career at D.H. Blair is challenging and requires dedication, hard work, and flexibility. Lifestyles vary depending on the individual's own goals as well as those of the group in which the banker works.

The Recruiting Process

Describe your recruiting process and the criteria by which you select candidates. Is prior experience necessary?

We seek people with a history of achievement and success. These candidates show a great deal of initiative and aggressiveness, as well as the requisite analytical skills and strong interpersonal skills. Many successful candidates have had previous work experience, although it is not required. Although grades are a meaningful criterion, each candidate is considered as a combination of many abilities, and no single one is dominant.

How many permanent associates and analysts do you hire in a typical year? How many summer interns do you expect to hire? If you have a formal summer program, please describe it. Please be sure to indicate whether the summer program is in place for all offices or just some.

D.H. Blair hires between two and four associates each year. Although D.H. Blair offers no formal training, there is very thorough on-the-job training.

D.H. Blair has no formal summer program. We hire summer associates, depending on availability and need, in investment banking and brokerage.

Donaldson, Lufkin & Jenrette

277 Park Avenue
New York, NY 10172
(212) 892-3000
Web site: www.dlj.com

MBA Recruiting Contact(s):
Investment Banking:
Elizabeth Derby, Senior Vice President
(212) 892-7217
Investment Services Group, Fixed Income and Equities:
Gladys Chen, Vice President
(212) 892-3904
Fax: (212) 892-2265

Company Description

Describe your firm's business and the types of clients served by your finance group(s).

Donaldson, Lufkin & Jenrette (DLJ) is a top-ranked, full service investment and merchant bank. Founded in 1959 by three entrepreneurial Harvard MBAs as a research boutique specializing in institutional equity analysis, DLJ has developed premier franchises in research, sales, trading, and underwriting of equity and fixed income securities. These franchises extend to all major sectors of the capital markets and complement the firm's expertise in merchant banking, high yield financings, initial public offerings, and mergers and acquisitions. Furthermore, DLJ has expanded its international presence, particularly in Europe, Latin America, and Asia.

DLJ has successfully grown its businesses by focusing on transactions in which the quality of ideas and execution skills can make a difference in our clients' performance. DLJ has focused on high-margin businesses. DLJ serves a wide variety of domestic and international clients, ranging from small start-ups to Fortune 500 companies.

Describe your ownership structure.

In 1985, DLJ was acquired by The Equitable Life Assurance Society of the United States. In turn, the AXA Group, one of France's largest insurance concerns, owns 60% of The Equitable. The Equitable's current ownership interest is approximately 71%.

How does your approach to finance differ from that of other firms, and what do you consider to be your strengths and distinctive capabilities?

DLJ's approach to capital raising, merchant banking, and venture capital investing has yielded superior results for our clients and portfolio companies. We believe that no transaction is easy or routine; each requires the personal attention and commitment of senior professionals. DLJ encourages teamwork to leverage the diverse talents of our various departments. DLJ values close client relationships, innovative solutions, and high quality transactions, and utilizes the intelligent employment of capital, our distinctive research strength, and strong institutional distribution capabilities.

Discuss changes in your firm's revenues (both domestic and international) and professional staff over the past year; over the past five years.

Total revenues climbed 32% in 1999 to a record $5.6 billion, compared to $3.9 billion in 1998, and $2.0 billion in 1995. As of January 2000, DLJ employed approximately 10,200 people worldwide, up from 8,500 last year. DLJ maintains offices in 13 cities in the United States and 16 cities in Europe, Latin America, and Asia. The firm's growth has contributed directly to high profitability per professional and has created many opportunities for new MBAs joining the firm.

The Finance MBA's Job Description

Describe the career path and corresponding responsibilities for an MBA at your firm.

Investment Banking

Each associate's career path is largely a function of his/her unique strengths and talents. Compensation and advancement are based solely on merit and achievement.

Immediate Responsibility and Breadth and Depth of Coverage. Associates assume immediate responsibility, working with DLJ's senior professionals and our clients' senior management. DLJ is committed to providing exposure to a wide range of transactions in a very CEO-intensive, value-added and dynamic work environment. An associate may work on four or five assignments simultaneously. By the end of the first year, associates are expected to assume a high degree of responsibility for both project management and client maintenance. Due to the full service orientation and broad industry/product coverage of all our offices, associates work on all phases of a transaction and receive the breadth and depth that is critical for career development.

Direct Input and Flexibility Regarding Career Path. Another differentiating factor is the level of input each DLJ associate has in determining his or her own career. DLJ has a flexible program whereby an associate can begin his or her career in any one of our hiring offices, including: Boston, Chicago, Dallas, Hong Kong, Houston, London, Los Angeles, Menlo Park, Mexico City, New York, San Francisco, São Paulo, Seoul, and Taipei. Furthermore, one can become a generalist or specialist from the start. In New York there are opportunities to specialize in one of several product/industry groups, including: Chemicals, Consolidating Industries, Debt Capital Markets, Diversified Large Cap, Energy and Power, Equity Capital Markets, FIG, M&A, Metals and Mining, Private Placements, Real Estate Capital Partners, Real Estate and Home Building, Satellites, and Transportation. Other regional offices afford a specialty focus as well (Houston—Energy and Power; and Menlo Park—Technology).

Institutional Equity Research

The entry-level associate (MBA) is given immediate responsibility for coverage of a mutually agreed upon industry. The position entails development of specialized analytical skills, frequent interviews with senior corporate managers, company visits, secondary research, and ultimately, intensive interpersonal marketing. A group of senior analysts will be fully accessible to, and will assist in the development of, the new analyst. Ultimately it is the individual's responsibility to build a franchise of authority and expertise within the investment community through his or her written product and client interaction.

Institutional Equity Sales

Sales professionals are responsible for transmitting research recommendations produced by analysts and banking products generated by the Investment Banking Division to analysts and portfolio managers at institutional firms. Sales associates will spend the first six months in an Equities Division training program that incorporates rotation on various desks, meetings with research analysts, a research department project, and weekly meetings with senior sales professionals. Following training, a new associate takes on direct account responsibility.

Investment Services Group (ISG)

ISG professionals provide high-net-worth individuals, family groups, and smaller institutional accounts access to the very same array of products and services as DLJ's largest and most sophisticated institutional clients. Upon joining the firm, each class of new Associates will participate in a four and one-half month comprehensive and demanding training program that will focus on product knowledge, selling skills, and business building techniques. ISG professionals become expert in a comprehensive range of investments, including domestic and international equity and fixed income securities, derivatives, restricted stock, and direct private investments. Typically working individually or in a team, ISG representatives have expertise in advising our private clients on the optimal asset allocation designed to protect and grow their wealth.

Fixed Income

The Fixed Income Division recruits MBAs for its sales, trading, and research areas. In the sales and trading area, new MBAs are assigned to work closely with experienced professionals for the first six months to obtain product knowledge. They then assume responsibility for smaller accounts in order to build their own book. In research, new MBAs work directly with senior professionals in a specific product group (high yield, quantitative research, investment grade, or real estate). DLJ has the most respected fixed income research on Wall Street and has earned more first-place citations than any other Wall Street firm in *Institutional Investor* magazine's annual "All-America Fixed-Income Research Team" survey.

Describe the opportunities for professional mobility between the various departments in your firm.

DLJ hires associates directly into the various departments described above. There is no pre-planned mobility among departments, but if interest is expressed and the individual has demonstrated competence, there is some opportunity to move to a different area of specialization. In Investment Banking, associates are able to move between and among specialty groups and offices. There is an active Associate Development Program that provides career guidance and a mechanism for mobility. Recently, several Investment Banking associates have had the opportunity to work in our London and Hong Kong offices. DLJ believes that its most valuable assets are its people and wants its professionals to be happy. As a result, DLJ has a very high retention rate.

Discuss the lifestyle aspects of a career with your firm (i.e., average hours per week, amount of travel, flexibility to change offices, corporate culture, etc.).

The lifestyle aspects of a career with DLJ vary from department to department. Nevertheless, some career choices place large demands on an individual's time and require much travel. The amount of work is comparable to that at other major investment banks; however, the level of responsibility is greater.

DLJ's culture is collegial, teamwork-oriented, meritocratic, non-bureaucratic and non-hierarchical, open-doored, flexible, intellectually stimulating, supportive, opportunistic and refreshing. DLJ's corporate culture emphasizes excellence, informality, team work, and initiative. Growth is a key aspect of DLJ's culture, and senior management actively and opportunistically manages our growth. Growth creates opportunities to identify new markets and help build new businesses.

Furthermore, we want our associates to take pride in personal and corporate accomplishments, assuming responsibility early without losing sight of our traditional final corporate objective: to have fun!

The Recruiting Process

Describe your recruiting process and the criteria by which you select candidates. Is prior experience necessary?

Students should visit our Career Opportunities Web site at www.dlj.com and must submit a résumé to the appropriate contact.

New MBAs are hired into Investment Banking, Investment Services Group (ISG), Equity or Fixed Income Research, and Equity or Fixed Income Sales and Trading.

DLJ has no predetermined formula for selecting candidates. Prior experience in finance, while helpful, is not required. More importantly, we look for individuals with demonstrated intelligence, initiative, excellence, and creativity.

How many permanent associates and analysts do you hire in a typical year? How many summer interns do you expect to hire? If you have a formal summer program, please describe it. Please be sure to indicate whether the summer program is in place for all offices or just some.

DLJ anticipates hiring 110 Class of 2000 associates worldwide for our Equities, Fixed Income, Investment Banking, and Investment Services Groups. In addition, we expect to hire approximately 175 analysts.

DLJ anticipates hiring 100 Class of 2001 summer associates worldwide and 60 summer analysts. Investment

Banking, Investment Services Group (private client services), and Fixed Income have formal summer associate programs. DLJ considers its summer associates integral and active members of its professional team and provides each with an experience that is truly reflective of full-time employment. We maintain a relatively small summer program to ensure the best possible experience and believe in hiring summer associates whom we envision having as full-time professionals.

Investment Banking expects to hire 50 class of 2001 summer associates worldwide with opportunities in Chicago, London, Los Angeles, Menlo Park, New York, and San Francisco. While the majority of summer associates are generalists, DLJ offers direct specialty group positions in New York in Debt Capital Markets, Equity Capital Markets, Energy and Power, Financial Institutions, Mergers and Acquisitions, Private Funds, Private Placements, Real Estate, Real Estate Capital Partners, and Structured Products. ISG anticipates hiring 35 summer associates in various regional offices and Fixed Income expects to hire 15 summer associates for the New York office.

What international opportunities does your firm offer for U.S. citizens? For foreign nationals?

DLJ has taken important steps since 1995 to build its presence in select international markets and has targeted Asia, Europe, and Latin America. As a result, there are growing international opportunities at DLJ. Please visit DLJ's Career Opportunities Web site for updated information regarding international positions.

In Investment Banking, we have opportunities for associates in Buenos Aires, Hong Kong, London, Mexico City, Seoul, and Taipei. For European positions, we prefer that candidates be EU work authorized. For Asian and Latin American opportunities, we are open to U.S. citizens and foreign nationals with appropriate language fluency.

Our Equities and Fixed Income Departments have leading international franchises in Geneva, Hong Kong, London, Lugano, Paris, and Tokyo. In 1997, DLJ acquired London Global Securities, a firm specializing in securities lending. This purchase strengthened the European presence of Pershing, the leading clearing firm in the United Kingdom.

DLJ established a London base for its first overseas private client services office, catering to the investment needs of high-net-worth individuals.

Ewing Monroe Bemiss & Co.

Riverfront Plaza, West Tower
901 East Byrd Street, Suite 1650
Richmond, VA 23219
(804) 780-1900
Fax: (804) 780-1901

MBA Recruiting Contact(s):
Susan D. Livingston
(804) 780-1916

Location of Offices:
Richmond, VA

Total Number of Professionals (U.S. and worldwide):
17

Company Description

Describe your firm's business and the types of clients served by your finance group(s).

Ewing Monroe Bemiss & Co. is a private investment banking firm specializing in mergers and acquisitions and raising private capital. EMB&Co. serves the corporate middle market in transactions ranging in size from $10 to $300 million. EMB&Co.'s clients include Fortune 100 corporations, mid-sized public and private companies, and private equity firms across the U.S.

Describe your ownership structure.

EMB&Co. is a private corporation owned by its managing directors.

How does your approach to finance differ from that of other firms, and what do you consider to be your strengths and distinctive capabilities?

EMB&Co. is one of the largest privately owned firms in its regional area dedicated solely to producing excellent results for its clients through a broad array of merger and acquisition services. Its clients receive a relationship-focused level of expertise, advice, and service that only a privately owned firm can offer. The firm will invest side-by-side with its clients, and it offers each associate the opportunity to participate. Every EMB&Co. professional has a feeling of ownership in the company, and every associate is expected to become a partner. Each of the com-

pany's five principals has approximately 15 years of merger and acquisition experience, working with private and public companies ranging from start-ups to Fortune 100 corporations to private equity firms. While EMB&Co. takes a generalist approach, it is naturally developing certain industry concentrations. The firm assigns at least four professionals to every assignment and prides itself on its ability to work in a team fashion, internally and with the client. Our distinctive capabilities are maturity, breadth of advice, and excellence in execution with a relationship-based, long-term focus.

Discuss changes in your firm's revenues (both domestic and international) and professional staff over the past year; over the past five years.

EMB&Co. has experienced rapid growth in revenues and profitability. Since its founding in 1993, the firm has grown from two to five partners and from four to seventeen total professionals.

The Finance MBA's Job Description

Describe the career path and corresponding responsibilities for an MBA at your firm.

Associates at EMB&Co. manage projects related to mergers and acquisitions, private placements, and other financial advisory assignments. Responsibilities include writing confidential memoranda, creating marketing presentations, structuring and modeling financial projections, overseeing analysts on financial analysis or industry research, contacting potential buyers or investors, assisting potential buyers or investors with the due diligence process, and developing a new market territory.

Because of the company's size, an EMB&Co. associate has the opportunity to quickly assume as much responsibility as he or she can handle and to have a noticeable impact. An associate joining EMB&Co. is assigned immediately to transactions in progress and has a high degree of contact with the firm's partners.

EMB&Co. has a flexible reporting structure. Most project teams consist of one partner, one vice president, one associate, and one analyst. Again, EMB&Co. expects every associate to become a partner, and the typical career path for successful individuals is advancement from associate to vice president to director to partner within five to seven years. EMB&Co. is interested in aggressive associates who are willing to make a long-term commitment to the firm and the merger and acquisition business and who have a relationship, entrepreneurial, and merchant banking mentality.

Describe the opportunities for professional mobility between the various departments in your firm.

Associates have the opportunity to work on a variety of transactions, including sell- and buy-side assignments and acquisition and equity financing, for a wide range of clients. EMB&Co. rotates members of project teams to enable each professional to work on different types of transactions in various industries. Consequently, its professionals become generalists with expertise in managing any investment banking assignment. Associates receive a market-rate bonus, a contribution to a profit sharing plan, and other benefits. In addition, they may participate in certain private equity investments well before becoming a partner.

Discuss the lifestyle aspects of a career with your firm (i.e., average hours per week, amount of travel, flexibility to change offices, corporate culture, etc.)

EMB&Co. requires a serious level of commitment and a degree of sacrifice from every professional, while recognizing the importance of each associate's life outside the firm and encouraging community service. The firm's principals are dedicated to their families and expect this from associates. Associates work long hours and travel on a regular basis regionally and nationally on active assignments. Each associate is assigned a business development territory.

The Recruiting Process

Describe your recruiting process and the criteria by which you select candidates. Is prior experience necessary?

EMB&Co. seeks professionals with a significant talent for and a long-term interest in investment banking, who would like to live in the Southeast. Prior investment banking experience is helpful but not required. The firm is building a team of professionals who are quite successful and who enjoy the business and each other's company.

How many permanent associates and analysts do you hire in a typical year? How many summer interns do you expect to hire? If you have a formal summer program, please describe it.

EMB&Co. plans to double the size of the firm in the next five years. We anticipate hiring two to four associates and four analysts in the coming year. The firm does not have a formal summer program.

What international opportunities does your firm offer for U.S. citizens? For foreign nationals?

EMB&Co. has a national practice with clients throughout the U.S. We contact international buyers, sellers, and private equity firms regularly, and certain projects occasionally take us outside the U.S. The firm's team includes two foreign nationals.

First Union Securities, Inc.

101 South Tryon Street, 40th Floor
Charlotte, NC 28280
(704) 348-1000
Fax: (704) 348-1099

MBA Recruiting Contact(s):
Claudius E. "Bud" Watts IV
(704) 348-1051
Todd R. Newnam
(704) 348-1128

Company Description

Describe your firm's business and the types of clients served by your finance group(s).

First Union Securities, Inc., is a leading provider of full service investment banking services to growing companies. We have created a leadership position in this market by providing superior advice and capital solutions to our clients. First Union Securities, Inc. is the key strategic platform driving the growth of First Union Corporation, the nation's sixth largest bank holding company.

We offer the full range of investment banking products and services, including M&A advisory, public and private equity, high yield and investment grade debt, loan syndications, and structured finance to our expansive corporate and private equity group client base. At First Union Securities, Inc., our products and capabilities are designed and orchestrated as part of financing strategies intended to optimize a company's operating performance. We engineer creative solutions that integrate multiple disciplines to give our clients a distinct and lasting competitive advantage.

Our organization has evolved quickly and maintains an entrepreneurial culture that rewards initiative and performance at all levels. We began to develop our investment banking effort in 1994, and since then, we have built an organization with over 2,500 professionals and pre-tax earnings of over $1.5 billion. Given the talent of our client relationships, we are exceptionally well positioned to continue our strong growth trajectory and become a dominant capital markets service provider of growing companies.

The following is a brief overview of the firm's organization and activities.

Mergers and Acquisitions and Private Equity Group Coverage

Mergers and Acquisitions. The M&A group, originally the investment banking firm of Bowles Hollowell Conner & Co., specializes in merger and acquisition advisory services for large corporations, middle market companies, and private equity groups. With over 100 investment bankers, First Union Securities, Inc., is the nation's leading M&A advisor for transactions less than $250 million.

First Union Securities, Inc. provides the full range of M&A services, including sell-side and buy-side advisory, strategic financial advisory, fairness opinions, and takeover defense. We have dedicated resources covering a broad range of industries and coordinate closely with the Corporate Finance coverage effort. In partnership with the dedicated Private Equity Group coverage team, the M&A group also covers many of the nation's established private equity investors.

Private Equity Group Coverage. Our dedicated Private Equity Group coverage team markets the full range of capital markets products, including M&A advisory, public equity, high yield and investment grade debt, mezzanine finance, equity co-investments, loan syndications, and structured finance to First Union Securities, Inc.'s private equity group client base. First Union Securities, Inc., has a particularly strong following among leading private equity investors and has well-established relationships with nearly 400 different private equity groups. In 1998, over 60% of our M&A transactions involved a private equity group as either the seller or acquirer/principal investor.

Corporate Finance

Our Corporate Finance groups serve as the primary client coverage and business origination source for First Union Securities, Inc.'s top-tier and priority corporate clients. First Union Securities, Inc.'s Corporate Finance effort has over 200 professionals who are responsible for client coverage and are aligned by the industries we cover. These professionals are responsible for marshalling and directing a unified investment banking effort to identify capital markets needs and ensure that we provide cohesive one-stop investment banking solutions to our clients. Corporate Finance consists of 18 specific industry coverage groups. Each industry group brings extensive experience and understanding of issues confronting growing companies, as well as a team of experts to provide strategic and capital formation advice in a timely manner. Each group has a specific managing director who functions as the group head and directs each group's efforts. Corporate Finance professionals also work closely with each of the various product specialists from M&A and the Investment Banking Product groups to provide clients with timely and flawless execution. First Union Securities, Inc., places a strong emphasis on team effort and each member is expected to play a significant role in every transaction.

Equity Research

Our equity research analysts provide institutional equity research and analysis for public companies in targeted industries, as well as support the equity sales and trading and investment banking initiatives to generate business. We have over 75 equity research analysts covering over 500 companies to support our clients. Our focus of coverage is broken down much like our Corporate Finance industry coverage groups.

Equity Research works closely with all of Investment Banking to maximize business opportunities for our clients. We hold numerous institutional conferences throughout the year. In addition, we host one of the most significant annual conferences of any investment bank, held on Nantucket Island, to which we invite more than 130 companies from all of our industries, as well as buy-side analysts and institutional investors.

Our research analysts, through relationships built with the management of the companies we follow, are in a prime position to introduce new business opportunities to our corporate finance bankers. Research and Corporate Finance combine talent to pursue investment banking opportunities in the areas of equity offerings, mergers and acquisitions, and debt finance.

Investment Banking Products

First Union Securities, Inc., offers the full range of investment banking financing capabilities including senior debt, high yield and mezzanine securities, and public and private equity.

Leveraged Finance. Leveraged Finance focuses on structuring and underwriting complex transactions, including acquisition financing, leveraged buyouts, recapitalizations, and expansion opportunities for private equity groups and corporate clients. The product groups within Leveraged Finance include High Yield Debt, Loan Syndications, and Private Placements. Collectively, the Leverage Finance group, in coordination with other areas of Investment Banking, delivers integrated financing solutions for corporate transactions.

High Yield Debt. Our High Yield effort has over 50 experienced professionals engaged in origination, sales,

trading, and research of non-investment grade securities. The group provides clients with the ability to issue and trade a full range of public and 144A securities. Importantly, this group has the capability to provide over $1 billion of bridge capital to our corporate and private equity group clients to ensure that their strategic objectives are met, regardless of short-term fluctuations in the markets. This group has grown substantially, rising to tenth in the league tables, and is of critical importance and focus for the success of capital markets.

Loan Syndications. Our Loan Syndications team has over 100 experienced professionals organized in three areas: Origination, Loan Distribution, and Trading and Research. The group provides clients with a full range of floating rate loan products as well as secondary market knowledge and liquidity and has the capability to provide over $1 billion of capital in a single transaction. In 1998, First Union Securities, Inc. ranked fifth in the number of completed agent/co-agent deals by completing 368 deals worth over $185 billion.

Middle Market Capital. Middle Market Capital was formed in January 1999 to provide one-stop financing solutions to private equity sponsors and middle market clients. The group focuses on providing non-investment grade private capital through a combination of senior debt, subordinated debt, and preferred equity to support leveraged buyouts, leveraged recapitalizations, and fuel future growth needs. The group also identifies larger transactions and helps to deliver integrated financing solutions in conjunction with Leveraged Finance to provide the requisite capital and help leverage the client's equity returns.

Equity Capital Markets. First Union Securities, Inc. began offering a comprehensive array of public equity and equity-related capital markets solutions in February 1998, when we acquired Wheat First Butcher Singer, one of the leading stock underwriters and advisors to growing companies in the eastern United States. In May 1999, we announced the acquisition of Everen Securities, a Chicago-based full service brokerage firm that complements our existing equity capabilities and provides us with a national platform to better serve our clients. As a result of these strategic acquisitions and the hiring of numerous Wall Street-experienced professionals, First Union Securities, Inc., now ranks seventh in middle market equity underwritings in the United States and sixth in terms of the size of our retail distribution system.

First Union Capital Partners. First Union Capital Partners is a private equity investment group that makes direct equity and mezzanine investments in both private and publicly held companies. Capital Partners' investments are primarily directed to growing businesses that require capital to fund acquisitions or consummate significant capital expenditure plans. In addition, Capital Partners also pursues investments in leveraged transactions in partnership with management teams. Since 1988, Capital Partners has deployed over $1 billion in capital in over 100 different companies while achieving an aggregate internal rate of return in excess of 40%.

Investment Grade Debt. Our Investment Grade Debt team has over 200 experienced professionals involved in origination, underwriting, research, sales, and trading. The team provides sophisticated service, efficient execution, secondary market support, and long-term commitment to our clients. As a result, we have grown substantially over the last several years and continue to gain market share. In 1998, we ranked eleventh by managing or co-managing 45 deals worth over $12.1 billion and are on pace to exceed this in 1999.

Structured Finance and Real Estate Capital Markets

Structured Finance and Real Estate Capital Markets originates and executes all structured finance investment banking transactions for both First Union Securities, Inc.'s clients, as well as for all areas of First Union Corporation. With over 300 professionals, Structured Finance and Real Estate Capital Markets is a leading underwriter of asset-backed securities and commercial mortgage-backed securities. During 1998, we were lead manager on over $20.6 billion in asset-backed and commercial mortgage-backed securities.

Asset Securitization Division. This division provides corporate clients with a comprehensive offering of structured finance investment banking services. ASD provides complete financing solutions for clients by integrating our activities as a principal to bridge clients to the asset-backed capital markets. We combine our proprietary asset-backed funds with our distribution strength in underwriting asset-backed securities in both the public and 144A capital markets to offer clients a seamless, fully integrated capital markets funding program. In 1998, ASD executed transactions totaling in excess of $20 billion, ranked eleventh by arranging $8 billion in asset-backed securities, and managed the ninth largest asset-backed commercial paper vehicle in the U.S. with $9 billion in outstandings. We serve both domestic and international clients across a wide range of industry sectors.

Real Estate Capital Markets. This division is responsible for all real estate investment banking activities by First Union Securities, Inc. RECM is comprised of seven groups specializing in providing capital to the real estate industry. We are vertically integrated in commercial real estate lending and provide integrated debt and equity products for Real Estate Investment Trusts and other real estate clients. We offer short-term, interim and construction lending, origination and funding of non-recourse loans, advisory services, underwriting and distribution of debt and equity securities, as well as various off-balance sheet financing products. Last year, First Union Securities, Inc., closed over $13 billion in real estate transactions.

The Finance MBA's Job Description

Describe the career path and corresponding responsibilities for an MBA at your firm.

Associates are an integral part of the investment banking team. We target candidates with strong analytical skills, the ability to work on small deal teams, the initiative to take on significant responsibilities for multiple concurrent transactions, proven leadership skills, written and oral communication skills, and the marketing abilities necessary to interact with the senior management of First Union Securities, Inc.'s client base. In addition, we look for individuals with two or more years of meaningful work experience and a master's or other graduate degree from a leading university. Our environment is fast-paced and energetic, offering personal and professional challenges and providing continuous learning opportunities.

Associates will participate in a three-week formal training program to introduce them to the organizational structure, culture, and products of investment banking. Classroom education will consist of group exercises and casework that will mirror the team environment of each division. Emphasis is placed on developing core analytical skills as well as relationships throughout the organization. Upon completion of the program, successful associates will assist in delivering our full range of products and services to clients formulating financial strategy and policy with our clients' top management, developing and managing client relationships, and designing and executing innovative financing packages.

Discuss the lifestyle aspects of a career with your firm (i.e., average hours per week, amount of travel, flexibility to change offices, corporate culture, etc.).

First Union Securities, Inc.'s business requires a great deal of hard work, dedication, and sacrifice. A high level of commitment is necessary to deliver financial expertise of the highest quality in the timeliest manner. Because over 70% of our assignments are outside the southeastern United States, an associate will be required to travel regularly throughout the country on firm business. Nevertheless, since First Union Securities, Inc., is seeking to recruit future managing directors with a long-term career horizon, the firm respects the requirements of each individual for personal time and the importance of developing interests outside the firm. First Union Securities, Inc., encourages outside interests and activities, particularly within the community, early in its associates' careers.

First Union Securities, Inc.'s Charlotte headquarters is currently the group's primary office and where we will focus the majority of our recruiting. However, we also have offices in New York, Los Angeles, and Richmond, VA. New York and Los Angeles are predominantly private equity marketing coverage locations and will continue to be staffed and developed over the next several years. We expect our associate candidates who are interested in these locations and private equity coverage to have the opportunity to work at these offices.

The Recruiting Process

Describe your recruiting process and the criteria by which you select candidates. Is prior experience necessary?

First Union Securities, Inc., is looking for MBAs who have a demonstrated capability for the analytical analysis, strategic thinking, and written and oral communication requirements for the associate role, as well as an aptitude to perform as a managing director of the firm who will be responsible for generating and executing transactions. We look for academic achievement, intellectual ability, demonstrated leadership abilities, personal integrity, and the ability to communicate ideas and recommendations effectively, both orally and in writing. Although not a strict requirement, we look for individuals with two to four years of meaningful work experience.

How many permanent associates and analysts do you hire in a typical year? How many summer interns do you expect to hire? If you have a formal summer program, please describe it. Please be sure to indicate whether the summer program is in place for all offices or just some.

First Union Securities, Inc., expects to hire approximately 30 associates and 70 analysts in the coming year. The firm has brief, formal training programs for both associates and analysts but strongly favors on-the-job training. Associates and analysts are expected to become productive members of the firm quickly. In addition, First Union Securities, Inc., expects to hire twenty-five summer associates to work in Charlotte for approximately ten weeks.

FMC Corporation

200 East Randolph Drive
Chicago, IL 60601
(312) 861-6000
Fax: (312) 861-5913
Web site: www.fmc.com

MBA Recruiting Contact(s):
FMC College Relations

Company Description

Describe your firm's business and the types of clients served by your finance group(s).

FMC is a New York Stock Exchange–listed, $5 billion, Chicago-based multinational corporation producing machinery and chemicals for industry, agriculture, and government. Our worldwide work force of 22,000 staffs 115 manufacturing facilities and mines in 24 countries.

Our competitive edge in manufacturing excellence, technological innovation, cost control, and customer satisfaction has made us a leader in the global markets we serve. Earning a consistently high real return on shareholder equity is a challenge and an imperative. At FMC, the finance function is committed to increasing value today while positioning the company for future profitable growth and strategic development.

FMC is a corporate leader in developing and implementing state-of-the-art analytical techniques for financial planning, performance measurement, and resource allocation. For example, FMC recapitalized in 1986, doubling shareholder value, while enabling FMC to continue its vigorous program of internal development, capital investment, and research and development. We have also adopted an innovative current cost accounting system to assist top management in evaluating performance and strategic investment decision making. At one of our plants, we are implementing a new activity-based costing, which will give our management a deeper understanding of our product costs.

This philosophy of financial innovation pervades the entire corporation. Financial managers are active leaders of the management team and are required to think and act strategically. They are involved in all facets of managing FMC's complex businesses, from product planning to international investment decisions. Therefore, we seek highly motivated individuals who will become both our future financial leaders and future general managers.

The Finance MBA's Job Description

Describe the career path and corresponding responsibilities for an MBA at your firm.

Financial Business analysts begin their careers in a variety of corporate and site locations, where they are responsible for analyzing, monitoring, and tracking the performance of specific business segments. Analysts also work with line management on a variety of projects that affect management decisions and business performance. After 12–18 months, most analysts assume positions in financial management in one of our line organizations. It is also possible for analysts to pursue other functions at this point. Their choices often depend on their career focus: specializing in a functional discipline or taking advantage of FMC's opportunities for cross-functional career growth. In addition, Financial Business analysts are in demand for a wide variety of offshore opportunities.

The Recruiting Process

How many permanent associates and analysts do you hire in a typical year? How many summer interns do you expect to hire? If you have a formal summer program, please describe it. Please be sure to indicate whether the summer program is in place for all offices or just some.

FMC recruits at eight to ten major business schools. Typically, we hire 15 to 25 full-time MBAs and 12 to 20 interns each year in the Planning, Manufacturing, Human Resources, and Finance functions.

Ford Motor Company

World Headquarters Building
11th Floor—East Wing
The American Road
Dearborn, MI 48121
(313) 323-0850
Web site: www.ford.com/recruiting

MBA Recruiting Contact(s):
Kathleen Gallagher

Company Description

Describe your firm's business and the types of clients served by your finance group(s).

Ford is the world's second-largest industrial corporation and the second-largest producer of cars and trucks. It also ranks among the largest providers of financial services in the United States. Approximately 350,000 form a Ford team dedicated to delivering outstanding value to our customers and shareholders.

Our two core businesses are Automotive and Financial Services. Our vision is to become the world's leading consumer company that provides automotive products and services.

Our Finance Organization serves a broad range of internal and external clients. The primary focus of Finance at Ford is on providing timely and accurate financial analysis to company management in order to support a wide range of business decisions.

Describe your ownership structure.

Ford Motor Company is a widely held, publicly traded corporation. Approximately 40 percent of the voting shares in the corporation are controlled by the Class B stock—controlled by the Ford family.

How does your approach to finance differ from that of other firms, and what do you consider to be your strengths and distinctive capabilities?

Historically, finance has played a very strong role in the automobile industry, particularly at Ford. In fact, in a survey conducted by CFO magazine, over 200 financial executives, executive recruiters, bankers, and consultants identified Ford Motor Company as one of the three companies that best prepares financial managers for the chief financial officer chair.

Finance professionals are involved in every aspect of the company's operations—product development, manufacturing, sales and marketing, e-commerce, customer service, and financial services—as well as the traditional finance functions, such as treasury, financial planning, and operations analysis. Typically, finance professionals move frequently among the company's different components, developing into well-rounded managers who can fill top-level positions in the Finance organization or in general management.

Finance MBAs at Ford can expect a wide variety of challenging assignments that expose them to all the functional areas of the corporation. At Ford, finance is not about abstract theories; it is about real decisions that affect the viability of a multibillion-dollar new car platform, the investment in hundreds of millions of dollars' worth of plant and equipment, or the pricing strategy of a major product line.

The Finance MBA's Job Description

Describe the career path and corresponding responsibilities for an MBA at your firm.

The Career Foundation Development Program is a flexible, individualized, fast-start program offering several core finance experiences in two major business units during the first three to four years of employment. Examples of core experiences include new product program financial analysis, benchmarking and competitive analysis, financial planning and business development, and corporate treasury.

Career paths could lead in multiple directions to senior positions in finance and general management.

Discuss the lifestyle aspects of a career with your firm (i.e., average hours per week, amount of travel, flexibility to change offices, corporate culture, etc.).

The finance culture at Ford is reflective of the people we hire: highly analytical, aggressive, motivated, and career oriented—with a strong desire to win. Professional development is an integral part of our corporate culture. At Ford, we view our people as an investment, not an expense.

While the Ford culture is known to prize work ethic and top-notch commitment to the business, increasing attention and commitment from senior management has been given to work/life balance, flexible job design, and related employee needs. The results are clearly a win-win.

The Recruiting Process

Describe your recruiting process and the criteria by which you select candidates. Is prior experience necessary?

Ford is looking for aggressive, intelligent, highly motivated men and women who are looking for a challenge in an exciting, highly competitive industry. As Ford enters the twenty-first century, we face many challenges: globalization, trade barriers, increased regulation, excess capacity, and stiff competition, to name a few. We are looking for people to help us meet these challenges.

Prior technical experience or education is helpful but certainly not essential. A healthy interest in, and a willingness to get close to, our products is more essential to long-term success at Ford.

Our recruiting process includes a recruiting briefing in the fall followed by on-campus interviews in the winter. A second-round interview on-site follows a successful on-campus interview. Candidates with offers are given an opportunity to spend a day with an MBA who has worked at Ford for two or three years. He or she will show you what a typical day is like and introduce you to the SE Michigan area.

How many summer interns do you expect to hire? If you have a formal summer program, please describe it. Please be sure to indicate whether the summer program is in place for all offices or just some.

Ford plans to continue to seek a limited number of talented individuals for a variety of summer positions. Summer positions are designed to provide a challenging short-term assignment that will give an accurate perspective on a full-time career at Ford. The process and qualifications for summer applicants are similar to those for full-time positions.

What international opportunities does your firm offer for U.S. citizens? For foreign nationals?

Ford derives about 35 percent of its revenues from international operations, offering abundant opportunities for international experience. Overseas assignments, if desired, are possible after completion of the Foundation Development Program. Many Ford executives have had international experience at some point in their careers.

Ford recruits MBAs who are U.S. citizens or are authorized to work full time in the United States.

General Motors Corporation
New York Treasurer's Office

GM Building
767 Fifth Avenue
New York, NY 10153
(212) 418-6100
Web site: www.gm.com

MBA Recruiting Contact(s):
Niharika Taskar, HBS 1996
Christopher Morris

Company Description

Describe your firm's business and the types of clients served by your finance group(s).

General Motors designs, manufactures, and sells automobiles, trucks, vans, locomotives, and other equipment and components related to the worldwide transportation industry. The corporation also designs and manufactures satellites and integrated circuits and provides automotive, mortgage, and other financial services.

The global automobile industry is progressing into an era of unprecedented competition. At General Motors, we are approaching this challenge with a commitment to remaining the premier manufacturer of cars and trucks in North America and the rest of the world. As has been well documented in the press, this commitment has resulted in a period of incredible change, with the entire GM organization being scrutinized and restructured. This process is placing emphasis on the ability of GM's employees to manage its operations and finances effectively.

GM's New York Treasurer's Office plays a vital role in the decisions that affect both the current operations of the corporation and its future direction. The office is extensively responsible for a broad range of financial, strategic planning, and other business matters leading to the execution of transactions, including new business ventures, domestic and international subsidiary financings, investments, divestitures, capital planning, and foreign exchange trading. In addition to developing and executing action plans for senior management, the Treasurer's Office is also responsible for presenting such action plans and other information to the Board of Directors and its Finance, Audit, Incentive and Compensation, and Nomi-

nating Committees. As such, GM's New York Treasurer's Office distinguishes itself from other corporate treasury staffs by providing individuals with the opportunity to develop and practice corporate finance, consulting, and general management skills.

Furthermore, the appeal of the Treasurer's Office extends beyond that provided by traditional treasury functions. Specifically, GM's Treasurer's Office also functions as GM's in-house consulting firm. As such, the office's responsibilities include developing, assessing, negotiating, and implementing strategic business initiatives of the corporation. Reflecting the Treasurer's Office objectives of developing both the financial and general business acumen of its employees, many alumni have progressed to top financial and general management positions throughout the United States and virtually all of our international locations, including Europe, Asia, and South America.

The Finance MBA's Job Description

Describe the career path and corresponding responsibilities for an MBA at your firm.

A senior financial analyst in the office is exposed to a wide range of strategic and financial assignments that can be matched by very few other companies. For example, a typical business school graduate could immediately be engaged in any of several activities, including structuring an international subsidiary or joint venture, developing an entirely new form of equity or debt offering, managing GM's multibillion-dollar cash portfolio, or trading foreign currency on a global basis. Newly hired MBAs are provided with the opportunity to practice a wide range of corporate finance activities. In this regard, individuals in the Treasurer's Office are rotated from section to section in order to develop their breadth of expertise fully. Senior analysts would typically follow a rotational assignment system through several of nine office sections, which places emphasis on developing general managers proficient in many areas of finance. While the responsibilities of each section and position vary, analysts are expected to develop a broad knowledge of GM's operations, its products, and its markets on a worldwide basis. Key responsibilities within the sections include:

Business Development (Overseas & Domestic)

- Analysis of potential acquisitions, mergers & divestitures

- Structuring and negotiating alliances, partnerships & joint ventures

- Devise workout strategies for financially distressed GM suppliers

Capital Planning

- Corporate change initiatives focused on asset management and financial performance accountability

- Forecast & analysis of GM capital structure, cash flows & related strategies

- Structured finance and balance sheet management

Investor Relations

- Communication with Wall Street analysts, rating agencies & global investor community

- Competitive analysis of other major automobile manufacturers

Domestic Finance

- Analysis & implementation of both debt & equity issuances for corporate funding purposes

- Management of interest rate risk via utilizing derivative products

- Investment of corporation's multibillion-dollar cash portfolio

- Foreign exchange/commodities analysis & hedging

- Manage stock buyback program

Worldwide Pension Funding & Analysis

- Development of funding strategies for worldwide pension & benefit plans

- National negotiations with the United Auto Workers union

- Design & analysis of benefit & compensation plans

Overseas Finance

- Overseas capital planning & liquidity management, including cash repatriation

- Funding for Latin American & Mid-East/African operations

- Export & trade finance

- Global financial policies

Regional Treasury Centers—RTCs (Satellite Offices in Brussels, Singapore & Beijing)

- Foreign exchange & interest rate exposure management of GM's European subsidiaries

- Cash management for European operations

- Risk management advisory work for Asian subsidiaries

- Funding for Asian & European operations

- Corporate finance advisory for Asian & European operations

- Venture development & financing of Chinese projects

Outlined below are the job classifications within the New York Treasurer's Office and the average time at each level:

Job Classification	Average Years in Level
Senior Financial Analyst	2–3 years
Manager (typically supervises 3 or 4 analysts)	2–3 years
Section Director (responsible for 2 to 4 managers and 4 to 8 analysts)	2 years

Describe the opportunities for professional mobility between the various departments in your firm.

In addition to promotions leading to a successful and rewarding experience at the Treasurer's Office in New York, numerous financial openings occur for Treasurer's Office employees at the regional treasury centers, and in overseas and domestic subsidiaries and divisions (e.g., eGM [GM's Internet strategy and venture group], GM Hughes Electronics, NUMMI [GM's joint venture with Toyota in Fremont, CA], GMAC, Saturn, GM-Europe, and GM's North American Operations). Furthermore, many opportunities are available outside the financial side of the business, including general management, personnel, industrial relations, manufacturing, industry-government relations, and our worldwide trading corporation.

The Recruiting Process

Describe your recruiting process and the criteria by which you select candidates. Is prior experience necessary?

GM's Treasurer's Office is staffed with approximately 50 MBAs from the nation's top schools and from around the globe. We seek individuals with initiative and a willingness to assume a demanding work load in a challenging environment, as new analysts are expected to assume a significant amount of responsibility within a very short period of time. A typical senior financial analyst has a strong academic background, with particular emphasis on finance; a background in economics, accounting, engineering, or operations is also valuable. Attractive candidates demonstrate strong analytical and organizational abilities, as well as effective oral and written communication skills. Importantly, they also have a high level of interpersonal skills and an ability to function effectively as part of a team.

How many permanent associates and analysts do you hire in a typical year? How many summer interns do you expect to hire? If you have a formal summer program, please describe it. Please be sure to indicate whether the summer program is in place for all offices or just some.

GM's Treasurer's Office has an excellent summer program that allows students between years of business school to learn about the New York office and gain valuable knowledge and skills in a particular section. GM's Treasurer's Office has also offered summer internships in Brussels, Singapore, and Brazil in recent years. Many of our recent summer analysts have elected to return to the Treasurer's Office upon graduating.

Goldman Sachs & Co.

85 Broad Street
New York, NY 10004
(212) 902-1000
Web site: www.gs.com

MBA Recruiting Contact(s):
Tamara Eden, Associate
Equities

Wendy Doyle, Associate
Fixed Income, Currency and Commodities

Anne Marie O'Reilly, Associate
Global Investment Research

Penny Petrow, Associate
Investment Banking

Christina Schmittner, Associate
Investment Management (Asset Management
Candidates)

Sarah McNamara, Vice President
Investment Management (Wealth Management
Candidates)

Elizabeth Burban, Vice President
Merchant Banking

Company Description

*Describe your firm's business and the types of clients
served by your finance group(s).*

Goldman Sachs is a full-service international investment
banking and securities firm headquartered in New York
City. Offices are located in New York, London, Tokyo,
Atlanta, Bangkok, Beijing, Boston, Buenos Aires, Chi-
cago, Dallas, Frankfurt, George Town, Hong Kong,
Houston, Johannesburg, Los Angeles, Madrid, Memphis,
Menlo Park, Mumbai, Paris, Philadelphia, San Francisco,
Sao Paolo, Seoul, Shanghai, Singapore, Stockholm, Syd-
ney, Taipei, Tampa, Toronto, Vancouver, Washington,
D.C., and Zurich.

The firm is a leader in virtually every aspect of financing
and investing, serving corporations, institutions, governments and individuals worldwide. Our leadership derives
principally from the dedication, talent and professional-

ism of our people. We recruit and train the very best
graduates from leading colleges and universities. These
individuals become part of our noted team effort, which
provides the closely integrated financial skills and services necessary to help our clients meet diverse goals and
new challenges in global markets. We were rated this year
as #9 on Fortune's "100 Best Companies To Work For"
and #2 on Fortune's "America's Most Admired Companies in the Financial and Securities Industry."

The following is a brief overview of the firm's organization and activities.

Investment Banking Division

The Investment Banking Division assists corporations,
financial institutions, and governments in planning and
executing financial strategies in the global capital
markets.

Corporate Finance Department. Our Corporate Finance Department advises clients worldwide on structuring and executing innovative financial strategies to meet
their strategic and financial objectives. Client teams execute debt and equity offerings and, where appropriate, derivative transactions to manage risks related to volatility
in securities and currency markets. Some professionals
also work on merger-related projects with the Mergers &
Acquisitions Department.

Communications, Media & Entertainment Group.
The Communications, Media & Entertainment Group applies broad-based experience and knowledge to assist
telecommunications, cable, publishing, broadcasting, and
entertainment companies as well as emerging telecommunications wireless, and telecommunications equipment businesses. Services include the full spectrum of
financing products as well as mergers and acquisitions
and other strategic advice.

Energy & Power Group. The Energy & Power Group
provides financing, merger and acquisition, and other services to clients in the oil and gas, natural gas pipeline, and
utilities industries worldwide. Coverage of these major
global industries is provided to support the significant
needs of clients and to assist them in planning and executing financial strategies.

Financial Institutions Group. Professionals in the Financial Institutions Group provide comprehensive investment banking services to the financial services industry.
The Group serves many of the largest commercial banks
and insurance companies as well as investment managers,
finance companies, and financial services–related technology companies worldwide. In addition to traditional

financing and merger activities, the group works closely with other areas of the firm on asset restructuring as both agent and principal.

Healthcare Group. The Healthcare Group provides comprehensive investment banking services across the various sectors of the healthcare industry, which includes pharmaceuticals, biotechnology, medical technology and devices, managed care, and information technology. The industry is in the midst of major consolidation as well as major technological advancement.

High Technology Group. High Technology Group professionals provide financing, merger and acquisition, and other investment banking services to the high technology industry. The group, comprised of professionals on both the east and west coasts, has a global base of high-quality clients in various sectors of the technology industry, which include Internet technology and services, computer hardware and software, telecommunications and data networking equipment, IT services, semiconductors, and semiconductor equipment.

Leveraged Finance Group. Leveraged Finance Group professionals work closely with Corporate Finance and other industry coverage groups of the division to provide comprehensive financing services, as well as capital structure guidance and credit assistance primarily to non-investment grade companies globally. The group, comprised of professionals in New York and London, advises clients and commits capital in conjunction with complex senior banking and high-yield debt financings related to leveraged buyouts, recapitalizations, refinancings, and other corporate restructurings. The group is structured as a joint venture between the Investment Banking and Fixed Income, Currency, and Commodities divisions.

Mergers & Acquisitions Department. The Mergers and Acquisitions Department, consistently a leading advisor in major merger transactions, provides strategic advice worldwide regarding acquisitions, divestitures, joint ventures, recapitalizations, leveraged buyouts, and takeover attempts. The merger and acquisition process frequently involves soliciting transactions; analyzing the business dynamics of companies and industries; valuing businesses; determining likely buyers and sellers; and marketing, negotiating, and closing transactions. Professionals work with public and private companies in many industries.

Real Estate Department. The Real Estate Department provides complex and innovative investment banking services worldwide to the leading real estate companies. Clients include real estate investment trusts, the hospitality industry, and a variety of Fortune 500 companies. The de-

partment structures debt and equity financing, executes merger and disposition transactions, provides strategic advisory services, securitizes portfolios of commercial mortgages.

Investment Banking Services Department. The Investment Banking Services Department is the marketing arm of the Investment Banking Division. Professionals are responsible for maintaining and strengthening client relationships and developing new relationships and business. When a particular client need is identified, these professionals assemble the appropriate team of specialists and lead them through strategy development and implementation.

Fixed Income, Currency and Commodities Division

The Fixed Income, Currency and Commodities Division serves clients worldwide. The division assumes risk and trades as principal for the firm in fixed income instruments, foreign exchange, and commodities. Specific products include government and government agency securities, corporate debt, high-yield securities, emerging market debt, money market instruments, mortgage and asset-backed securities, futures, options, swaps and other derivative instruments, currencies, crude oil, natural gas, gold, silver, base metals, municipal securities, and the Goldman Sachs Commodity Index.

Sales. The Sales professional role is twofold: building and maintaining the trust of our clients and creating solutions to their investment needs. Professionals are involved in designing strategies to take advantage of market changes, including highly sophisticated portfolio restructuring and hedging and arbitrage transactions. There are opportunities to work with portfolio managers, research analysts, and traders at pension funds, mutual funds, insurance companies, hedge funds, money management firms, and major commodities producers and customers.

Trading. Trading professionals are responsible for making a market in their specialized product area—to customers in the sales force and to other counterparts in the markets. Professionals commit the firm's capital and are responsible for managing any positions that result from their market activities. They monitor the world for any changes that affect the markets, from economic news, to industry trends, to shifts in foreign exchange and interest rates, and advise professionals in the investment banking and other areas of the firm on the pricing, structuring, and timing of new issues.

Fixed Income Research Department. The Fixed Income Research Department uses sophisticated analytical, mathematical, and computer capabilities to develop new ideas, products, and approaches for trading, hedging, and investment strategies as well as for asset-liability management. Professionals work in specialized sections covering debt options, trading systems, asset-liability management, risk management, sales support, financial modeling, hedging, portfolio optimization, new product development, and research.

Finance. Finance professionals work in an advisory and marketing capacity with issuers of securities, linking clients with the financial markets. Professionals develop strategies for debt and equity hybrid issuances, derivatives, liability management, and new product development. Clients include Fortune 500 companies, U.S. government agencies, sovereign and supranational entities, and large international corporations. Specific areas within Finance include Debt Capital Markets, Loan Syndication and Trading, Whole Loan Trading and Principal Finance, Municipal Finance, Asset-Backed Finance, Distressed Debt Trading and the Financial Institutions Industry Resource Group.

Equities Division

Through its Equities Division, Goldman, Sachs underwrites, distributes, and trades equity securities and derivative products on a worldwide basis. Goldman, Sachs' leadership position in the global equities marketplace results from its product innovation, distribution capability, and willingness to commit capital in response to clients' needs. The division has long-standing relationships with many of the world's major financial institutions, corporations and governments.

As a member of several stock exchanges around the world, Goldman Sachs is a trader and market maker in U.S. European, U.K., Japanese and other global equities.

Institutional Investor Services Department. The Institutional Investor Services Department provides trading and research coverage, through product focused specialists, to institutional clients, including public and private pension funds, insurance companies, mutual funds, hedge funds, banks, investment advisors, endowments, and foundations in the United States, Europe, and Asia.

Equities Arbitrage. Professionals in this area conduct risk arbitrage in the securities of companies involved in domestic and international mergers, acquisitions, recapitalizations and divestitures where Goldman Sachs is not acting as advisor or agent at the time of investment.

Equity Capital Markets Department. Equity Capital Markets professionals work closely with professionals in Investment Banking, Global Investment Research, and the Equities sales and trading force to design, structure, and execute equity and equity-linked financing transactions. These transactions include private equity financings, structured equity products, and investments in real estate, foreign exchange, precious metals, and other commodities.

Private Client Services Department. The Private Client Services Department provides comprehensive equity, fixed income, and cash management services, as well as securities safekeeping, margin lending, portfolio reporting, and principal investment opportunities to wealthy family groups, medium-size institutions, corporations, and professional investors worldwide.

Global Securities Services (GSS) Department. The GSS Department provides a comprehensive range of sophisticated investment support services to institutional investors. Professionals assist clients in borrowing and lending securities, custody and safekeeping, managing multiple accounts, financing positions, clearing and settling trades, and administering offshore funds.

Investment Management Division

The Investment Management Division is comprised of two major businesses—Asset Management and Wealth Management. The Asset Management Group structures and manages customized portfolios for institutional clients, as well as develops and manages institutional and retail mutual funds. The Wealth Management Group provides wealthy individuals and families with investment advisory services, including portfolio strategy.

Global Investment Research Division

Global Investment Research professionals research and analyze more than 2,000 companies in over 20 markets. They develop investment ideas and strategies that are used by clients in structuring and managing investment portfolios, provide data and analysis on interest rates, currencies, and other developments that affect economic conditions, as well as market investment data, opinions, and strategy to our sales and trading professionals and our clients through research reports, electronic delivery systems, and investor meetings.

Operations, Finance and Resources

Professionals in the division are closely involved with nearly all of the firm's activities. Departments within the division include:

Global Operations. The Global Operations professional is responsible for processing, clearing, and settling trades in a timely and accurate manner, as well as providing integrated operations services in a highly controlled environment.

Controllers Department. The Controllers Department designs and monitors all internal financial functions. The department is responsible for internal financial analysis and consulting, external financial reporting, monitoring internal trading positions and regulatory compliance, and general accounting for the firm.

Credit Department. The Credit Department approves and monitors the credit/exposure limits of many companies with which Goldman Sachs does business. Professionals help ensure the continued profitability and efficiency of the firm's businesses and make sure that those business practices are in keeping with financial and regulatory requirements worldwide. The department participates in the solicitation, structuring, and selling of commercial paper and conducts due diligence investigations.

Treasury Department. Worldwide funding of the firm's operations is the responsibility of the Treasury Department. The firm is rated A1+, the highest ranking for commercial paper issuers assigned by Standard & Poor's.

Human Resources

The Human Resources professional ensures that Goldman Sachs maintains the highest standards in all human resources activities. Functional areas include benefits, compensation, employee relations, training and professional development, information management, recruitment, global information services, and relocation and international assignments.

Describe your ownership structure.

Founded in 1869, we are one of the oldest and largest investment banking firms. After more than a century as a private partnership, our firm became a public company in 1999.

How does your approach to finance differ from that of other firms, and what do you consider to be your strengths and distinctive capabilities?

Commitment to client interest and teamwork are the most distinctive characteristics of our approach to investment banking. We emphasize relationships rather than the completion of individual transactions. Our success is directly related to our ability to provide our clients with exceptional service. Among our key strengths are the following:

- The skill, experience, and dedication of our people

- Leadership in financial markets worldwide

- Strong capital position

- Technological resources

- Reputation for excellence

Most important, we believe our ability to integrate all facets of the firm's areas of excellence through teamwork is unique in the industry.

The Finance MBA's Job Description

Describe the career path and corresponding responsibilities for an MBA at your firm.

The firm recruits MBAs for career positions in most divisions and operating entities. Initial training will depend on the new associate's background and functional area. Training emphasizes on-the-job learning, which is complemented by formal instruction. Professionals throughout the firm serve as instructors and mentors. During training, associates prepare for any registration exams that may be required for their specialization. They begin training in their functional areas after they complete those exams. Associates are encouraged to assume as much responsibility in their assignments as they can handle.

Associates play an integral role in planning, structuring, and executing transactions that range from a single private placement of equity or debt to a major portfolio restructuring or corporate reorganization. They work with managing directors, vice presidents, other associates, and analysts in an open atmosphere in which ideas are shared and creative thinking is encouraged. Because the firm has only three levels of professionals, new associates have significant contact with its senior members.

Describe the opportunities for professional mobility between the various departments in your firm.

As part of career development, we foster a working environment in which professionals are encouraged to explore their interests and develop their skills continuously. Believing that diversity of experience is beneficial not only to our professionals but also to the firm and its clients, we provide opportunities to work in other areas of the firm and to transfer to other departments, divisions, or offices.

We are diligent in evaluating professionals for career advancement and financial reward. Yearly reviews are made by teams of superiors and peers to ensure thoroughness and objectivity.

Discuss the lifestyle aspects of a career with your firm (i.e., average hours per week, amount of travel, flexibility to change offices, corporate culture, etc.).

A career at Goldman Sachs is a challenging one that places significant demands on time and energy. Professionals are encouraged to make their lifestyle decisions within the context of doing the best job possible. The amount of travel varies greatly. In areas requiring the most travel, our professionals can average two or three days on the road each week.

As a result of our care in hiring, developing, challenging, and rewarding our people, the turnover rate for our professionals has consistently been one of the lowest in the industry.

The Recruiting Process

Describe your recruiting process and the criteria by which you select candidates. Is prior experience necessary?

In recruiting, we look for professionals who will flourish in a team-oriented environment. There is no single type of individual who fits in at Goldman Sachs. We are an amalgam of people from around the world with different cultural and educational backgrounds and professional orientations. What we have in common are creativity, the confidence and willingness to take initiative and responsibility, an interest in being a part of a highly motivated group, and a desire to achieve beyond the norm.

Although each area of specialization requires certain qualities, most of our professionals demonstrate a keen interest in the financial markets; strong interpersonal, analytic, and communication skills; and an ability to respond creatively and quickly in a fast-paced, changing environment.

We believe that academic achievement is a good indication of potential, but it is not the most important criterion. Prior experience is usually not a major consideration for MBAs.

How many permanent associates and analysts do you hire in a typical year? How many summer interns do you expect to hire? If you have a formal summer program, please describe it. Please be sure to indicate whether the summer program is in place for all offices or just some.

Each year, we hire a significant number of college graduates throughout the firm. As with MBAs, most of the training of college graduates is on the job. Many of our analysts earn an MBA and return to the firm as associates.

The firm actively recruits for its summer associate programs. Our summer associates gain broad exposure to many areas of our business, and many return as full-time employees.

What international opportunities does your firm offer for U.S. citizens? For foreign nationals?

Investment banking has become an international business and Goldman Sachs is fully committed to the business on a worldwide basis. We have 41 offices in 23 countries around the world. Consequently, we offer many international opportunities for both U.S. citizens and foreign nationals.

Harris Williams & Co.

707 East Main Street, 19th Floor
Richmond, VA 23219
(804) 648-0072
Fax: (804) 648-0073

One Montgomery Street, Suite 2250
San Francisco, CA 94104
(415) 288-4260
Fax: (415) 288-4269

MBA Recruiting Contact(s):
Giles Tucker (804) 648-0072
E-mail: gtucker@harriswilliams.com

Company Description

Describe your firm's business and the types of clients served by your finance groups.

Founded in Richmond in 1991, Harris Williams & Co. is a 56-person mergers and acquisitions advisory firm specializing in middle market transactions with enterprise values of $20–350 million. We serve the needs of many of the nation's most prominent private equity groups (including Florida Capital Partners, BancBoston Capital, Code Hennessy & Simmons, Citicorp Venture Capital, and Metapoint Partners) in the sale of portfolio companies and Fortune 500 companies (including Procter & Gamble, International Paper, Schering-Plough, and Dover Corporation) in the divestiture of divisions. Privately held companies, including those that are family-owned, represent another important segment of our client base. By drawing upon our broad base of knowledge, we add value in each of our transactions—value that is apparent to our clients.

Describe your ownership structure.

Harris Williams & Co. became part of The FINOVA Group, Inc. in 1999. FINOVA is a diversified specialty finance company based in Phoenix, Arizona with a market capitalization and total assets of approximately $1.7 billion and $11.6 billion, respectively.

How does your approach to finance differ from that of other firms, and what do you consider to be your strengths and distinctive capabilities?

Expertise. Commitment. Service. Results. At Harris Williams & Co., we consistently deliver all four. That's why we have become one of the nation's leading middle-market investment banking firms. We bring to our market place a level of expertise typically found only in much larger transactions. We are committed to the middle market because we know that these companies need and deserve experienced mergers and acquisitions advice. Finally, our level of service is second to none, with senior level attention on every transaction and active participation on every assignment by each team member.

Discuss changes in your firm's revenues and professional staff over the past year; over the past five years.

Since its founding in 1991, Harris Williams & Co. has generated record levels of revenue and profitability each year. In 1999, the company enjoyed its best year on record and 2000 is on track to again continue the string of record performances. The increase in the number of employees at the firm mirrors the tremendous growth of revenue and profitability. Since 1994, HW&Co. has increased the number of employees from four to fifty-six, making the company one of the largest firms in the United States focused solely on mergers and acquisitions.

The Finance MBA's Job Description

Describe the career path and corresponding responsibilities for an MBA at your firm.

Associates at HW&Co. play an integral role in all of the firm's merger and acquisition advisory activities. Each new associate is expected to experience rapid professional growth to the vice president and partner level. Associates are encouraged to handle a high level of responsibility on transaction teams and are very important to the execution of the transaction. In this role, Associates are expected to actively contribute during every phase of the deal process. Associates lead the writing and development of both initial pitch material and descriptive memoranda, and are expected to actively participate in drafting sessions and due diligence meetings. Associates are also responsible for the integrity of the valuation analyses and merger and acquisition models developed in concert with the financial analysts. In addition, associates are encouraged to participate actively in new business development. Upon joining the firm, each associate is assigned to a marketing team covering a specific geographic territory, with responsibility for maintaining existing or establishing new client relationships.

Describe the opportunities for professional mobility between the various departments in your firm.

Because the firm is devoted exclusively to mergers and acquisitions advisory services to middle market companies, each new professional is developed as an industry generalist working on a variety of assignments and in various teams within the firm.

Discuss the lifestyle aspects of a career with your firm (i.e., average hours per week, amount of travel, flexibility to change offices, corporate culture, etc.).

The business of the firm requires a great deal of motivation, dedication, and sacrifice. A high level of commitment is necessary to deliver mergers and acquisitions advisory services of the highest quality in the timeliest manner. Because over half of our assignments are outside the southeastern United States, an associate will be required to travel regularly throughout the country on firm business. Nevertheless, the firm respects the requirements of each individual for personal time away from the office and the importance of developing interests outside the firm.

In addition, HW&Co. is committed to the importance of community service. HW&Co. is dedicated to finding local volunteer community service activities for the firm, as well as creating social activities for staff members. Examples include Habitat for Humanity, athletic fundraising events, tutoring, weekly basketball games, and social outings at local gathering spots. Involvement in outside activities within the community is viewed as an important aspect of an associate's development, and members of the firm are encouraged to participate in a variety of external community activities.

The Recruiting Process

Describe your recruiting process and the criteria by which you select candidates. Is prior experience necessary?

Harris Williams &Co. dedicates a great deal of effort to hiring individuals who have demonstrated outstanding academic achievement and a proven track record of performance excellence, both in and out of the classroom. In addition, each new associate is expected to develop into a partner. An associate candidate should possess strong oral and written communication skills, attention to detail, the ability to work well under pressure, and a willingness to work long hours. No specific academic major is a prerequisite; however, a strong finance and accounting background is desired.

How many permanent associates and analysts do you hire in a typical year? How many summer interns do you expect to hire? If you have a formal summer program, please describe it. Please be sure to indicate whether the summer program is in place for all offices or just some.

HW&Co. expects to hire four to six associates for full-time positions during the 2000–2001 recruiting year. In the past, we have successfully recruited and hired outstanding associates from such schools as Harvard, Kellogg, Tuck, and Kenan-Flagler. HW&Co. also offers a summer internship program.

Hewlett-Packard Company

Employment Response Center
3000 Hanover Street/ms: 20APP
Palo Alto, CA 94304-1181
Web sites: www.hp.com or www.jobs.hp.com
(415) 852-8473

MBA Recruiting Contact(s):
Employment Response Center

Company Description

Describe your firm's business and the types of clients served by your finance group(s).

Hewlett-Packard Company (HP), a leading global provider of computing and imaging solutions and services for business and home, is focused on capitalizing on the opportunities of the Internet and the proliferation of electronic services.

HP plans to spin off Agilent Technologies and distribute its shares to HP shareowners by mid-calendar year 2000. Agilent consists of HP's test and measurement business, semiconductor products, chemical analysis and healthcare solutions businesses, and has leading positions in multiple market segments.

HP has 85,400 employees worldwide and had total revenue from continuing operations of $42.4 billion in its 1999 fiscal year. Information about HP, its products, and the company's Year 2000 program can be found on the World Wide Web at http://www.hp.com.

Describe your ownership structure.

HP is a publicly owned company and is one of the fifty largest industrial companies in the America. HP stock is traded on the New York Stock Exchange.

How does your approach to finance differ from that of other firms, and what do you consider to be your strengths and distinctive capabilities?

HP's combination of strength and structure enables us to offer a broad spectrum of financial career opportunities and early responsibility.

HP's unique corporate culture, often referred to as the "HP Way," is a combination of organizational values, cor-

porate objectives, and company practices. The company is built upon values such as honesty, teamwork, and respect that are reflected in everything we do.

One of our guiding objectives as a company is profit. The profit we generate from our operations is the ultimate source of the funds we need to prosper and grow. It is the one absolutely essential measure of our corporate performance over the long term. Without profit, the company is unable to grow or fulfill the rest of its objectives.

Our long-standing policy has been to reinvest most of our profits and to depend on this reinvestment, plus funds from employee stock purchases and other cash flow items, to finance our growth.

The day-to-day performance of each individual adds to— or subtracts from—our profit. Profit is seen as the responsibility of all HP employees.

Discuss changes in your firm's revenues (both domestic and international) and professional staff over the past year; over the past five years.

HP's revenue from continued operations grew to $42.4 billion in its 1999 fiscal year.

HP employs approximately 85,400 employees worldwide. HP was the #32 Employer among the Fortune 500 U.S. industrial and service corporations (based on number of employees) (April 26, 1999).

The Finance MBA's Job Description

Describe the career path and corresponding responsibilities for an MBA at your firm.

Financial analyst positions are typically in HP product divisions, field sales organizations, or corporate functions. These initial experiences lead to careers in financial management or in other functional areas such as marketing and manufacturing.

In the divisions, financial analysts work closely with other functional areas. Tasks may include product/process cost analysis, financial planning and reporting, product pricing and profitability analysis, asset evaluation, and the design and implementation of financial models that will simulate division operations.

Financial analysts in the sales regions are responsible for financial planning and reporting, customer leasing arrangements, credit analysis and accounts receivable management, inventory analysis and control, and contracts and order administration.

In our corporate headquarters, responsibilities may include many of the activities described above plus cash, debt, and foreign exchange management; pensions and investment analysis; coordination of long-range plans; the development of corporate financial policy; external shareholder and Securities and Exchange Commission reporting; and internal audit tasks.

Describe the opportunities for professional mobility between the various departments in your firm.

The company is committed to giving people the flexibility to reach well-defined goals. HP believes that freedom encourages the creativity and initiative of every employee. Career paths are not defined formally at HP; rather, they are flexible by design. We strive to help our people succeed and move on to greater challenges and responsibilities. An extensive internal job posting system allows employees to change jobs within their site (both within their function and across functions) and to move to other sites.

Discuss the lifestyle aspects of a career with your firm (i.e., average hours per week, amount of travel, flexibility to change offices, corporate culture, etc.).

HP trusts individuals and believes that people are committed to doing a good job given the right environment. To create this environment, HP offers pay based on performance, pleasant and open work environments, flexible work hours, cash profit sharing, and recognition for achievement.

The Recruiting Process

Describe your recruiting process and the criteria by which you select candidates. Is prior experience necessary?

HP recruits highly motivated, successful MBAs with initiative and a strong desire to make a significant impact on our business. Prior experience is preferred although not mandatory. Candidates must have a thorough knowledge of financial and accounting principles and proficiency in PC-based analytical tools. We look for outstanding analytical and problem-solving ability, as well as flexibility and excellent communication skills.

How many permanent associates and analysts do you hire in a typical year? How many summer interns do you expect to hire? If you have a formal summer program, please describe it. Please be sure to indicate whether the summer program is in place for all offices or just some.

The number of openings varies from year to year, but we typically have several finance openings distributed among many of our operations.

HP's Student Employment and Educational Development (SEED) Program enables students who have completed their first year in business school to gain hands-on experience as contributing members of our Finance team.

What international opportunities does your firm offer for U.S. citizens? For foreign nationals?

International employment opportunities are limited primarily to foreign nationals.

IBM Corporation

IBM Staffing Services
3808 Six Forks Road
Raleigh, NC 27609
(800) 964-4473
Web site: www.ibm.com

Company Description

Describe your firm's business and the types of clients served by your finance group(s).

IBM is a unique organization—a major multinational corporation that takes pride in its small-team atmosphere.

Consider that the company stands at the leading edge of one of the world's most dynamic industries: information processing. Consider that it does business in over 130 countries.

Consider, also, that IBM is an organization known worldwide for its respect for the individual and its environment for personal and professional growth. Consider that it is a market-driven company dedicated to providing the best possible customer service and that it is committed to excellence in all activities. Consider that it is a dynamic organization constantly striving to be competitive, to be responsive, to push decision making down to manageable levels.

In fact, IBM is a number of things. It is products and services designed to help customers solve problems through the application of information solutions. It is mainframe, mid-range, and personal computer systems; software for systems, applications, communications, and application development; telecommunications products; office systems; and related supplies and services. All are products and services designed to help record, process, store, retrieve, and communicate information.

In addition, IBM is a technological leader—an innovator with over 32,000 patents worldwide and major contributions at all levels of information processing. The company invented FORTRAN, RAMAC, the floppy disk, the relational database concept, systems network architecture, RISC technology, and much more. It has continually increased the density of circuit packaging, recently producing the first 4-million-bit chip. IBM scientists have earned Nobel Prizes for advances in superconductivity and scanning tunneling microscopy. The company is exploring sub-half-micron lithography, optical storage, speech recognition, artificial intelligence—and a host of other technologies.

But IBM is also open communications channels and respect for privacy, career flexibility and promotion on merit, personal growth and recognition, shared employee/company responsibility, a balance of work and personal life, corporate citizenship, and a benefits program considered one of the finest in industry. In other words, IBM is a special place to work.

Within IBM, Finance is its own team, a function that cuts across organizational lines. A cadre of over 5,000 professionals in the United States, IBM Finance offers opportunities at U.S. plant, laboratory, marketing, and subsidiary locations, as well as at headquarters facilities. Joint ventures and business alliances are also mutually staffed with an IBM and partner financial team.

Working in IBM Finance, you will gain exposure to all aspects of the business. Financial decisions affect research, engineering, manufacturing, programming, marketing, administration, personnel, communications—all the basic functions of the company. As a member of an IBM financial team, you will be in frequent contact with senior management early in your career. From the start, you will also interact with your counterparts at other locations.

In the process, you will gain an understanding of the business and what makes it work. To build a career in IBM Finance, you need a perspective that cuts across functional lines. A pricing decision in Raleigh, NC, can affect accounting controls in Boca Raton, FL. Financial planning for the IBM Credit Corporation can affect the treasury function at corporate headquarters in Armonk, NY. Equity investments can have worldwide implications.

The Finance MBA's Job Description

Describe the career path and corresponding responsibilities for an MBA at your firm.

Career paths in IBM Finance are characterized by a variety of experience and responsibilities, with advancement on merit. The path you follow depends on your objectives and how well you do in the variety of job responsibilities you will be given. You can move ahead as fast as your capabilities permit.

You will most likely start in financial planning or accounting—with later assignments in these areas plus pricing, treasury, and controllership—and rotate assignments for balanced experience. You could start as a cost accounting analyst, become a planning manager, move on to be a product pricer in an international headquarters in Paris—all while moving up in your career. An assignment in the IBM Credit Corporation might be in the picture. Ideally, your performance will lead you to first-line management in an operation unit, then on toward executive positions in financial or general management or increased professional staff responsibility.

Throughout your career, training will be largely on the job, enriched by formal classroom work within and outside the company. In fact, your training and education will never stop.

Looking Ahead with Financial Planning
A major entry-level area is financial planning—the development of basic financial strategies by which IBM runs its business. Financial planning is to IBM management what flowcharting is to the programmer. It establishes short-range projections of income and expense—the operating plan—and long-range strategic planning for the business environment.

IBM financial planning starts with determination of the goals and objectives of the business deliberately set at challenging but realistically attainable levels. Basic inputs are the following: customer requirements, competitive analysis, industry opportunity, technology trends, and available resources (both dollars and people). From goals and objectives, financial planners develop strategies for the business. This demands analysis of the company's current position and the availability of alternate strategies for the future.

In this area, you will work hand-in-hand with the IBM engineering, manufacturing, marketing, and general management communities to understand requirements, analyze IBM's and competitors' strengths and weaknesses, and realistically assess opportunities. You will interact closely with product planners; forecasters; and development, marketing, and service organizations. You may develop business models with desired returns, do portfolio analysis, or make investment decisions.

Aside from overall short- and long-term evaluations, your work can extend to specific IBM lines of business. Here the focus is on discrete markets and products, including the impact of competition. Developing, implementing, and controlling IBM financial plans calls for rigorous objectivity. Every recommendation must be judged by one basic criterion: Is this a sound business decision for IBM?

Financial planning at IBM helps convert goals to reality. Your experience in this area can make a real difference.

You will develop creative ability, business judgment, and strong communications skills.

Accounting: The Language of the Business
A function of the office of the controller, accounting also offers a range of opportunities. State-of-the-art tools and technologies are used to collect, record, and report the company's economic transactions; the accountant's skills are used to interpret past business performance and to present recommendations for management decisions. The function is highly communications-oriented, with data consolidated from many sources for analysis and reporting in commonly understood terms.

Accounting fills many roles at IBM, from measurements and planning to government reporting and preparation of financial statements. Schedules are sensitive and demanding, logistics complex. The work demands teamwork and communication. You must accurately record financial results, comply with government regulations, and report earnings in a variety of ways. You must also ensure consistent presentation of accounting data and compliance with generally accepted accounting principles.

Accounting plays a vital, creative role in the management decision-making process at IBM. In an accounting position, you not only affect all basic operational areas—engineering, programming, marketing, administration—but also play a key role with IBM Treasury, international operations, and internal business partnership arrangements.

IBM also offers internal education to help you prepare for and take the Certified Management Accountant (CMA) exams. IBM is a corporate leader in the number of CMA certificates in its financial ranks.

IBM Pricing: Much More Than Finance
The pricing of IBM products and services is one of the most important responsibilities of the business. It is much more than finance—it is business itself. To ensure an adequate profit and return on investment, the pricing function must manage a product or service throughout its life, from conception to withdrawal from the market.

In simple terms, the role of pricing is to select IBM offerings and their prices to maximize the corporation's profitability. The major challenge is to ensure recovery of all costs and expenses, direct or indirect, associated with the development, manufacture, marketing, and maintenance of IBM products and services. In addition, IBM hardware, software, and service offerings must be understood within the context of a global marketplace where product strategies vary from country to country.

In fact, the pricing area is instrumental in initial selection of IBM products to be developed. Pricing analysts work side by side with the product management and marketing teams to ensure that new product offerings will meet the needs of IBM customers. The pricing function takes a financial and general management role in the decision about a program's financial viability and match to IBM's strategic objectives.

Pricing has an impact on all stages of a product's life. In the introduction stage, price selection, and terms and conditions involve detailed analysis of several areas: business area opportunity, product function, strategy, positioning, price elasticity, supply constraints, cost trends in technologies, manufacturing process, research and development strengths, marketing support plans, and selection of cost-effective distribution channels. The product must be positioned with respect to competition, with respect to the needs of the customer, and within IBM's product line.

Once introduced, a product is open to competitive moves: new products, price cuts, discounting, creative marketing, and promotional tactics. Pricing's responsibility is to anticipate these actions and prepare appropriate responses. During the growth stage of the product life cycle, the generation of sales is paramount. This often means that competitive bid situations, existing prices, terms, conditions, and methodologies are constantly subject to review and fine tuning.

If you work in this area, you will draw on the full repertoire of financial skills acquired in business school. You will coordinate the efforts of many groups, including product managers, market requirements specialists, business planning managers, and product forecasters. It is a unique opportunity for cross-disciplinary exposure within IBM and excellent experience in the IBM Finance career.

Treasury: Providing Capital for the Business
The IBM Treasury function is responsible for managing the company's capital structure and securing funds needed to operate the business. This demands reliable forecasting of cash receipts and disbursements, up-to-the-minute knowledge of international money markets, selection of funding vehicles, and maintenance of relationships with investment banking and commercial banking institutions.

In effect, Treasury is a focal point for the evaluation of a broad range of complex financial alternatives. IBM is concerned with worldwide liquidity, asset safety, currency management, tax optimization and compliance, risk/insurance management, optimal capital structure, investor perceptions, portfolio returns, and cost of capital.

The worldwide nature of IBM's business also requires techniques to protect the company from fluctuation in the value of foreign currencies. The ultimate objective is to optimize the use of cash, to keep any excess funds appropriately invested until needed, and to ensure access to funds when needed at the most favorable terms possible.

Other activities within the Treasury organization include internal audit, retirement fund management, short-term investment supervision, intercompany relations, and IBM's corporate citizenship programs.

Opportunities in the IBM Credit Corporation
Opportunities are also available for recent graduates in the IBM Credit Corporation, a wholly owned corporate subsidiary. By helping customers acquire IBM products and services through competitive financing offerings, IBM Credit plays a pivotal role in providing complete customer solutions.

IBM Credit provides leases and other financing products, remarketing services, end-of-lease options, and—for IBM Business Partners—inventory financing programs. It also provides IBM employees with financial services such as a money market account and mutual funds.

IBM Credit contributes significantly to the corporation's competitiveness and to the growth and stability of IBM earnings.

Since IBM Credit's products are financing offerings, financial professionals are involved in every stage of product development and delivery. These stages include the following:

- Development of new financial offerings that respond to customer requirements and competitive opportunities

- Assessments of credit risk and recovery of investment in high-risk situations

- Pricing of specific customer proposals for financing, including unique terms and conditions and competitive tactics

- Borrowing of debt funds via commercial paper, medium-term notes, and bond issues; relationships with investment-banking advisors

- Managing capital structure, including asset and liability matching and relations with the principal rating agencies

• Planning, accounting, and modeling financial performance, including publication of annual reports and supporting external financial communications

The Recruiting Process

Describe your recruiting process and the criteria by which you select candidates. Is prior experience necessary?

Within this environment, IBM Finance needs talented people with MBA degrees. The qualities sought are leadership, intelligence and awareness, interpersonal skills, creativity and ingenuity, energy, business maturity and judgment, integrity, personal enthusiasm, a goal-setting outlook, a desire to compete among the best—and the ability to be yourself.

ING Baring Furman Selz LLC

55 East 52nd Street
35th Floor
New York, NY 10055
(212) 409-1000
Web Site: www.furmanselz.com

MBA Recruiting Contacts:
Investment Banking
Terri Reinhart
Recruiting Coordinator
(212) 808-2190
Fax: (212) 808-2189

Tracy Baker
Recruiting Assistant
(212) 808-2713
Fax: (212) 808-2189

Company Description

Describe your firm's business and the types of clients served by your finance group(s).

ING Baring Furman Selz is a financial services firm that provides investment banking, brokerage, and asset management services to corporations, governments, and individuals. Our firm includes nearly 10,000 people in more than fifty locations worldwide. We are active in all major sectors of finance and are one of the largest financial services firms in the world.

How does your approach to finance differ from that of other firms, and what do you consider to be your strengths and distinctive capabilities?

ING Baring Furman Selz is focused on differentiating itself by providing thoughtful, cutting-edge advice while at the same time delivering personal service. The firm maintains an entrepreneurial feel. We focus on selected industries including: financial institutions, health care, industrial manufacturing, information services, media, real estate, retail, technology, telecom, and transportation.

The Finance MBA's Job Description

Describe the career path and corresponding responsibilities for an MBA at your firm.

As a member of the Investment Banking Group, associates are responsible for creating and managing the quantitative financial analysis as well as the qualitative document issues related to the execution of debt, equity, and merger and acquisition transactions on behalf of corporations, financial institutions, and government entities. Associates work with senior investment bankers in the marketing of ING Baring Furman Selz services and client development. Assignments will provide exposure to a variety of specialized industry teams and capital markets products within Investment Banking.

Discuss the lifestyle aspects of a career with your firm (i.e., average hours per week, amount of travel, flexibility to change offices, corporate culture, etc.).

ING Baring Furman Selz prides itself on employee satisfaction. Average hours per week and amount of travel vary by industry group. ING Baring Furman Selz strives to create a positive environment for all employees.

The Recruiting Process

Describe your recruiting process and the criteria by which you select candidates. Is prior experience necessary?

When evaluating candidates, the firm looks for individuals with strong quantitative and analytic aptitudes, demonstrated leadership ability, excellent writing and presentation skills, and a long-term view of the business. The work of an associate demands a high degree of self-motivation, dedication, and commitment to Investment Banking. Candidates are first interviewed on campus with some invited back to be interviewed by senior management during a Super Saturday.

How many permanent associates do you hire in a typical year? How many summer interns do you expect to hire? If you have a formal summer program, please describe it. Please be sure to indicate whether the summer program is in place for all offices or just some.

Each year the firm hires ten to fifteen new associates in Investment Banking.

ING Baring Furman Selz hires eight to ten summer associates per year for the New York office in Investment Banking. The Summer Program starts in early June and lasts eight to ten weeks.

J.P. Morgan & Co. Incorporated

60 Wall Street
New York, NY 10260
Web site: www.jpmorgan.com

MBA Recruiting Contact(s):
Alison Trumbower, Associate
Investment Banking

Gladys Chen, Associate
Markets (Sales, Trading & Research)

Michelle Bucaria (nee Wright), Vice President
Private Client Group and
Investment Management

Company Description

Describe your firm's business and the types of clients served by your finance group(s).

J.P. Morgan is a leading global financial firm that serves the critical needs of a diverse community of clients. They include corporations, governments, financial institutions, private firms, not-for-profit institutions, and wealthy individuals throughout the world. For these clients, Morgan provides a broad range of complex, interrelated activities that are grouped into three business sectors: finance and advisory, market making, and asset management and servicing. In addition, the firm manages equity investments and invests and trades for its own accounts. Our client and proprietary activities complement and reinforce each other.

Finance and advisory. Morgan helps clients advance their strategic goals. We structure and raise equity and debt capital, counsel on business and financing strategy, and execute transactions, including mergers, acquisitions, divestitures, and privatizations. Our global presence and experience are increasingly important to our advisory business as cross-border transactions grow in number and importance for clients.

Market making. Morgan provides clients with access to the world's financial markets, both established and emerging. We deal in securities, currencies, commodities, loan syndications, and derivative instruments to help clients meet their investment, trading, and risk management needs.

Asset management and servicing. Morgan manages financial assets entrusted to us by institutions and individuals using separately managed portfolios and investment funds. For private clients, we offer a range of investment, advisory, banking, brokerage, and fiduciary services. Morgan also serves the global business community by acting as a futures and options broker on exchanges worldwide and by operating the Euroclear system that clears global securities for its member institutions.

Equity investments. Morgan manages its own diversified portfolio of equity investments. We invest in privately held growth companies, management buyouts, privatizations, and recapitalizations, turning our global knowledge and experience into a comparative investment advantage for stockholders.

Proprietary investing and trading. Morgan actively manages market positions for its own account, with varying investment and trading horizons, diversified across a spectrum of markets and instruments. We use our global market knowledge and resources to manage the firm's capital and liquidity profiles.

How does your approach to finance differ from that of other firms, and what do you consider to be your strengths and distinctive capabilities?

What differentiates Morgan in the financial arena is the way we do business. We are guided by a few long-standing and fundamental beliefs: objectivity, fairness, and integrity. We always put our clients' long-term interests first. We use a team approach in serving them, drawing on our global network of colleagues. This approach gives our clients the benefit of the breadth of our capabilities and expertise. All our business activities are supported by strong, objective research. Clients rely on our sound rigorous analysis and recommendations. We are committed to maintaining the highest standard of conduct and operate always with the belief that our reputation for fair dealing is our greatest asset.

Discuss changes in your firm's revenue (both domestic and international) and professional staff over the past year; over the past five years.

During the past ten years, Morgan has expanded its capabilities in the United States, adding investment and merchant banking capabilities to its commercial banking and investment management businesses. Our global experience in these areas gave us the momentum to reach leadership positions in debt and equity underwriting and M&A activity in less than ten years. Now positioned as a leader in every arena, Morgan's strategy is to be the leading global financial firm of the next century.

The Finance MBA's Job Description

Describe the career path and corresponding responsibilities for an MBA at your firm.

MBA graduates join the firm as associates in specific positions in four business areas: Investment Banking, Markets (sales, trading, and research), the Private Client Group, and Investment Management. Opportunities generally arise for Morgan professionals to work in a variety of positions within their business area and sometimes in other areas during the course of their careers. This mobility factor underscores Morgan's commitment to developing its people. Also, by serving in a variety of functions, individuals better understand our clients' needs and can maximize the firm's ability to meet those needs.

Investment Banking. Associates in Investment Banking initially work with client and product teams on the marketing, structuring, and execution of financing and advisory assignments. As associates develop a broad and solid base of knowledge and experience, they move into positions as product specialists and work closely with experienced client managers to ensure the optimal execution and delivery of products and services that match a client's business and financial strategy.

Markets (sales, trading, and research). Associates are hired for sales, trading, or research positions in Equities, Fixed Income, Foreign Exchange, or Emerging Markets. Responsibilities vary based on the individual's specific assignment and function within the group. They could include compiling research, technical analysis, and market commentaries for the sales and syndicate desks; managing risk, liquidity, and interest rate exposure on a trading desk; developing and maintaining relationships with institutional investors and marketing Morgan products and capabilities to them; and developing views on prospects and stock prices.

Private Client Group. Associates focus on one of two functions: client advisory or securities sales. Client advisors, acting as financial planners and working with a team of experts, focus on optimizing wealth for high-net-worth clients; they coordinate the overall delivery of Morgan's services to these clients. Securities sales associates are investment specialists who provide access to Morgan's securities research, advice, products, and trade execution in

markets worldwide for clients who manage their own portfolios.

Investment Management. Responsibilities vary depending on the associate's assignment and could include conducting original, fundamental research and valuing companies; executing securities; analyzing investment performance; assisting in the construction, management, and monitoring of portfolios; or marketing products and servicing clients.

The Recruiting Process

Describe your recruiting process and the criteria by which you select candidates. Is prior experience necessary?

All four groups—Investment Banking, Markets, Private Client Group, and Investment Management—conduct on-campus interviews for full-time and summer positions. Morgan seeks outstanding, creative, analytical, and committed individuals who work well with others and are willing to assume responsibility. The firm offers hard-working individuals the opportunity to make a significant contribution quickly. Morgan operates with a team approach, which promotes an open discussion of ideas and enables its professionals to learn about parts of Morgan's business outside their own areas. Members of the firm stress dealing honorably and responsibly with others to maintain the firm's high-quality work environment and high standard of integrity. Prior experience in the financial services industry is not required or expected. Foreign language skills are considered an asset but are not a requirement.

How many permanent associates and analysts do you hire in a typical year? How many summer interns do you expect to hire? If you have a formal summer program, please describe it. Please be sure to indicate whether the summer program is in place for all offices or just some.

Morgan has an extensive summer program for MBAs who are between their first and second years of business school. Summer associates are hired to work in one of the four recruiting areas based on their interests, skills, past experience, and the needs of the firm. However, the program provides summer associates with a broad exposure to the firm and all its businesses through presentations by managers. Members of Morgan's senior management also meet with summer associates to brief them on the firm's strategy and management philosophy. Summer associates are encouraged to meet with officers throughout the firm to identify areas for further exploration.

Candidates for the summer associate program should have a serious interest in finance and the financial markets. Most positions are in New York. They last ten to twelve weeks and are scheduled between mid-May and mid-September.

What international opportunities does your firm offer for U.S. citizens? For foreign nationals?

Morgan recruits MBAs primarily for positions in New York but does hire MBAs with the right to work in countries in Europe, Asia, and Latin America.

Lehman Brothers

Three World Financial Center
New York, NY 10285
(212) 526-7000
Web site: www.lehman.com

MBA Recruiting Contact(s):
Joseph Valenti
Global Debt and Capital Markets
(212) 526-2555

Kristin Williams
Sales, Trading & Research
(212) 526-4843

Company Description

Describe your firm's business and the types of clients served by your finance group(s).

Company Description

Lehman Brothers is a global investment bank with leadership positions in corporate finance, advisory services, municipal finance, merchant banking, and fixed income and equity sales, trading, and research. Lehman Brothers serves the financial needs of corporate, government, and institutional clients, and high-net-worth individuals through offices in major financial centers worldwide.

Lehman Brothers has major operating centers in New York, London, and Tokyo, and over 33 additional offices worldwide.

Describe your ownership structure.

Lehman Brothers, which is celebrating its 150th anniversary this year, has been a publicly traded company since May 1994. As of the end of 1999, approximately 33% of Lehman Brothers' common stock was employee-owned.

How does your approach to finance differ from that of other firms, and what do you consider to be your strengths and distinctive capabilities?

Lehman Brothers differs from its competitors in the following five ways:

Our Franchise
Founded in 1850, Lehman Brothers has long been one of Wall Street's premier investment banking firms. Our global presence provides us with access to the most significant issuers and investors worldwide.

Our Future
Lehman Brothers' rich history and tradition provide a strong foundation as we continue to expand our business in high-growth markets. We are leveraging technology to be a leader in e-commerce and were the first investment bank to conduct a corporate bond offering entirely over the Internet.

Our Strategy
Our strategy is client-driven. Lehman Brothers professionals understand that providing the highest level of service to our clients is the core of our business strategy.

Our Culture
Lehman Brothers operates on a "One Firm" philosophy that emphasizes integration and teamwork across all businesses worldwide. Working together as "One Firm" enables us to deliver a full range of products and services to our clients in a seamless manner.

Our People
Our professionals have a bias for action and a desire to make a difference. At Lehman Brothers, you will join a highly talented and motivated group of people who want to build a long and successful career at the firm.

Discuss changes in your firm's revenues (both domestic and international) and professional staff over the past year; over the past five years.

Lehman Brothers' net revenues for the 12 month reporting period ended November 30, 1999 totaled $5.3 billion. Net operating income was a record $1,132 million for the full fiscal year 1999, an increase of 54% over 1998. The firm strengthened its market position in key sectors such as equity and investment banking, while fortifying its already strong place in the fixed income markets.

Over the past five years, Lehman Brothers has posted a revenue growth rate of 16% per year and has increased its earnings at a rate of 47% per year. Our return on equity has increased to 21.8% from 7.1% in 1995.

Lehman Brothers achieved the following accomplishments in 1999:

- Sourced approximately 40% of revenues from our European and Asian activities with 30% of our employees based outside the U.S., making Lehman Brothers one of the most internationally-oriented of the major investment banks;

- Raised a $350 million Venture Capital fund to invest in mid- to latter-stage pre-IPO companies across all growth sectors. Lehman Brothers also initiated fund raising for the Communications Fund which will also make venture investments in early-stage communications companies;

- Received numerous "Deal of the Year" awards for our role in various transactions across products, sectors, and geographies, including Olivetti/Telecom Italia, MediaOne/AT&T, China.com IPO, and WalMart bond offering;

- Announced a groundbreaking alliance with Fidelity Investments which provides Lehman with retail distribution of our lead managed financings to Fidelity's 6.5 million customers, who also have access to our equity and fixed income research;

- Lead-managed over $6 billion of IPOs for 44 clients around the globe. Of our 22 lead managed Internet IPOs, the stock prices increased an average of 291%;

- Raised $195 billion in debt and equity underwritings for clients worldwide as lead manager;

- Ranked #4 in Fixed Income Trading by *Institutional Investor* across all products in 1999;

- Completed $179 billion of M&A transactions and announced $312 billion; and,

- Our "10 Uncommon Values" stock picks had a 23.9% return through January 19, 2000, outperforming the S&P 500s 6.1% through the same date. Launched the "Virtual Economy Portfolio" economic model.

The Finance MBA's Job Description

Describe the career path and corresponding responsibilities for an MBA at your firm.

Lehman Brothers prides itself on the variety of backgrounds and range of achievements represented by its professionals. Before joining the firm, many Lehman Brothers' professionals had careers in areas such as law, medicine, the military and other public service, and private industry, as well as in finance. This diversity instills creativity in and provides depth to the firm.

Lehman Brothers is committed to developing well-rounded professionals and encourages associates to take on as much responsibility as they can handle. Each associate is given the opportunity to build a broad base of skills, and the firm constantly monitors each associate's development, working with him or her to help achieve specific career goals.

All Investment Banking, and Sales, Trading & Research associates begin their career at Lehman Brothers participating in a "One Firm" training program that introduces them to Lehman Brothers, its clients, products, and services. Classroom training during the first six weeks enables associates to hone their skills in finance and accounting and to develop the analytical tools they will use throughout their careers. Specific training is also provided in fixed income, equity, and derivative products. In addition, associates share in team-building activities and social events. This strategy helps build internal networks and working relationships among professionals throughout the organization.

Following the training program, Investment Banking associates rotate through various industry coverage or product specialty groups. During the rotation, they will gain exposure to three groups within Investment Banking and are able to apply the analytical tools developed during the training program. The rotation is followed by a placement in a specific group. International associates benefit from the same training and rotation as U.S. associates. At the end of an 18-month period in Lehman Brothers' New York headquarters, the international associates begin their permanent assignments in Lehman Brothers' international offices.

Associates for Sales, Trading & Research move from the training program into a six-week generalist rotation. There they will be exposed to a variety of product areas before joining a specific business. High Net Worth Sales associates also benefit from the generalist rotation, prior to joining Private Client Services. International Sales, Trading & Research associates also begin their careers in Lehman Brothers' New York headquarters. Following classroom training, associates complete a rotation through various product areas. This rotation may take place in New York, the international offices, or both, and provides associates with an overview of the product areas.

After completing the training program, Public Finance associates serve as generalists during their entire first year, working with a variety of municipal clients. Associates then join either a specialty group, such as Housing, Education, or Health Care, or a regional group covering a geographically defined area of the United States.

The Recruiting Process

Describe your recruiting process and the criteria by which you select candidates. Is prior experience necessary?

In our recruiting efforts we look for individuals who possess a keen intellect, a powerful desire to succeed, and the resourcefulness to produce results. Because of the emphasis on teamwork, we also want people who can cooperate and leverage one another's skills while encouraging each individual's unique creativity and entrepreneurial spirit.

How many permanent associates and analysts do you hire in a typical year? How many summer interns do you expect to hire? If you have a formal summer program, please describe it. Please be sure to indicate whether the summer program is in place for all offices or just some.

Lehman Brothers' Summer Associate Program provides students at the midpoint of their graduate school education an opportunity to evaluate the working environment and career opportunities at the firm. The summer associate program is available at many of the offices around the world.

Investment Banking and Pubic Finance summer associates work as full members of client teams on a variety of transactions. They also enjoy extensive contact with Lehman Brothers' professionals at all levels through discussion groups, seminars, and informal social functions.

Sales and Trading summer associates are assigned to two five-week placements, one in fixed income and one in equity. Additionally, they spend one day of each week in different product areas, covering a variety of businesses over the course of the summer. Finally, they attend lectures by senior professionals and participate in weekly market update sessions.

Merrill Lynch & Co., Inc.

World Financial Center
250 Vesey Street
New York, NY 10281-1331
(212) 449-4374
Web site: www.ml.com

MBA Recruiting Contact(s):
Andrea C. Beldecos
Director & Manager
Corporate & Institutional Client Group Recruiting

Company Description

Describe your firm's business and the types of clients served by your finance group(s).

Merrill Lynch is one of the world's leading financial management and advisory companies with offices in more than forty countries and total client assets exceeding $1.7 trillion. As an investment bank, it is the top global underwriter and market maker of debt and equity securities and a leading strategic advisor to corporations, governments, institutions, and individuals worldwide. Through Merrill Lynch Asset Management and Merrill Lynch Mercury Asset Management, the company is one of the world's largest managers of financial assets with assets under management exceeding $550 billion.

Merrill Lynch acts as principal, agent, underwriter, market maker, broker, and financial advisor to its clients. The firm is fundamentally client driven, bringing together issuers and investors.

Our Corporate and Institutional Client Group (CICG) provides investment banking and strategic merger and acquisition advisory services, as well as equity and debt trading and capital markets services, to corporations, financial institutions, and governments around the world. CICG raises capital for its clients on favorable terms through securities underwriting, private placements, and loan syndication.

Headquartered in New York, CICG trades securities, currencies, and other products, and writes over-the-counter derivatives to satisfy customer demand for these instruments. With more than 2,000 equity research professionals and equity trading activities in over twenty countries, Merrill Lynch maintains one of the most powerful equity trading and underwriting capabilities of any firm in the world. Through its expertise in government and corporate debt trading, CICG is also the leader in global distribution of new issue and secondary debt securities. CICG's client-focused strategy provides investors with opportunities to diversify their portfolios, manage risk, and enhance returns by tailoring investments and structuring derivatives to meet clients' customized needs.

Merrill Lynch's non-U.S. operations are organized into six geographic regions: Europe, Middle East, and Africa; Asia Pacific; Australia and New Zealand; Japan; Canada; and Latin America.

Describe your ownership structure.

Merrill Lynch & Co., Inc. is a holding company that provides investment, financing, insurance, and related services to individuals and institutions on a global basis through its broker, dealer, banking, insurance, and other financial services subsidiaries. The common stock of Merrill Lynch is listed on the New York Stock Exchange, the Chicago Stock Exchange, the Pacific Exchange, Paris Bourse, the London Stock Exchange, and the Tokyo Stock Exchange.

How does your approach to finance differ from that of other firms, and what do you consider to be your strengths and distinctive capabilities?

The strength of our organization is based on leadership in both the institutional and retail sectors. Merrill Lynch's ability to capitalize on the synergies that exist between these sectors—specifically, a strong distribution function complementing an origination and trading capability—distinguishes its strategy from that of its competitors. With the largest distribution capabilities on Wall Street and an integrated global network, the firm has the unique ability to place deals and facilitate transactions worldwide.

Discuss changes in your firm's revenues (both domestic and international) and professional staff over the past year; over the past five years.

Earnings for 1999 were a record $2.6 billion, up 69% from the $1.5 billion reported in 1998. Our corporate and institutional businesses had a record year, led by robust M&A, underwriting, and market-making activity. The strategic investments we have made to build our businesses globally—in asset management, investment banking, private client and the debt and equity markets—are producing strong results, with a growing proportion of our business coming from outside the U.S.

The Finance MBA's Job Description

Describe the career path and corresponding responsibilities for an MBA at your firm.

Merrill Lynch invests substantial resources in identifying and recruiting superior candidates. In the graduating class of 1999, CICG hired approximately over 130 associates.

The following businesses recruit the most MBAs:

- Investment Banking is responsible for corporate and institutional client relationships worldwide. Through the delivery of advisory services and financial products, the division focuses on the needs of issuer clients. Included in this division are mergers and acquisitions, leveraged buyout fund management, real estate, project financing, relationship management, and several specialty functions.

- Debt Markets offers issuing and investing clients a complete array of debt financing alternatives in short-, medium-, and long-term debt products. The division is integrated vertically to include origination, trading, fixed income, marketing, research, and new product development. Major product areas are money markets, global debt financing, mortgage capital, financial futures and options, U.S. governments and agencies, foreign exchange, and municipal markets.

- Equity Markets is structured to provide institutional investor clients with origination, trading, syndication, and wholesale services worldwide. The division also works with investment banking in serving corporate and government issuers.

- Municipal Markets encompasses all activities related to the origination, pricing, sales, and trading of tax-exempt debt instruments. These include fixed rate bonds and notes, commercial paper and other variable rate products, interest rate swaps, hedges, and embedded derivative products.

Career paths and corresponding responsibilities vary depending on the business division. An MBA joining Investment Banking, for example, typically enters as an associate, responsible for the details of executing transactions and preparing proposals. After approximately four years, associates are eligible for promotion to vice president. Vice presidents manage the execution of transactions and identify new opportunities with clients. About three years later, vice presidents become eligible for promotion to director, or the more senior title of managing director. Directors and managing directors are responsible for maintenance of client relationships and identification of new business opportunities.

New CICG associates generally join the firm in early August and complete a six-week firmwide development training program; besides serving as an orientation to Merrill Lynch, the program builds strong ties among the participants. The academic component includes team assignments, case studies, simulations, and hands-on interaction with trading games.

Describe the opportunities for professional mobility between the various departments in your firm.

New associates work in a specific department, though they have much contact throughout the firm. As their interests change and as our businesses evolve, new opportunities are often available firmwide.

Discuss the lifestyle aspects of a career with your firm (i.e., average hours per week, amount of travel, flexibility to change offices, corporate culture, etc.).

Lifestyles vary depending on which business unit an MBA joins. Requirements for each division are typical for the financial services industry.

The Recruiting Process

Describe your recruiting process and the criteria by which you select candidates. Is prior experience necessary?

Merrill Lynch participates in on-campus presentations and events and on-campus interviews. Successful candidates are called back for final interviews in New York.

We seek individuals with a record of achievement and excellence. Successful candidates have strong analytical skills and an understanding of strategic issues. They communicate effectively, think creatively, work well with others, and act decisively. Academic performance and prior work experience are also important criteria, though prior work in the industry is not necessary.

How many permanent associates and analysts do you hire in a typical year? How many summer interns do you expect to hire? If you have a formal summer program, please describe it. Please be sure to indicate whether the summer program is in place for all offices or just some.

Hiring is based on the needs of each business division, and recruiting goals are set early in the fall for the coming recruiting season. In 1999, we hired over 130 full-time associates.

Summer associates have significant responsibilities and are involved with a variety of transactions. Scheduled activities and seminars with senior management offer summer associates frequent exposure and the opportunity to expand their knowledge of the firm. In 1999, 134 summer associates were hired in CICG worldwide.

Morgan Stanley Dean Witter

1585 Broadway, 16th Floor
New York, NY 10036
(212) 761-4000
Fax: (212) 761-0290
Web site: www.msdw.com/career/recruiting

MBA Recruiting Contact(s):
North America Recruiting Contacts:
1585 Broadway, 16th Floor
New York, NY 10036
Attn: *Division of Interest*

Firmwide Recruiting
Katie Leonard

Investment Banking Recruiting
Patricia Palumbo, Vice President

Fixed Income Sales, Trading and Research Recruiting
Jennifer Edwards, Recruiting Manager

Institutional Equity, Equity Research, Equity Financing Services
Erica Weiner

Private Wealth Management
Courtney Phillips

Institutional Investment Management, Private Equity, Capital Partners
Maria Hurley

European Recruiting Contact(s):
25 Cabot Square, Canary Wharf
London, E14 4QA, England

Firmwide Recruiting
Rebecca Neale

Investment Banking
Charlotte Thatcher

Equity Sales & Trading
Donna Gardner

Fixed Income Sales, Trading & Research
Frances Bailey

Private Wealth Management
Sarah Scott

Southeast Asia Recruiting Contact:
Morgan Stanley Dean Witter Asia Ltd.
Recruiting Manager, Human Resources
30th Floor, 3 Exchange Square
Hong Kong

Japan Recruiting Contact:
MSDW Japan, Ltd.
Recruiting Manager, Human Resources
Yebisu Garden Place Tower
20-3, Ebisu 4 Chome
Shibuyu-Ku, Tokyo 150, Japan

Locations of Offices:
550 offices in 25 countries (56 principal offices)

Total Number of Professionals (U.S. and worldwide):
Over 52,000 worldwide

Company Description

Describe your firm's business and the types of clients served by your finance group(s).

Morgan Stanley Dean Witter & Co. is a preeminent global financial services firm that engages in a full range of financial services businesses with leading market positions in securities, asset management, and credit services. The firm's businesses include corporate finance, mergers and acquisitions, equity and fixed income institutional sales and trading, foreign exchange and commodities trading, asset management, equity financing services, public finance, and services to private clients—each of which offers many products and services. Morgan Stanley Dean Witter is organized as three main businesses: securities, asset management, and credit services.

Morgan Stanley Dean Witter's finance groups provide the following services to our clients:

Equity Research
Equity Research provides timely, high-quality, in-depth analysis to enhance the performance of Morgan Stanley Dean Witter's clients' global portfolios. Using economic market, industry, and company studies, Equity Research analysts, economists, and strategists strive to anticipate developments that will affect security values worldwide. New Research analysts are assigned to a specific industry at the very outset. Our program is designed to develop proficiency in one to two years, with the ultimate goal of our analysts becoming recognized experts in their re-

spective industries. Equity Research professionals analyze company financial data, industry trends, and macroeconomics factors; forecast earnings and stock prices; write research reports and updates on companies and industries; and make independent buy and sell recommendations. Research analysts work closely with Equity salespeople and traders, Investment Banking professionals, clients, and institutional investors.

Equity Sales and Trading

The Equity Division provides Morgan Stanley Dean Witter clients with global distribution capabilities, liquidity, and a high level of trading expertise in all major world markets. It also offers sophisticated analyses and ready access to a broad range of equity products and issues. Associates in Equity Sales and Trading are involved in the worldwide selling and trading of equity and equity derivative securities. After a three-month training program conducted in New York, associates immediately go to work on their assigned desk covering either the traditional stock business, equity derivatives, or convertible securities. New associates are assigned their own accounts and act as backup to some of our major accounts; they also have the opportunity to work with many different investors, products, and areas of the firm.

The Equity Division consists of three major areas:

Core Equity. Core Equity consists of the traditional stock business and encompasses the sales and trading of equity securities around the world. Customers include banks, insurance companies, private pension funds, mutual funds, investment advisors, endowments, foundations, and hedge funds. There are two main sources of revenue: sales and primary and secondary offerings, and trading commissions (which customers pay in return for liquidity, the firm's trading expertise, and access to equity research).

Convertible Securities. Convertible Securities plays a leading role in both the primary and secondary markets in global convertible securities, one of the earliest forms of equity derivative instruments. Through its operations in New York, London, Tokyo, and Hong Kong, Morgan Stanley Dean Witter is able to exercise its expertise in domestic and global markets.

Equity Derivatives. Equity Derivatives executes stock index futures and options on a global basis. In addition, it executes customer trading programs for institutions wishing to liquidate, invest, or restructure large equity portfolios. The group offers a range of services in synthetic equity products, including executions of long-dated options, index-linked bonds, and equity swaps. The global equity derivatives sales force advises institutional clients on the use of listed equity derivatives portfolio trading strategies and synthetic equity products to meet their unique risk profiles. Our equity derivative sales and trading activities have increased substantially in recent years and will continue to expand to meet the changing needs of our client base. The group now reaches all major international listed markets, while also supporting the latest techniques in structured financial engineering.

Fixed Income Sales, Trading, and Research

Morgan Stanley's Fixed Income Division offers clients a wide range of products and services. The division's sales and distribution teams are organized geographically and supported by product specialists. Using a broad and growing range of financial products, Fixed Income associates working in sales assist institutional investors in planning and implementing portfolio strategies. Associates working as traders commit the Firm's capital to ensure liquidity for our clients. Research associates provide fixed income strategy, corporate credit research, develop quantitative models and analytical support.

The Fixed Income Division consists of the following principal global product areas:

Derivative Products. The Derivative Products Group originates, markets and trades structured products, currency and interest rate swaps, and synthetic securities. The group advises corporate, government agency and sovereign issuers, and institutional investors on customized investments, asset liability management and hedging transactions. In joint ventures with other Morgan Stanley Dean Witter departments, the Derivative Products Group also focuses on mortgage derivatives and global high yield derivatives.

Global High Yield and Emerging Markets. The Global High Yield / Emerging Markets group focuses on non-investment grade debt of domestic and international corporations and sovereign debt of emerging market countries. The group is expert in global distribution, market making and analytics in complex high-yield securities, issued for both start-up and mature companies across all industries and countries.

Government Debt. The Government Debt group takes proprietary positions and makes markets in U.S. Treasury and agency securities on a global basis, around the clock. Client coverage extends through the group's New York, London and Tokyo trading desks, as well as through its online DBD electronic marketing system. Primary activities include making secondary markets in all U.S. Treasury and agency securities, taking proprietary positions, participating in Treasury auctions, and distributing agency new issues.

Investment Grade Debt. The Investment Grade Debt group includes intermediate and long-term corporate debt, medium-term notes, commercial paper, floating-rate notes, certificates of deposits and preferred stock for industrial corporations, utilities, banks, thrifts and finance companies. The group's primary activities include underwriting and trading these instruments in the U.S., Europe and Asia in a broad range of currencies.

Securitized Products Group. The Securitized Products Group engages in a wide array of activities, from structuring and underwriting collateralized securities to writing loans collateralized by real properties, consumer loans, and many other financial assets. Opportunities are available in client coverage, principal activities, capital markets and secondary trading. With professionals in New York, London, Tokyo and Hong Kong, the group covers clients and securitization opportunities around the world.

Foreign Exchange. The Foreign Exchange (FX) group provides a wide range of services to institutional and high-net-worth individual clients around the world. The group is a leading market maker in spot and forward currencies, as well as options, including exotics. The sales team provides 'one stop shopping' for clients who need 24-hour coverage for trading, research and analytics in the world's financial centers. In addition, the trading desk leverages the Firm's capital to take proprietary positions. The FX department plays a major role in facilitating global capital flows including financing, mergers and acquisitions, and cross-border trading in fixed income and equity securities.

Municipal Bonds and Public Finance Securities Division. The Municipal and Public Finance Securities Division provides sales, trading, underwriting, derivatives, capital markets, and investment banking services for issuers, investors, dealers, traders and arbitrageurs participating in the $200+ billion tax-exempt fixed income market. The group's major investor clients include mutual funds, hedge funds, insurance companies, commercial banks, and corporations. Typical issuer client categories include States, Counties, Cities, other municipal entities, Real Estate developers (single family, multi-family, municipal mortgage backed originators), Student Loan originators, Project Finance, Stadiums, Convention Centers, Hospitals (standalone and health care systems, HMOs), Universities (public and private), major Not-For-Profits (museums, libraries, foundations, etc.), Public Utilities (electric, water, waste treatment, resource recovery), Public/Private partnerships, Airports, Ports, and Surface Transportation (Toll Roads, Freeways, Mass Transit, High Speed Rail, etc.).

Summer Associate Program. The program is ten weeks in duration, during which time summer associates are assigned to specific trading or research desk; they work to identify market opportunities and assist traders, salespeople, and researchers in the analysis and evaluation of securities. Summer Associates are also given the opportunity to rotate among the various areas in Fixed Income and Foreign Exchange sales, trading and research.

Investment Banking

Morgan Stanley Dean Witter's Investment Banking Division utilizes both traditional and innovative financing techniques to help corporations and governments around the world make and execute decisions regarding their capital. New associates begin in Investment Banking as generalists, gaining broad exposure to a variety of the division's products, services, and clients. Associates work on a mix of assignments ranging from transaction execution to business development initiatives. Associates have the opportunity to work directly with the senior-level financial and strategic decision-makers of some of the world's largest corporations, as well as with smaller, emerging growth clients. After a one-year generalist experience, associates begin to specialize in either an industry, product area, or geographic region.

The Investment Banking Division consists of five closely related business units: Corporate Finance; Mergers, Acquisitions and Restructuring; Morgan Stanley Realty; Debt Capital Market Services; and Equity Capital Markets Services.

Corporate Finance. Corporate Finance is responsible for initiating, developing, and maintaining the firm's investment banking relationships with clients worldwide; for providing financial advice; and, in partnership with other specialized areas of the firm, for executing specific client transactions. The Corporate Finance Department is organized into teams of regional and industry specialists. The regional coverage groups provide a strong Morgan Stanley Dean Witter presence in the United States, Canada, Western and Eastern Europe, Latin America, the Middle East, the Far East, and Australia. The industry groups provide special expertise in the following sectors: commercial banking, financial entrepreneurs, food and consumer products, health care, insurance, media, natural resources, public utilities, retail, technology, telecommunications, and transportation. Within Corporate Finance, there is the Client Services Group (CSG), which is responsible for the execution of all equity offerings, complex debt issuances, and other capital markets-related business. We also advise government and private sector clients on the privatization of state-owned enterprises.

Mergers, Acquisitions and Restructuring (MARD). MARD provides corporate and financial clients with financial advisory services in situations involving mergers, acquisitions, defenses, proxy contests, divestitures, spin-offs, joint ventures, and restructuring. Many of our MARD assignments involve complex, competitive situations that require a high degree of creativity, analytical skills, and judgment. M&A professionals must be proficient in a wide range of technical skills (e.g., legal, tax, and accounting) and understand an extensive number of strategic alternatives in the context of any particular transaction. Within MARD is the Private Investment Group, which manages an investment partnership, Princes Gates Investors, L.P. This partnership invests globally in special situations that help to facilitate the strategic or financial objectives of companies.

Morgan Stanley Realty (MSR). MSR is a full service real estate investment banking group that provides a broad range of financial services to public and private clients. With offices in New York, San Francisco, London, Tokyo, and Hong Kong, MSR's real estate activities are focused in three primary areas: Advisory Services; Principal Investing; and Real Estate Debt Capital Markets (REDCM). MSR's Advisory Services include: commercial property portfolio and asset sales; mergers, acquisitions and restructurings; and debt and equity underwritings. Principal Investing is done through the Morgan Stanley Real Estate Funds, which have raised over $2.0 billion of discretionary capital and invest in real estate operating companies, property and mortgage portfolios, discrete assets, new developments, and international opportunities. REDCM is an MSR/Fixed Income Division joint venture that focuses exclusively on the origination, distribution, and trading of whole loans and commercial mortgage-backed securities.

Debt Capital Markets Services (DCMS). DCMS is responsible for the solicitation and execution of Morgan Stanley Dean Witter's primary debt and related products business. The group consists of Syndicate, Continuously Offered Products, Market Coverage, High Yield, Private Placements, Asset and Equipment Finance, Tax Products, Liability Management, and Preferred Stock. Together these groups provide a sophisticated global capital markets service, including product development, marketing, and execution from Morgan Stanley Dean Witter offices in New York, London, Hong Kong, Tokyo, Frankfurt, and Paris.

Equity Capital Markets Services (ECMS). ECMS has global product responsibility for corporate equity-related

transactions, including common stock, initial public offerings, subsidiary initial public offerings, convertibles, warrants, and share repurchases in the domestic and global markets. The specific functions of the group include product development, syndicate (execution of transactions), business development, and strategic advice from Morgan Stanley Dean Witter offices in London, Tokyo, Hong Kong, and New York.

Private Wealth Management (PWM). PWM is a financial advisory group that provides solutions to individuals, families, and foundations who control significant pools of wealth and liquidity. PWM offers its clients the same expertise and quality of services that the firm provides to its largest and most sophisticated institutional and corporate clients. After a five-month training program new investment representatives will develop their own investment advisory and asset management businesses with the support of the firm's sales, trading, research, and advisory resources. Investment representatives work closely with clients to tailor portfolios, identify opportunities, and evaluate and execute investment strategies. Investment representatives sell and manage products in every asset class including global equities, fixed income securities, currencies, and commodities.

Describe your ownership structure.

The common stock of Morgan Stanley, Dean Witter, Discover & Co. is listed on the New York Stock Exchange ("MWD") and the Pacific Stock Exchange. Employees and directors of the company own approximately 20 percent of the common stock.

The Finance MBA's Job Description

Describe the career path and corresponding responsibilities for an MBA at your firm.

Regardless of the business area in which one works, most Morgan Stanley Dean Witter careers share similar characteristics. New hires spend their initial years learning about our technology, products, services, and clients. Thereafter, they take on more operational responsibility and coach the junior people who are entering the business. We encourage professionals to start developing new business opportunities and client relationships, whether those clients are external or internal, as soon as their abilities permit.

The firm is committed to the recruitment of MBAs and to creating an environment for individuals to achieve professional and personal growth in the context of diverse career challenges and opportunities. When it makes sense, we encourage specialization—but we do not mandate it. We have a tradition of developing our people and matching our best people with our best opportunities, relying on the transferability of skills among businesses.

The Recruiting Process

Describe your recruiting process and the criteria by which you select candidates. Is prior experience necessary?

Each year the firm seeks to recruit and hire a diverse group of highly motivated, intelligent MBAs to join us in a number of business areas. Prior experience in the investment banking industry is not a prerequisite. We typically conduct a traditional recruiting process including campus presentations and interviews followed by final round in-office interviews for selected students.

How many permanent associates and analysts do you hire in a typical year? How many summer interns do you expect to hire? If you have a formal summer program, please describe it. Please be sure to indicate whether the summer program is in place for all offices or just some.

In addition to full-time hires, many areas of the firm seek to hire summer interns. Full-time position initial placement and summer internships are generally available in New York, London, Tokyo, and Hong Kong, although availability varies by business area. International opportunities exist both initially and later in one's career based on the firm's needs and individual qualifications.

The firm works through the school's placement office and interested students should look for our advertisements and announcements both there and in the campus newspaper.

Morgan Stanley Dean Witter is an Equal Opportunity Employer.

National Bank Financial Inc.

The Exchange Tower
2 First Canadian Place
Suite 3200, Box 21
Toronto, Ontario M5X 1J9
Canada
(416) 869-3707
Web site: www.nbfinancial.com

MBA Recruiting Contact(s):
Peter Jelley, Mergers and Acquisitions

Company Description

Describe your firm's business and the types of clients served by your finance group(s).

National Bank Financial is a subsidiary of the National Bank of Canada, created by the September 8, 1999, merger of Lévesque Beaubien Geoffrion and First Marathon Inc. National Bank Financial has brought together the strengths and traditions of two highly successful, but different, investment firms to form a major new, and truly national, firm. National Bank Financial has a substantial presence in all regions of Canada and yet remains unique among major Canadian firms for the depth of its services in Quebec. The new firm not only plays a leading role in all major Canadian investment markets, but is also active in certain specialized and rapidly growing investment businesses. National Bank Financial not only benefits from melding the best of these two exceptional firms, it also gains strength from its links with National Bank of Canada, Canada's sixth largest bank. With about 2,700 employees and 86 offices, National Bank Financial is one of the largest investment dealers in Canada. Its pro-forma annual revenues of approximately $600 million place it among the leaders in the Canadian investment industry. In addition, client assets of approximately $27 billion held for nearly 250,000 individual clients indicate the extensive reach of its operations.

Investment Banking

In selecting an investment bank, clients look for experienced professionals who understand their specific needs and the issues particular to their industry, and who can respond promptly, creatively, and professionally. In order to do so, National Bank Financial's investment banking department is organized into 14 dedicated industry groups, which focus on developing close working relationships with clients and on putting to work the group's specialized expertise in the wide range of industries.

National Bank Financial's 66 investment banking professionals, located in offices in Montreal, Toronto, Calgary, and Vancouver, constitute one of Canada's larger investment banking departments. In 1998, National Bank Financial (through its predecessor companies) participated in 134 equity financings having a total value of $14.1 billion. In 33 of these transactions, it was lead or co-lead. In that year, National Bank Financial also participated in $9.0 billion of corporate debt offerings, of which it was a lead or co-manager in 46 transactions. In addition, National Bank Financial acted as a lead or co-manager in $31.9 billion of fixed-income financings on behalf of governments.

In addition to raising capital on behalf of corporations and governments, National Bank Financial's investment banking division provides merger and acquisition, restructuring, and other advisory services, including fairness opinions and valuations. Nine of its professional staff are fully dedicated to this activity. When providing financial advisory services, National Bank Financial's industry expertise; knowledge of regulatory requirements; and structuring, negotiation, and execution expertise have all assisted a growing client base. In addition, its ability to place, on a timely basis, the difficult and complex financings which sometimes arise from such transactions has assisted clients who require financing in conjunction with acquisitions. National Bank Financial has also demonstrated a unique understanding of the industrial, economic, and financial fabric of Quebec. This expertise often yields a competitive advantage in the acquisition or sale of a Quebec-based company.

Institutional Equity Services

National Bank Financial fields one of the leading equity teams in Canada, with 27 investment analysts and economists and 20 research associates located in Montreal, Toronto, Winnipeg, Calgary, and Vancouver. Institutional and other clients demand quality investment advice which must be based on superior investment research and timely recommendations. Our predecessor firms were each successful because they placed primary emphasis on the quality of research—this will continue. Analysts focus on identifying trends, industries, and companies that promise outstanding relative investment returns as a result of growing sales, earnings or cash flow, changing technology or consumer preferences, the superiority of a competitive franchise or assets, and/or the quality of management.

Based on recent surveys of institutional clients and Investment Advisors, National Bank Financial's new consolidated research department would have been rated among the leaders in the country. For example, according to the 1999 Brendan Wood International industry survey, ten of National Bank Financial's analysts are considered all-stars, having been ranked by institutions within the top three in their industries. These analysts cover the following industry sectors: auto parts, biotechnology & pharmaceuticals, consumer products, industrial products, merchandising, precious metals & diamonds, printing, publishing & broadcasting, pipelines & energy utilities, and telecommunications & cable. In addition, the department boasts the best economics and strategy team in Canada, benefiting not only equity investors but also fixed income clients, corporations, and governments.

Institutional Fixed Income

National Bank Financial's fixed income market share more than tripled in the last five years, and the firm is today a major factor in Canadian fixed income markets. In 1998, approximately $650 billion in fixed income securities were traded either as principal or on behalf of clients. The institutional fixed income group consists of over 80 professionals located in Montreal, Toronto, Vancouver, New York, and London.

National Bank Financial is a major trader of Government of Canada fixed-income securities. In 1998, its 11% share of market gave it the second highest level of provincial bond secondary market trading. In addition to being alternating lead manager for other provinces, it is the lead manager for the Province of Quebec and Hydro-Quebec. In addition, besides being the leading secondary market trader of municipal bonds in 1998, with a 36% market share, National Bank Financial commanded a 34% share of all financings by Canadian municipalities. National Bank Financial also had a substantial share of corporate bond trading and participated as a lead or co-manager in 38% of all Canadian corporate debt financings during 1998. In addition, National Bank Financial participates in 28 medium-term corporate note programs, and a further 20 for government agencies and crown corporations.

The National Bank of Canada's money market operations were recently integrated with those of National Bank Financial. This department has 20 professionals with extensive experience in sales and trading of money market instruments. National Bank Financial is one of just ten Government of Canada primary money market distributors and has an approximate 11% share of Government of Canada primary auctions. With 11 futures traders, National Bank Financial also enjoys an exceptionally strong presence in Montreal Exchange futures markets, recently ranking first or second in execution, trading, and clearing. National Bank Financial has also established a specialized high-yield department, staffed with experienced professionals, which will research and trade non-investment grade fixed income securities. This group provides an important link between investors seeking potentially higher overall investment returns from fixed income securities and issuers of such securities.

Merchant Banking

National Bank Financial recently established NB Capital Partners, a merchant bank, to take advantage of the growing Canadian demand for merchant banking capital. NB Capital Partners' strategy is to achieve superior investment returns by employing a professional, aggressive, entrepreneurial approach to investing and by leveraging National Bank Financial's established relationships, capabilities, and resources. National Bank Financial's merchant banking activity both broadens and enhances the services it now provides to its investment banking clients, as well as increasing the range of investment products made available to its investor clients. National Bank Financial and National Bank of Canada have committed a minimum of $75 million in capital to this business, and are presently raising funds from other parties to invest alongside them in merchant banking partnerships. These partnerships will make equity and equity-like investments in private, and occasionally, public companies.

How does your approach to finance differ from that of other firms, and what do you consider to be your strengths and distinctive capabilities?

National Bank Financial's success has been based upon developing specialized areas of expertise where its substantial experience, knowledge of the industries involved, and in-depth research and trading coverage allow for superior responsiveness to client needs. A major source of value for both issuing and investor clients is our commitment to provide research coverage and liquidity to issuers and investors after financings are completed. In this regard, National Bank Financial's exceptional trading capability and strong relationships with leading institutional investors, as well as its broad retail distribution capability, have been of great benefit to issuing clients, both in pricing new issues and in ensuring liquid after-market trading conditions. Furthermore, National Bank Financial's ability to quickly deploy its substantial capital resources has been a feature of many underwritings and will grow in importance in future years

National Bank Financial's unique knowledge of the Quebec market is an asset that distinguishes it from other Canadian investment houses. This enables it to offer clients better-informed advice and appropriate investment strategies. In fact, National Bank Financial is the most important independent source of financial information on political and economic events in Quebec.

In addition to its strong team of analysts and economists, National Bank Financial has one of the most highly ranked institutional equity trading and sales teams in Canada. Well staffed and highly experienced equity trading desks are located in Montreal, Toronto, and Vancouver. Specialized trading coverage is given to certain key industries and financial instruments. Similarly, an institutional sales team with extensive experience is located in these offices and in Halifax. Distribution and secondary market trading of Canadian securities is also facilitated by National Bank Financial's offices in New York, London, and Geneva. With exceptional client service experience and unusual depth in both sector and client specializations, National Bank Financial's trading and sales capability is an asset, not only to clients trading in secondary markets, but also to issuers of securities.

The MBA's Job Description

Describe the career path and corresponding responsibilities for an MBA at your firm.

The company recruits MBAs for career positions in our Investment Banking Division (consisting of Corporate Finance, Mergers and Acquisitions, and Syndication) and for our Merchant Bank. Associates are both encouraged and expected to assume as much responsibility in their projects as they can handle. Over time, increased levels of responsibility and decision making will naturally accrue to the individual.

Associates work with other associates, analysts, vice presidents, and managing directors. Transaction teams are typically small and consist of two to three professionals. Our philosophy of promoting people based on merit and proven performance is consistent with the entrepreneurial, nonbureaucratic culture of the firm.

Discuss the lifestyle aspects of a career with your firm (i.e., average hours per week, amount of travel, flexibility to change offices, corporate culture, etc.).

A career in finance can be very demanding, while financially and intellectually rewarding. Our commitment to professionalism, client satisfaction, and respect for each other creates a dynamic and challenging environment that requires all members of the team to frequently work long hours. Travel can be an important part of the job, but it varies from four-day roadshow segments or due diligence trips, to day trips for client meetings. Generally, due to the transactional basis of our business, there are natural peaks in the demands placed on one's time.

The Recruiting Process

Describe your recruiting process and the criteria by which you select candidates. Is prior experience necessary?

Recruiting efforts focus on on-campus activities during the fall recruiting season. Finalists are flown to Toronto and/or Montreal to meet with other members of the team.

All candidates should have strong financial, business, communication, and interpersonal skills. Prior industry work experience is preferred but not necessary. A strong interest in finance and capital markets is essential, as well as the desire and ability to work in a fast-paced and challenging environment.

How many permanent associates do you hire in a typical year? How many summer interns do you expect to hire?

National Bank Financial has full-time associate opportunities in Vancouver, Calgary, Montreal, and Toronto and will consider summer positions for the right candidates.

What international opportunities does your firm offer for U.S. citizens? For foreign nationals?

All candidates should meet the necessary requirements to work in Canada before applying.

NM Rothschild & Sons Canada Limited

1 First Canadian Place
Suite 3800
P.O. Box 77
Toronto, Ontario M5X 1B1
Canada
(416) 369-9600
Fax: (416) 864-1261

MBA Recruiting Contact(s):
Stephen L. Shapiro
Vice President

Company Description

Describe your firm's business and the types of clients served by your finance group(s).

NMR Canada provides independent investment banking, corporate finance, and financial advisory services to selected Canadian and international clients in Canada, and offers the global capability and expertise of the Rothschild Group around the world. Our range of experiences includes advising on acquisitions, mergers, divestitures, reorganizations, financings, spin-offs, privatizations, and restructurings. In addition, NMR Canada is involved in valuing and selling, both nationally and globally, private and public companies as a whole, operating units of large companies, and, in some cases, specific assets.

NMR Canada works with the other offices in the Rothschild Group to identify target companies for acquisition or investment purposes for current and prospective clients. There is a steady flow of ideas between Rothschild's offices with respect to opportunities in the mergers and acquisitions market in Canada and internationally.

As part of our long-term relationships with our clients, we advise them on their ongoing corporate and financial strategies, corporate finance activities, and on the implementation of their strategic plans.

The Rothschild Group has organized itself into industry specific groups that are focused on our experiences and on opportunities presented by the M&A environment.

NMR Canada is not associated with commercial banks, financial institutions, or industrial groups in Canada, nor does it engage in public underwriting, market trading, arbitrage, or principal investing. NMR Canada is able to provide unbiased judgments free from potential conflicts of interest.

Describe your ownership structure.

NMR Canada is the Canadian member of one of the world's leading independent merchant banking organizations, the Rothschild Group. The main operating companies of the Rothschild Group are N M Rothschild & Sons Limited, the merchant bank that has been based at New Court in the City of London for over 200 years, Rothschild & Cie. in Paris and Rothschild Inc. in New York. The Rothschild Group has expanded globally to meet the increasingly diverse needs of its clients and now has offices in over thirty countries worldwide. The Canadian office was opened in 1990 and has grown each year.

How does your approach to finance differ from that of other firms, and what do you consider to be your strengths and distinctive capabilities?

NMR Canada's independence and professional client-related approach to its focused business of providing advisory services differentiates it from its competitors in Canada. In addition, the international reach of the Rothschild Group allows it to offer truly global investment banking services.

The Finance MBA's Job Description

Describe the career path and corresponding responsibilities for an MBA at your firm.

A new member of the investment banking team has the opportunity to gain experience quickly in a vast number of transactions. Our experience to date has covered all major industries in Canada and a wide range of various types of transactions. Our professionals generally begin to specialize in industrial sectors after having an opportunity to develop a broad base of product-related skills. All professionals begin as generalists, gathering as wide a portfolio of experiences as possible. As the firm grows, professionals naturally develop areas of particular expertise upon which the Canadian office, as well as our international group, will draw in dealing with various clients' needs.

Describe the opportunities for professional mobility between the various departments in your firm.

There are opportunities to meet and work with professionals from Rothschild's other offices, or the Rothschild Group, as well as opportunities to consider extended assignments in other offices.

Discuss the lifestyle aspects of a career with your firm (i.e., average hours per week, amount of travel, flexibility to change offices, corporate culture, etc.).

While the lifestyle of an investment banker is renowned for its hard work and long hours, NMR Canada maintains a friendly and cooperative atmosphere. Within a very short period, every new associate will have worked with all members of the office. The professionals are relatively young and this allows for common interests and non work-related activities.

The Recruiting Process

Describe your recruiting process and the criteria by which you select candidates. Is prior experience necessary?

The recruiting process at NMR Canada has identified certain characteristics that we feel are crucial to having a successful long-term career in investment banking. While strong academic performance is not in itself a requirement, it does tend to indicate the dedication and commitment that recruits have made in their past endeavours. Experience in the industry or in related fields will also act as guidance in identifying those recruits who have decided to make investment banking their career choice. A third requirement, of course, is recruits familiarity with and knowledge of the Canadian business environment and ability to work in Canada.

Nomura Securities International, Inc.

2 World Financial Center
Building B
New York, NY 10281
Web site: www.nomurany.com

MBA Recruiting Contact(s):
Human Resources Department

Company Description

Describe your firm's business and the types of clients served by your finance group(s).

Nomura Securities International, Inc. (NSI) is a wholly owned subsidiary of the Nomura Securities Co., Ltd. (Nomura), the world's largest securities firm. With shareholder equity exceeding $14 billion and total assets of more than $23.2 billion, Nomura is the most profitable financial institution in the world.

A medium-sized investment banking company, NSI employs more than 800 people in the United States. NSI has evolved from a company handling primarily Japanese-related securities into a full-fledged member of the American financial community and also is a member of the major securities and commodities exchanges, as well as a primary dealer in U.S. Treasury securities. U.S. operations, which began in 1927, have expanded to include two branch offices in Chicago and one in Los Angeles. Today, NSI offers a wide range of products and services: sales, trading, investment banking, mutual funds, and portfolio and asset management.

NSI is continually in a state of evolution as the firm works to develop new businesses, such as the high-yield and Latin American departments. Two years ago, 80% of NSI's investment banking revenues were due to Japanese-related business (country funds distributed in Japan, Tokyo Stock Exchange listing fees, etc.). This past year over 40% of revenues were from non-Japan-related business (Compania Cervecerias Unidas S.A., Chic by H.I.S., and JAFCO II). Our investment banking group was active with numerous initial public offerings and private placements and created innovative financing structures such as ROSA II and Ivory.

In addition to its financial strength and the breadth of its capabilities, Nomura is internationally renowned for its innovation in finance:

- Nomura introduced and popularized the Gensaki, a Japanese bond sale and repurchase agreement that has developed into an important short-term investment instrument.

- Nomura pioneered the expansion of the Japanese financial community by introducing foreign companies to the country's rapidly growing capital markets. The firm designs and implements investor relations programs for client companies and arranges the listing of their shares on the Tokyo Stock Exchange. In the past, Nomura has listed Anheuser-Busch, AT&T, General Electric, Kraft, and J.P. Morgan, among others.

- With the increase in global investing, more and more institutional and individual investors rely on Nomura's international research, sales, and trading capabilities. Nomura's leadership position in the Japanese market as a broker/dealer and market maker provides an unparalleled resource for investors.

- Working to meet clients' needs, Nomura has established relationships with financial institutions to help ensure the development of innovative products in the areas of leveraged leasing, project financing, real estate investing within the United States, and mergers and acquisitions.

- NSI's Equity Derivatives group is constantly at the top of the New York Stock Exchange chart of 15 most active firms in program trading volume.

The growing importance of investment management has led NSI to form additional companies to provide service to clients. Nomura Corporate Research and Asset Management (NCRAM) is a money management firm with a worldwide client base specializing in high-yield bond investments. Combining the credit expertise of NCRAM with Nomura's tremendous capital base and global distribution capability has helped the firm to achieve a preeminent position in asset management. Expertise in corporate credit also provides the foundation for our aggressive worldwide expansion into proprietary trading, structured finance, and other related merchant and investment banking activities.

With our mortgage-backed securities business continuing to grow, Nomura created a subsidiary, Nomura Asset Capital Corporation (NACC), to conduct our real estate and nonagency trading and financing. NACC, though initially focusing on commercial mortgages, will transact in the commercial and residential loan markets, as well as the asset-backed securities market.

Emphasizing an empirical, problem-solving approach to its studies, Nomura Research Institutes conducts fundamental research on a wide range of socioeconomic and socioscientific issues, as well as on matters of long-term relevance to the securities industry.

The Finance MBA's Job Description

Describe the career path and corresponding responsibilities for an MBA at your firm.

Full-time associates receive global finance training in such areas as investment banking and sales and trading through our associates program. As a sales and trading associate, individuals undergo a six-month training program during which they rotate through various sales and trading areas and participate in intensive product training seminars. In investment banking, associates are expected to become a contributing member of the department immediately. Most of the training is conducted on the job by teaming senior executives in the department with the associates. Since the firm encourages initiative, the degree of responsibility of an associate's assignment is determined to a large extent by an individual's desire and ability to learn and contribute.

The Recruiting Process

Describe your recruiting process and the criteria by which you select candidates. Is prior experience necessary?

NSI seeks people with strong academic records and excellent analytical and communication skills. Demonstration of leadership, high levels of self-motivation, initiative, and commitment, and the ability to work effectively with others in an intense and demanding environment are crucial.

How many permanent associates and analysts do you hire in a typical year? How many summer interns do you expect to hire? If you have a formal summer program, please describe it. Please be sure to indicate whether the summer program is in place for all offices or just some.

NSI's summer associate program provides a select group of students with an intense, hands-on view of the securities industry, as well as the extensive global operations at Nomura. After choosing to work in one of the following areas—investment banking, derivative products or fixed income, or equity sales and trading—the summer associate is quickly integrated into the department's daily operations. In sales and trading, there is a rotation through the different sales and trading areas. Investment banking and derivative products tend to be more project oriented. Additionally, through a series of weekly seminars with senior managers, the MBAs have the opportunity to be exposed to the many facets of our business.

What international opportunities does your firm offer for U.S. citizens? For foreign nationals?

NSI does not recruit for the other overseas offices. Individuals interested in working internationally should contact NSI for additional information.

PaineWebber Incorporated

1285 Avenue of the Americas
New York, NY 10019
(212) 713-2000
Web site: www.painewebber.com
Recruiting Web site: www.painewebber.com/on-campus

MBA Recruiting Contact(s):
Investment Banking
Ashlee Gandy
(212) 713-3406
Fax: (212) 713-9719
E-mail: ashlee_gandy@painewebber.com

Public Finance
Stephanie Gammone
(212) 713-4657
Fax: (212) 713-6051
E-mail: sgammone@painewebber.com

Real Estate Investment Banking
Karen Larsen
(212) 713-8745
Fax: (212) 713-7947
E-mail: klarsen@painewebber.com

Company Description

Describe your firm's business and the types of clients served by your finance group(s).

PaineWebber is an independent, full service securities firm with a leadership position in individual and institutional businesses and a reputation for outstanding research and quality client service. With assets of over $54 billion, total capital in excess of $7.3 billion, and more than 17,767 employees in this country and seven offices overseas, PaineWebber services the investment and capital needs of over two million clients, including individuals, institutions, corporations, state and local governments, and public agencies in the United States and abroad. Among the firm's key businesses are private client brokerage, investment banking, public finance, real estate, institutional equity and fixed income sales and trading, research, asset management, and transaction services.

PaineWebber's core strengths set it apart from the competition. With a distribution capability that is one of the strongest in the industry, PaineWebber is uniquely posi-tioned to quickly and fully meet the needs of both its institutional and retail clients. Our renowned Research Group keeps a close watch on nearly 800 companies in 50 industries, and serves as a vital resource for Investment Banking, the Private Client Group, and Capital Markets.

The Finance MBA's Job Description

Describe the career path and corresponding responsibilities for an MBA at your firm.

Investment Banking
PaineWebber's Investment Banking Division is built on a strong client-oriented philosophy. We keep apprised of the fast-moving financial markets, enabling us to serve our clients' increasingly diverse and complex needs. We concentrate our resources in specifically targeted industries—notably consumer products/retailing, energy and natural resources, financial institutions, healthcare, media, telecommunications, and utilities—in order to leverage our full range of financial products, as well as our capabilities such as mergers and acquisitions advice.

Our strategy for the future is to continue to focus on those selected areas where we have achieved a competitive edge, bringing together for our corporate clients the resources we have developed in areas such as research, trading, and distribution, in addition to our investment banking expertise in these targeted industries.

After training, associates join industry and product groups based on their expressed interest and the needs of the specific groups. Associates participate in all aspects of a transaction and have the potential opportunity to play a key role in maintaining client relationships. In addition to research and financial analysis, associates help to develop new business proposals, work on structuring and documenting a deal, and learn to negotiate as well as close a transaction.

Public Finance
The role of an associate involves extensive client interaction. The associate advises clients on the most efficient way to access capital, assists in the creation and presentation of new ideas on innovative financing techniques for municipal issuers, and communicates with syndicate members, underwriting professionals, attorneys, and financial advisors. The associate's quantitative expertise will extend to cash flow, arbitrage, derivative product, and yield analysis. Each associate is assigned to a specific project team that best matches his or her own career interest.

Real Estate Investment Banking:

Associates and assistant vice presidents are the point persons on the transaction. They interface with clients and manage the analysts on the deal team. Preparing accretion and dilution models are some tasks the associate would perform.

Describe the opportunities for professional mobility between the various departments in your firm.

Mobility between various departments in PaineWebber would be dealt with on a one-on-one basis between the associate and managing director.

Discuss the lifestyle aspects of a career with your firm (i.e., average hours per week, amount of travel, flexibility to change offices, corporate culture, etc.).

First year associates typically work 85–100 hours per week and hours decrease slightly with seniority. Real Estate Investment Banking opportunities are available in New York, Chicago, and San Francisco. The corporate culture at PaineWebber is team-oriented and a friendly environment. In addition, we have casual Fridays. Travel can be significant and is always a possibility, especially unplanned travel.

The Recruiting Process

Describe your recruiting process and the criteria by which you select candidates. Is prior experience necessary? If you have a formal summer program, please describe it. Please be sure to indicate whether the summer program is in place for all offices or just some.

Investment Banking

Investment Banking looks for approximately 10–15 individuals who demonstrate a high level of motivation, outstanding scholastic, extracurricular, and professional achievement, excellent communication and interpersonal skills, good judgment and the ability to take initiative. A background in finance or investment banking is preferred. Advancement is determined by individual performance. Normally associates are promoted to vice president after four years.

The Investment Banking Summer Associate Program serves as an introduction to the associate position. Summer associates act as generalists and are given similar responsibilities to those of a full-time associate during their 11 weeks. Each summer associate is staffed on several transactions in a broad range of industries and product areas. All summer associates work out of the New York office.

Public Finance

The Municipal Securities Group hires about 3–4 associates out of business school who go through an intensive 10-week Municipal training program. The training program is taught by PaineWebber employees and well respected industry experts, and is one of the most renowned on Wall Street. Quantitative experience along with prior public finance or finance experience is requested.

Real Estate

Prior real estate experience is not a necessity but is an asset. The process involves resume review, looking at majors, past experience, cover letter stating interest in Real Estate, GPA, and undergraduate school.

Typically Real Estate hires 2–4 full-time and summer associates. The program is for all three offices. The summer program is 12 weeks of life as a first year associate. The hours are demanding and the candidate is treated as if he or she were permanent. Travel flexibility is mandatory. There is no training program for summer associates.

Foreign nationals are assisted in obtaining proper visa status.

Peter J. Solomon Company

767 Fifth Avenue, 26th Floor
New York, NY 10153
(212) 508-1600
Web site: www.pjsolomon.com

MBA Recruiting Contact(s):
Diane M. Coffey, Managing Director

Company Description

Describe your firm's business and the types of clients served by your finance group(s).

Peter J. Solomon Company (PJSC) is among the leading independent investment banking firms. Headquartered in New York City, the firm of fifty professionals including thirty-five bankers provides investment banking and senior advisory services to owners, chief executives, and senior management of public and private companies. PJSC initiates and completes merger and acquisition transactions, advises clients on raising public and private debt and equity capital, and assists creditors and owners of financially distressed companies with bankruptcy and re-structuring advice.

A Singular Focus

Every investment banking firm has its own unique culture that embodies its values and the way it approaches transactions. The characteristic that differentiates PJSC is a single-minded focus on our clients' strategic needs. Since we do not underwrite or trade securities or provide investment research, we are free to explore every conceivable way for our clients to accomplish their strategic goals. Our specialty is sound, unbiased advice. Our firm thrives on complexity and is recognized by our clients for original, creative thinking and an ability to deal with the most difficult, multi-faceted transactions. We approach every assignment with a fresh outlook. We seek innovative solutions. Finally, our degree of persistence is exceptional. PJSC bankers will stick with a difficult transaction for as long as it takes to get it done.

The Clients of Peter J. Solomon Company

Since its establishment in 1989, Peter J. Solomon Company has performed more than 150 advisory assignments for leading United States and foreign corporations in a wide range of industries. As such we have applied our strategic merger and acquisition, restructuring and corporate finance skills to transactions in the retail and consumer product industries, in media, communications and e-commerce, in health care, as well as real estate, paper, forest products, and diversified manufacturing industries. Indeed, our firm's keen understanding of influential individual and institutional shareholder concerns that affect corporate decisions is equally acute in shaping strategies for young entrepreneurial concerns and family-owned or -controlled businesses where special sensitivity to intergenerational and intra-family issues is both welcome and needed.

Describe your ownership structure.

Founded in 1989 by Peter J. Solomon, whose distinguished career spans more than thirty-five years in investment banking, the firm is privately owned.

With PJSC's extensive experience in mergers, acquisitions, recapitalizations, restructurings, accounting, and strategic analysis, each of our bankers provides a different and valuable perspective gained through their work at major investment banks and financial institutions including Goldman, Sachs & Co., Salomon Brothers, Credit Suisse First Boston, Lazard Freres, and GE Capital Corporation. In addition, PJSC's bankers bring established credentials from big six accounting firms, law firms, and corporations.

Peter Solomon's illustrious career, which includes two periods of government service—to the City of New York as Deputy Mayor for Economic Policy and Development under Mayor Edward I. Koch and to the federal government as Counselor to the United States Treasury under President Jimmy Carter—began at Lehman Brothers where he served in various capacities including Chairman of the Mergers and Acquisitions Department, Co-Chairman of the Investment Banking Group, Chairman of the Merchant Banking Group, and Vice Chairman of the firm. Mr. Solomon is also a frequent guest on CNN's *Ahead of the Curve,* where he provides regular commentary on merger activities.

How does your approach to finance differ from that of other firms, and what do you consider to be your strengths and distinctive capabilities?

From the beginning of an engagement a select team of our senior bankers focuses on meeting each client's special needs. That same team remains with that client throughout the relationship and is always available. As senior advisors, our bankers apply their expertise to understanding our clients' businesses and industries, long-term strategic and financial objectives, marketing and competitive environments, and to assessing the cost and feasibility of alternatives and opportunities. Often we function as unofficial members of our clients' management teams and in some instances we serve on their boards. Because of PJSC's size and the fact that we accept a limited number of assignments, senior bankers are not distracted by administrative concerns, allowing them to devote their undivided attention to client matters. This personal, highly responsive approach emphasizes *relationships,* not transactions, and is at the heart of our concept of investment banking.

Our strengths are many. Let's begin with our *independence:* since we are free from the potential conflicts of underwriting, research, and trading, our advice is candid and unbiased. Our *size* is optimal: large enough to field teams of experienced, senior-level people to work on major transactions, yet small enough to preserve our intense involvement with our clients. Unlike the integrated investment banking firms where separate groups focus on particular industry sectors, or transactions, our bankers interact easily, constantly sharing their ideas, judgments, and collective knowledge with one another. PJSC's size also permits a more rapid response to client needs, greater flexibility when market conditions require a change in strategy, and, of course, confidentiality. With fewer people aware of a deal, clients can be sure their discussions will remain confidential. Our *experience* in mergers, acquisitions, recapitalizations, restructurings, accounting, and strategic analysis is extensive and the quality of PJSC's bankers is exceptionally high.

The Finance MBA's Job Description

Describe the career path and corresponding responsibilities for an MBA at your firm.

The firm recruits associates from the nation's leading business schools and although career training is essentially on-the-job, it is coupled with formal instruction from professionals within and outside the firm. Associates also are provided ample time and opportunity to prepare for any required registration examinations. The size of our firm is particularly advantageous for associates as

it offers a rapid and diverse learning experience. Associates work in small client project teams, generally with a managing director of the firm and an analyst to plan, analyze, and execute a wide variety of investment banking and principal investment transactions. Because of the entrepreneurial nature of the firm, we encourage associates to assume increasing levels of responsibility commensurate with their abilities. As a result, we believe our associates develop significant client and deal experience earlier than at larger, more structured investment banking firms.

Our firm is assiduous in evaluating associates as well as senior bankers. Notwithstanding the excellence of our professionals, we are vigilant in seeking ways to improve ourselves and the quality of our work. Associates receive semiannual reviews by senior and junior members of the firm for objectivity as well as guidance. Advancement and financial reward are dependent on one's initiative, performance, and contribution to the firm. Again, the size of our firm permits considerable latitude for diversity in assignments as well as the opportunity to assume substantial responsibility.

Such responsibility is naturally accompanied by solid commitments of time and energy. An investment banking career at PSJC is intellectually and physically demanding yet exciting, stimulating and financially rewarding.

The Recruiting Process

Describe your recruiting process and the criteria by which you select candidates.

PJSC's philosophy is to pursue American citizens with diverse backgrounds and prior investment banking experience, who are highly motivated and possess exceptional interpersonal and analytical skills. Candidates should have demonstrated a talent for leadership, an ability to write well, and attention to detail. Those who can flourish in a team environment, who are flexible by nature and creative in their thinking, will thrive at our firm. As PJSC continues to expand, these are the types of individuals who will be welcome.

Raymond James Financial, Inc.

880 Carrillon Parkway
St. Perersburg, FL 33716
Web site: www.rjf.com

MBA Recruiting Contact:
Dave Meyrowitz, Assistant to the Chairman
E-mail: fflexer@exec.rjf.com

Company Description

Describe your firm's business and the types of clients served by your finance group(s).

Raymond James Financial is a diversified financial services holding company whose subsidiaries engage primarily in investment and financial planning, including investment banking, asset management, securities and insurance, brokerage, banking and cash management, and trust services. With more than 4,000 financial advisors in over 1,300 offices located throughout the United States and internationally, its broker-dealer subsidiaries provide their services to more than 1.1 million individual and institutional accounts. The firm's asset management subsidiaries manage in excess of $13.7 billion for individuals, pension plans, and municipalities.

Raymond James & Associates, a subsidiary of Raymond James Financial, provides investment banking services to emerging-growth companies throughout the United States. The primary emphasis is on companies within targeted industries such as information technology, healthcare/biotechnology, consumer, energy, among others, where sufficient industry knowledge has been developed to deliver an extremely high level of value-added service. Investment banking services include public underwritings, private placements; merger, acquisition, and divestiture representation; and various advisory services.

Describe your ownership structure.

Raymond James Financial is a publicly-traded corporation whose shares are traded on the New York Stock Exchange (NYSE: RJF).

How does your approach to finance differ from that of other firms, and what do you consider to be your strengths and distinctive capabilities?

Raymond James has developed a reputation for providing capital and advice to emerging-growth and medium-sized companies in targeted industries. Members of the Investment Banking Department work closely with our highly-acclaimed Research Department to develop an in-depth understanding of our clients and their businesses in order to provide the highest level of value-added services.

Discuss changes in your firm's revenues (both domestic and international) and professional staff over the past year; over the past five years.

Raymond James is one of the leading growth companies in the country with a compound growth rate in revenues and earnings in excess of 20% per year during most of the firm's history. In our most recently completed fiscal year, revenues exceeded $1.2 billion and profits totaled $85 million. All major areas of the firm have grown dramatically in the past five years, including expansion of our institutional sales effort to seven offices in Europe and investment banking and asset management activities through joint ventures in India, Turkey, and South America.

The Finance MBA's Job Description

Describe the career path and corresponding responsibilities for an MBA at your firm.

Raymond James hires MBAs for a variety of positions within the firm, including Investment Banking, Equity Research, Sales and Trading, Asset Management, Merchant Banking, and Office of the Chairman. By virtue of its growth and entrepreneurial environment, Raymond James provides a recently hired MBA more rapid exposure to transactions and client contact than other firms.

Describe the opportunities for professional mobility between the various departments in your firm.

There are numerous examples of MBAs moving from one department to another within the firm as their interests change. Our philosophy is to hire bright people who are focused on achieving a high quality of professional and personal life. Thus, we are flexible in meeting their needs over time in recognition of their contributions to the success of the firm.

Discuss the lifestyle aspects of a career with your firm (i.e., average hours per week, amount of travel, flexibility to change offices, corporate culture, etc.).

Raymond James offers an attractive alternative to the lifestyles offered by other firms. Most MBA positions are located at the firm's spacious headquarters in St. Petersburg. However, there are also limited opportunities for MBAs to work in other company offices. A typical work week is 60–70 hours, and travel ranges from 30% to 50% of the MBA's time. The real benefit is the warm climate of Florida, where many leisure activities can be pursued year-round, and the first class professionals who make the firm unique and exciting. The corporate culture at Raymond James can best be described as "work, work, play."

The Recruiting Process

Describe your recruiting process and the criteria by which you select candidates. Is prior experience necessary?

Raymond James conducts on-campus recruiting at several of the country's finest business schools for full-time positions in Investment Banking, Equity Research, Sales and Trading, Asset Management, Merchant Banking, and Office of the Chairman. In each of these departments, the firm seeks individuals with a track record of superior achievement who wish to work in an entrepreneurial environment. All aspects of a candidate's background are considered and measured against a high set of standards. Personality fit is also an important factor. Prior experience in financial services is not required.

How many permanent associates and analysts do you hire in a typical year? How many summer interns do you expect to hire? If you have a formal summer program, please describe it. Please be sure to indicate whether the summer program is in place for all offices or just some.

Each summer, Raymond James offers a number of summer internships in positions throughout the firm. These internships provide students with an opportunity to work alongside senior management on special projects that will have an impact on the ongoing success of the company.

RBC Dominion Securities Inc.

P.O. Box 50
Royal Bank Plaza, South Tower
Toronto, Ontario
M5J 2W7
Canada
(416) 842-7588
Fax: (416) 842-7555
Web site: www.rbcds.com

MBA Recruiting Contact(s):
Jim Fasano, Vice President

Company Description

Describe your firm's business and the types of clients served by your finance group(s).

RBC Dominion Securities is a fully integrated Canadian investment bank that enjoys a leading position in all segments of the securities business in Canada. Its principal investment banking activities are general corporate and government finance, mergers and acquisitions, corporate restructuring, real estate, fixed income and equity sales and trading, international financing, commercial paper, and foreign exchange. The firm has an extensive retail sales network of approximately 1,600 registered representatives located in over 70 cities across Canada. RBC Dominion Securities also has a strong international presence, with offices in New York, Boston, London, Paris, Lausanne, Hong Kong, and Tokyo.

RBC Dominion Securities has grown through a series of mergers over the past two decades to become one of the largest, most profitable investment banks in Canada. The firm's investment banking clients include most of Canada's largest and fastest-growing companies, as well as the 10 Canadian provinces, the federal government, and numerous government agencies. Over the past several years, RBC Dominion Securities has lead-managed over 25% of all public Canadian corporate debt and equity offerings in Canada. The firm has demonstrated a consistent ability to meet the changing needs of its many clients while maintaining a superior rate of return on its own capital. RBC Dominion Securities has been able to take advantage of its strong capital base and exceptional distribution capability to compete effectively and profitably in all aspects of investment banking.

The firm's corporate strategy is to be the leading investment bank to Canadian clients in both domestic and international markets and to be the leading investment bank to foreign clients in the Canadian market. The firm achieves this goal through its ability to view client interests as paramount and to deliver superior services that integrate the various areas of strength throughout the firm. This integrated, client-oriented approach has distinguished RBC Dominion Securities in terms of both its reputation and its performance over the past several years.

Describe your ownership structure.

As a consequence of financial services deregulation in Canada and certain acquisitions, the firm is wholly owned by the Royal Bank of Canada, Canada's largest commercial bank. The transaction provided the firm with access to the Royal's international network, as well as the financial backing of a major financial institution.

Although the corporate banking function is now under RBC Dominion Securities' management, a high level of independence of operations has been preserved. Career opportunities and compensation structures for professional staff have remained and will remain unchanged.

The Finance MBA's Job Description

Describe the career path and corresponding responsibilities for an MBA at your firm.

The firm employs approximately 120 investment banking professionals located in Toronto, Montreal, Calgary, Vancouver, Regina, and New York, as well as in London and other overseas offices. RBC Dominion Securities devotes a great deal of time and consideration to its search for associates. The firm's intention is to hire outstanding graduates who will continue with the firm throughout their careers. It has among the lowest turnover rates in the industry.

Associates who join the investment banking group at RBC Dominion Securities generally do not specialize in any one particular industry or product group. The firm prefers to develop well-rounded professionals who have participated in a wide variety of transactions, whether debt or equity, domestic or international, private or public. Associates are nevertheless encouraged to develop expertise in areas that interest them, and the firm makes every effort to satisfy a professional's ambitions in a particular specialty area. The firm is large enough to be able to offer both a generalist approach to the business and the opportunity to specialize in specific areas of interest but small enough to take a flexible approach in the career development of high-performing employees.

Other aspects of RBC Dominion Securities would be of interest to potential associates, including the firm's reputation for excellence, innovation, and high ethical standards. Moreover, there are comparatively few associates, which results in new professionals being given substantial responsibilities early in their careers. RBC Dominion Securities' position in the domestic underwriting league table affords new associates the deal flow necessary to develop well-rounded professional skills.

Discuss the lifestyle aspects of a career with your firm (i.e., average hours per week, amount of travel, flexibility to change offices, corporate culture, etc.).

An open and collegial atmosphere prevails throughout the firm. There is a genuine concern on the part of senior management that young professionals develop a number of outside interests and have the ability to devote a significant portion of time to their families. While the highest value is placed on productive output by professionals, the firm does not encourage long hours when they are unnecessary.

The Recruiting Process

Describe your recruiting process and the criteria by which you select candidates. Is prior experience necessary?

RBC Dominion Securities is highly selective in its hiring program. The firm has made a consistent commitment over the years to hire from the top business schools in both North America and Europe. A number of criteria are applied, including academic excellence, energetic presentation, evidence of strong outside interests, and overall fit with the firm. Grades by themselves are not given undue consideration. No prior investment banking experience is necessary, and the firm encourages applicants from a wide variety of academic disciplines and work experience. Successful candidates are typically persistent self-starters with a keen interest in financial markets and a good sense of humor.

How many permanent associates and analysts do you hire in a typical year? How many summer interns do you expect to hire? If you have a formal summer program, please describe it. Please be sure to indicate whether the summer program is in place for all offices or just some.

Each year three to five full-time associates and a smaller number of summer associates are hired into investment banking. Due to the limited number of job openings, employment opportunities are focused on those currently able to work in Canada. There is no formal training program. Associates are immediately assigned to client transaction teams to learn on the job.

The Robinson-Humphrey Company, LLC

Atlanta Financial Center
3333 Peachtree Road, NE
Atlanta, GA 30326
(404) 266-6000

MBA Recruiting Contact(s):
Pam Smith, Assistant
(404) 266-6919

Company Description

Describe your firm's business and the types of clients served by your finance group(s).

The Corporate Finance Department at Robinson-Humphrey consists of 70 professionals. The department is located at Robinson-Humphrey's headquarters in Atlanta. The firm also has offices in Boston and New York. Essentially, everyone in the Corporate Finance Department is regarded as a generalist in terms of product. Teams of professionals focus on certain industries (e.g., technology, health care, retailing, financial institutions), but a flexible approach to industry coverage is maintained at the junior level. Robinson-Humphrey attempts to position itself as a full-service investment banker to its clients. Robinson-Humphrey's primary corporate finance clientele is a group of middle-market, emerging-growth companies.

Describe your ownership structure.

The Robinson-Humphrey Company, Inc. was purchased by America Express in 1982 and operated as a wholly owned subsidiary of Shearson Lehman Brothers, Inc. As part of Primerica's acquisition of Shearson in 1993, Robinson-Humphrey operates today as an autonomous subsidiary of Salomon Smith Barney Inc.

How does your approach to finance differ from that of other firms, and what do you consider to be your strengths and distinctive capabilities?

Robinson-Humphrey positions itself as a full-service investment bank to emerging-growth and middle-market companies. Because of its outstanding retail distribution system (55 branches across 10 states), as well as its abil-

ity to tap the worldwide resources of Salomon Smith Barney, Robinson-Humphrey has capabilities unique among regional investment banking firms. The Corporate Finance Department has grown from approximately 30 to 70 professionals over the past six years. Robinson-Humphrey is the largest corporate finance and investment banking operation in the Southeast; an area realizing tremendous gains in economic growth and in the origination of capital.

Discuss changes in your firm's revenues (both domestic and international) and professional staff over the past year; over the past five years.

Robinson-Humphrey, like most other investment banking firms, has benefited over the past several years from the surge in public underwriting activity. Robinson-Humphrey has been a particularly active underwriter of new equity issues, both initial public offerings and issues for companies whose stocks are already publicly traded. The Corporate Finance Department, however, still maintains a balance between public underwriting and other activities, such as mergers and acquisitions and private capital raising. Over the past six years, merger and acquisition work has comprised approximately 40% of the department's business.

In the summer of 2000, our department will have five new associates. These additions continue the growth that the department has experienced during the past several years.

The Finance MBA's Job Description

Describe the career path and corresponding responsibilities for an MBA at your firm.

An associate works as a key member of transaction teams typically comprising two to three professionals. The associate's primary responsibilities consist of transaction execution duties, including financial analysis and project management. The associate also works with senior professionals to develop new business by meeting with and making presentations to prospective clients. An associate's degree of responsibility depends on the type and scope of project and on his or her particular capabilities.

Describe the opportunities for professional mobility between the various departments in your firm.

There is very little mobility between the various departments within Robinson-Humphrey, although Corporate Finance Associates are exposed to other areas of the firm on a regular basis.

Discuss the lifestyle aspects of a career with your firm (i.e., average hours per week, amount of travel, flexibility to change offices, corporate culture, etc.).

People who work at Robinson-Humphrey enjoy the lifestyle offered by a career with the firm and fostered by its location in the Southeast. In addition, the relatively small size of the department and of the firm, by Wall Street standards, tends to encourage close relationships among co-workers. While investment banking inevitably demands a significant time commitment, average hours worked and travel schedule will vary depending on market conditions and the number and types of projects on which an individual is working.

The Recruiting Process

Describe your recruiting process and the criteria by which you select candidates. Is prior experience necessary?

The company hires graduating MBAs to entry-level positions every year, depending on market conditions. Our annual recruiting effort usually begins in the fall, when we solicit cover letters and résumés from interested, qualified candidates. We are scheduled to conduct off-campus interviews in early November with a follow-on Super Saturday in Atlanta. Typically, an entering MBA will have some experience in investment banking or a closely related financial services business. All factors such as grades, prior experience, and personal attributes are taken into consideration in the decision process. However, final recruiting decisions are based on interviews with several people in the department who make judgments concerning a candidate's ability to make a meaningful contribution to the department.

How many permanent associates and analysts do you hire in a typical year? How many summer interns do you expect to hire? If you have a formal summer program, please describe it. Please be sure to indicate whether the summer program is in place for all offices or just some.

Hiring decisions are based solely on current and perceived market conditions and an assessment of the department's overall needs. The department has hired from two to six associates each of the past five years. Most likely, we will hire five to seven entry-level MBAs in the upcoming year.

Beginning in the summer of 2000, the firm is implementing a summer associate program for 2–3 summer associates in the Atlanta office. This program will be a generalist program and will be designed to give each summer associate optimum exposure to Robinson-Humphrey and middle-market investment banking.

Salomon Smith Barney

388 Greenwich St.
New York, NY 10013
(212) 816-6000

MBA Recruiting Contact(s):
Recruiting Manager
Investment Banking Recruiting

Susan H. Glendon, Vice President
Sales and Trading Recruiting
(212) 723-9541

Company Description

Describe your firm's business and the types of clients served by your finance group(s).

Salomon Smith Barney is a full-service financial institution engaged in investment banking, market making and trading of financial instruments, fixed income and equity market research, brokerage, and institutional money management. Salomon Smith Barney's services and activities include advisory services provided for mergers and acquisitions and financial restructurings; capital-raising activities, including the underwriting and distribution of debt, equity, and derivative securities; trading and arbitrage strategies using debt, equity, and derivative instruments; entering into contractual commitments, such as forward securities and currency agreements, interest rate swap cap, and floor agreements; options, warrants, and derivative products; fixed income and equity market research; institutional money management services; precious metals trading; and mortgage banking. Salomon Smith Barney conducts its business globally, with offices in Australia, Canada, France, Germany, Hong Kong, Japan, South Korea, Spain, Switzerland, Taiwan, Thailand, the United Kingdom, and the United States. Its customer base consists primarily of large- and medium-sized corporations, governments, financial institutions, and individuals.

Investment Banking
Salomon Smith Barney's investment banking activities consist principally of raising capital and providing strategic advisory services. Capital-raising activities include underwriting and distributing debt and equity securities and involve the development, underwriting, and distribution of derivative products. These products include warrants linked to a variety of instruments, such as debt securities, equity securities, baskets of equity securities, indexes based upon stock markets throughout the world, and commodities such as gold and oil. Strategic advisory services are provided in connection with mergers and acquisitions, leveraged buy-outs, financial restructurings, and privatizations.

Sales and Trading
Salomon Smith Barney is a major dealer in government securities in New York, Tokyo, London, and Frankfurt and is a member of all major international securities, financial futures, and options exchanges. It has extensive distribution capabilities and the largest capital base in the U.S. securities industry. Salomon Smith Barney is a major underwriter of securities for governments and high-grade primary issuers and is capable of executing trading strategies on behalf of its customers and for its own account requiring significant commitments of capital.

Salomon Smith Barney's trading expertise, which dates back more than 80 years, together with the ability to execute a high volume of transactions with counterparties, enables it to provide liquidity to investors across a broad range of markets and financial instruments. Salomon Smith Barney's ability to execute arbitrage strategies is enhanced not only by its established presence in international capital markets but also by its utilization of information technology, quantitative methods, and risk management tools; its research capabilities; and its leadership position in the development and use of financial derivative products.

How does your approach to finance differ from that of other firms, and what do you consider to be your strengths and distinctive capabilities?

Several areas of competence distinguish the businesses of Salomon Smith Barney: our ability and willingness to commit capital for our clients and for ourselves; our superior risk management and financial engineering capabilities; our geographic breadth, with strong customer and proprietary businesses on four continents; our first-class financial advisory and analytical skills and databases; and the character of our professionals.

Discuss changes in your firm's revenues (both domestic and international) and professional staff over the past year; over the past five years.

The financial services industry is characterized by change. Increasingly, the businesses of Salomon Smith Barney are becoming more global. A number of products, markets, and clients that contribute significantly to the revenue and profitability of Salomon Smith Barney today were nonexistent five years ago. The establishment of a

Tokyo office, where Salomon Smith Barney has become the leading non-Japanese competitor in terms of both revenue and profitability, and the development of its derivative product businesses are illustrative of such markets and products. A hallmark of Salomon Smith Barney has been its willingness to commit capital, both financial and human, to the development of promising emerging businesses such as these.

The Finance MBA's Job Description

Describe the career path and corresponding responsibilities for an MBA at your firm. Describe the opportunities for professional mobility between the various departments in your firm.

New associates, as well as senior investment bankers, have identified career mobility, cohesiveness, early professional responsibility, and comprehensive training as salient considerations in their decision to join Salomon Smith Barney.

Flexibility and Options

Flexibility is the hallmark of a professional career at Salomon Smith Barney. In Investment Banking, several options are available. In contrast with a number of other major investment banks, Salomon Smith Barney does not compel a candidate to choose a specific functional specialty in order to get an offer.

Associates who join Investment Banking enter the generalist associate program, where they have the opportunity to work with many product and coverage areas to develop a broad banking competence. During their first year at the firm, generalists typically spend approximately 25% of their time on financings, 30% on mergers and acquisitions assignments, 25% on financial advisory and restructuring work, and 20% on business development.

After their first one to two years in Investment Banking, associates usually select an initial specialization that best fits their interest and background. Areas of specialization include the following:

Capital Market Services (synthesizes the efforts of Corporate Finance, Sales, and Trading in new product development and public debt offerings)
Mergers and Acquisitions
Leveraged Finance
Specialty Industries (i.e., media, telecommunications and technology, forest products/paper, transportation, utilities, real estate, and consumer)

Specialty Finance Products (high yield, private funding, and project finance)
International (coverage of foreign and international corporations and governments: London, Tokyo, Frankfurt, Sydney, New York)
Financial Institutions (insurance coverage, depository institutions, diversified financials, student loans, electric commerce, and asset management insurance)

Similarly, Salomon Smith Barney takes the generalist approach in hiring for sales and trading. All interns are recruited for the training program and then choose their areas of specialty after exposure to all facets of sales and trading through our intensive training and rotation process. These areas of specialization include:

Corporate Bonds
Derivative Securities
Emerging Markets
Finance
Foreign Exchange
Government Bonds
High Yield
Mortgage Bonds
Syndicate
Equity Derivatives
Equity Convertibles
Equity Sales Trading
Equity Syndicates
Equity Block Trading
Equity Over the Counter

A career at Salomon Smith Barney is dynamic. Many of today's most important product lines and services either did not exist or were relatively small portions of our business a few years ago. Many of our people are now working in product areas that did not exist at the time they joined the firm. We are confident that Salomon Smith Barney's flexibility will enable the organization to continue to capitalize on emerging market opportunities and challenges.

Integration and Teamwork

The integration of the firm's investment banking, research, sales, and trading capabilities is responsible for Salomon Smith Barney's performance. Our achievements reflect the combined expertise of many areas within Finance, as well as contributions from other departments and our international network.

Teamwork is ingrained in Salomon Smith Barney's professionals. Investment Banking professionals work closely with members of the Sales, Trading, and Syndicate Departments on the trading floor, as well as with Research. For example, while working on an initial public offering, an associate will interact extensively with Syndicate, Equity Sales, and Equity Research.

Salomon's performance-based compensation policy underscores the fact that teamwork and cooperation are the basis of our business success. Unlike many of its competitors, Salomon Smith Barney does not pay commissions to sales and trading professionals. Instead, a broad group of senior managers carefully assesses each person's contributions to the firm's overall performance.

Responsibility and Participation
Although the number of professionals has grown to meet new market opportunities, Salomon Smith Barney remains committed to a leanly staffed organization. The firm emphasizes small working groups that give new associates room in which to operate and develop.

A first-year finance associate works closely with a managing director and a vice president on each of his or her important assignments. Rapid client responsibility is encouraged. We are anxious to bring new associates into client contact at the earliest possible stage so that they will cultivate the relationships that are critical to the firm's long-term success.

In Sales and Trading, a first-year associate's exposure to managing directors and vice presidents is also immediate. Sales units and trading desks are run by managing directors who spend most of their time on the sales or trading desk. Furthermore, sales units and trading desks are broken down into small subunits run by experienced vice presidents who act as mentors to train the young associates. Salespeople are given account assignments soon after their placement on a desk, and traders receive risk-taking responsibilities at a very rapid pace. Hands-on training and significant early responsibility are hallmarks of the Salomon Smith Barney sales and trading program.

The Recruiting Process

Describe your recruiting process and the criteria by which you select candidates. Is prior experience necessary?

Salomon Smith Barney's character is reflected in the diversity, talents, and various backgrounds of its new associates. Salomon Smith Barney recruits associates who have displayed exceptional talent at whatever they have set their minds to. Rather than seeking a particular résumé, experience, or personality, we look for individuals with a proven record of achievement, entrepreneurial initiative, outstanding integrity, and continuing desire to work hard and excel. Salomon Smith Barney's 1997 class includes representatives from a large number of business, law, and other graduate schools, of which a significant proportion were international.

Professional development has always been a top priority of the firm. New members of all departments—from Investment Banking and Research to Sales and Trading—complete the firm's training program, widely considered the broadest in scope and most challenging of its kind on Wall Street. The program has three basic components:

1. Two months of classroom training, which is conducted at the firm's New York headquarters for all new associates in Investment Banking and Sales and Trading worldwide. Senior managers provide instruction on all firm capabilities and organizations. Trainees are expected to complete assignments and rotate responsibilities for monitoring and summarizing market activities to the class each morning.
2. Rotation among sales and trading desks in key product areas to work alongside senior managers.
3. Preparation for the Registered Representative examination given by the National Association of Securities Dealers and the New York Stock Exchange.

Training modules continue for three weeks in Investment Banking and eight weeks in Sales and Trading.

Salomon Smith Barney's compensation policy reflects the firm's belief in a team approach to business. Bonuses and salaries are based on each professional's overall contribution to the firm's performance, which includes such factors as creativity and imagination, management potential, and the ability to train others within the firm.

How many permanent associates and analysts do you hire in a typical year? How many summer interns do you expect to hire? If you have a formal summer program, please describe it. Please be sure to indicate whether the summer program is in place for all offices or just some.

In 1998 our Investment Banking Department plans to hire approximately 40–45 summer and 65–70 full-time associates. In addition, our Sales and Trading Department estimates that it will hire 15 summer and 20–25 full-time MBA candidates.

The Salomon Smith Barney summer program is designed to identify candidates for full-time positions. More than 75% of Salomon Smith Barney summer associates have received offers, filling approximately half of our full-time hiring needs.

The Investment Banking summer program provides a realistic introduction to the firm and work experience comparable to that of a full-time associate. Summer professionals function as full-time associates and become integral team members working on financings, mergers and acquisitions, and new business presentations.

The Sales and Trading summer program is a flexible, unstructured program that allows associates to rotate to different areas of the firm in both equities and fixed income. Presentations and product-specific classes are an integral part of the program, giving the associate an introduction to a full range of security products, as well as a realistic experience in Sales and Trading.

What international opportunities does your firm offer for U.S. citizens? For foreign nationals?

Salomon Smith Barney's Investment Banking operations in Asia include offices in Bangkok, Beijing, Hong Kong, Jakarta, Melbourne, Osaka, Seoul, Singapore, Sydney, Taipei, and Tokyo. In addition, there are professionals based in our New York office who are dedicated to servicing the requirements of our Asian clients in the United States. This network enables Salomon Smith Barney to maintain regular contact with governments and major industrial and financial institutions throughout the region. These offices are staffed with Investment Banking professionals with both regional and product expertise, including capital markets, mergers and acquisitions, project and lease finance, and real estate.

Europe is a key component of Salomon Smith Barney's global investment banking network. Salomon Smith Barney's activities in Europe are headquartered in London, and Salomon Smith Barney is also supported by offices in Frankfurt, Madrid, Milan, Moscow, Paris, and Zurich. In Europe, Salomon Smith Barney provides a full range of investment banking services to corporations and to sovereign and supranational organizations. The Investment Banking group in London is staffed primarily by European nationals and includes individuals from over a dozen countries. Salomon Smith Barney's continuing commitment to Europe reflects the importance of the European economies on the world stage and the vital role Europe plays in the international financial markets.

Simmons & Company International

700 Louisiana, Suite 5000
Houston, Texas 77002
(713) 236-9999
Fax: (713) 223-7800

MBA Recruiting Contact(s):
Matthew R. Simmons, President
Frederick W. Charlton, Managing Director
Matthew G. Pilon, Director

Company Description

Describe your firm's business and the types of clients served by your finance group(s). Describe your ownership structure.

Simmons & Company International is a privately owned full-service investment banking firm based in Houston. The firm was founded in 1974 by Matt Simmons, an HBS graduate from the Class of 1967, to serve the financial needs of the worldwide oil and gas service and equipment industry. Twenty-five years later, Simmons & Company remains focused on providing investment banking services to the worldwide energy industry and its investment community.

Simmons & Company's corporate finance activities include merger and acquisition advisory services, private placements of equity and debt, financial restructuring advisory work, and a variety of strategic consulting assignments. The firm has worked with public and private participants in every sector of the energy service industry, from pre-exploration to downstream transportation and processing. The firm extended its practice in the downstream energy industry during 1996 through the addition of senior personnel with extensive sector experience. Simmons & Company has implemented over 400 transactions with an aggregate value of over $34 billion.

The firm established its Capital Markets division in 1992. Simmons & Company underwrites and co-manages public equity and debt offerings, provides equity research and institutional sales support, trades listed securities, and makes markets in selected over-the-counter stocks. Since mid-1993, Simmons & Company has co-managed thirty-nine equity offerings worth nearly $5.5 billion and has

received Institutional Investor's Best of Boutiques award for oil services and equipment research coverage.

In 1999, Simmons & Company opened its second office in Aberdeen, Scotland. Approximately one-third of the firm's clients are internationally headquartered. The Scottish office will focus on the firm's Eastern Hemisphere client base.

How does your approach to finance differ from that of other firms, and what do you consider to be your strengths and distinctive capabilities?

Simmons & Company's success is enhanced by its exclusive focus on the worldwide energy industry. Through industry specialization, the firm has a unique knowledge base of developments and trends in a historically volatile industry.

The firm's core specialty, the energy service sector, is large and diverse. It includes companies supplying products and services for the exploration, production, transportation, and processing of hydrocarbons. The industry is comprised of thousands of participants, including onshore and offshore manufacturing and service companies serving a range of geographical markets.

Five years ago, the firm expanded its investment banking focus to various other parts of the energy industry. In a short period of time, Simmons & Company is proving its value-added specialization to a growing list of major energy companies in the natural gas and petroleum, and electricity sectors of the energy industry.

Simmons & Company is considered the preeminent financial advisor to the energy service industry with its specialization serving as a distinctive competitive advantage over its competition, the large Wall Street investment banking firms. Since 1993, Simmons & Company has participated in over 50% of the M&A transactions in the energy service industry.

Several other aspects of the firm's business are different from the majority of its competitors. First, Simmons & Company has a team approach to its business, and in any given year, each associate has the opportunity to participate as a team member with virtually all other professionals in the firm. Second, the firm maintains strict control over the number and types of projects it undertakes, and has a close rate on committed projects that is as high as any other firm in its business.

Discuss changes in your firm's revenues and professional staff over the past year; over the past five years.

The energy industry has proved to be one of the more volatile segments of the world economy. Since 1980, the industry has experienced a boom and then a depression of a magnitude unprecedented in any other industry in any historical period. Recently, the operating environment for the industry has improved yet remained volatile as the price of oil reached a twelve-year low only to rebound strongly within a few months. This unparalleled volatility has created tremendous opportunities for Simmons & Company. Over the past five years, the firm has more than doubled its professional staff and revenue base, and increased the international component of its activities. Simmons & Company's staff now includes nine managing directors, forty-two other executives, and a support staff of approximately forty-five people.

The Finance MBA's Job Description

Describe the career path and corresponding responsibilities for an MBA at your firm.

The primary objective for an incoming associate is to gain the experience, judgment, and maturity necessary to assume a leadership role in managing the firm's projects and marketing the firm's services effectively. As an associate, an MBA can expect to progress through assignments of increasing responsibility toward partnership and ultimate ownership in the firm.

An MBA can expect to have immediate and substantial client contact, including written and oral presentations. Simmons & Company emphasizes analysis, so an associate should anticipate considerable quantitative work. All projects are organized on a team basis, with one or more associates and analysts supporting a managing director, who serves as project manager. In a typical year, an associate would work on between twenty and thirty projects and work with virtually every professional in the firm as a member of different project teams.

Discuss the lifestyle aspects of a career with your firm (i.e., average hours per week, amount of travel, flexibility to change offices, corporate culture, etc.).

One of Simmons & Company's enduring corporate goals is to offer a stimulating work environment for its professional staff and those who work with them. The work environment is fast-paced and engrossing, and domestic and international travel is involved; however, work hours and travel requirements do not preclude members of the firm from developing outside interests.

The Recruiting Process

Describe your recruiting process and the criteria by which you select candidates. Is prior experience necessary?

Simmons & Company seeks MBAs with two or more years of professional business experience, strong analytical ability, intellectual curiosity, an ability to work with others, a desire to keep on a fast learning curve, a sense of humor, and a commitment to excellence. A very important criterion for success is the chemistry fit with other members of the firm.

The firm's professionals come from remarkably diverse backgrounds. Prior exposure to the oil service industry is not required.

How many permanent associates and analysts do you hire in a typical year? How many summer interns do you expect to hire? If you have a formal summer program, please describe it. Please be sure to indicate whether the summer program is in place for all offices or just some.

Because Simmons & Company is a relatively small firm, recruiting for associates is limited. Recently, two to three associates have joined the firm each year. Simmons & Company also seeks one to two associates for summer internships, which provide exposure to all of the firm's corporate finance activities.

Stonebridge Associates, LLC

Ten Post Office Square
Suite 1330
Boston, MA 02109
(617) 357-1770
Fax: (617) 357-4933

MBA Recruiting Contact(s):
Patricia B. Davis, Vice President

Company Description

Describe your firm's business and the types of clients served by your finance group(s).

Stonebridge Associates, LLC is a private, Boston-based investment bank that specializes in providing a broad range of corporate finance services to middle market and emerging growth companies. Our primary areas of focus includes mergers and acquisitions, divestitures, and private placements of debt and equity securities as well as related corporate advisory services such as fairness opinions, valuations, and restructurings and recapitalizations.

Describe your ownership structure.

Stonebridge has been organized as a limited liability company ("LLC"). An LLC is an unincorporated organization owned by "members" who hold equity "interests" in the organization.

How does your approach to finance differ from that of other firms, and what do you consider to be your strengths and distinctive capabilities?

Stonebridge Associates offers the creativity, technical skills, professional expertise, and global perspective typically found only in large Wall Street investment banking firms. At the same time, we are an investment bank that has consciously chosen to limit the range of its activities and services in order to provide our clients with a level of attention and responsiveness that distinguishes us from larger competitors. The company has not engaged, nor does it intend to engage, in any investment banking services that involve the underwriting or trading of securities. This focus and our capabilities, combined with our structuring and placement skills and broad industry experience, provide us with a distinct advantage in servicing the unique needs of middle market and emerging growth companies.

Stonebridge's emphasis on developing an in-depth understanding of each client's business needs and objectives, committing the resources necessary to provide solutions for complex transactions, providing senior-level attention, commitment, and focus for every transaction, has enabled the company to develop a reputation as a valued and trusted advisor.

The Finance MBA's Job Description

Describe the career path and corresponding responsibilities for an MBA at your firm.

For those candidates possessing capability, commitment, and exhibiting strong performance, there is an opportunity to gain broad and detailed experience in analyzing, structuring, and negotiating client engagements. A successful candidate should be prepared to operate effectively in a team setting within diverse business environments and to ultimately advance in both compensation and responsibility. Responsibilities allocated to staff members are highly challenging and involve a high degree of accountability. The associate participates in every aspect of a transaction from the initial engagement, to the preparation of offering materials, and marketing of the engagements. There is broad-based exposure to investment banking as well as the opportunity to work closely with senior management.

Describe the opportunities for professional mobility between the various departments in your firm.

Given the small size of the firm and the participating role in all tasks, there is both a high degree of mobility and an unprecedented opportunity for exposure to diverse responsibilities and development of investment banking skills and knowledge.

Discuss the lifestyle aspects of a career with your firm (i.e., average hours per week, amount of travel, flexibility to change offices, corporate culture, etc.).

Stonebridge Associates promotes a positive working environment where professionals share a dedication and purpose for doing the best job possible. From time to time, and dependent on deal flow, demands can be intensive; however, the firm encourages a balanced lifestyle. Inasmuch as the firm has one office, transfer or office changes are not a consideration. Overall, there are reasonable travel requirements.

The Recruiting Process

Describe your recruiting process and the criteria by which you select candidates. Is prior experience necessary?

Our hiring needs and organizational structure are closely tied. We recruit through correspondence opportunities and on-campus interviews. We find the process of a successful recruiting program begins with a commitment to an annual recruiting effort. Our criteria by which we select candidates emphasizes proven written and oral communication skills, comfort and familiarity with quantitative analysis, emphasis on integrity, intelligence, interpersonal skills, willingness to work hard, and a teamwork orientation. Prior investment banking or consulting experience is essential and background in technology, engineering, or the healthcare/life science areas is preferred.

How many permanent associates and analysts do you hire in a typical year? How many summer interns do you expect to hire? If you have a formal summer program, please describe it. Please be sure to indicate whether the summer program is in place for all offices or just some.

In a typical year, one graduating MBA student is hired for the associate position and one pre-MBA financial analyst is recruited. We do not offer summer assignments.

TD Securities Inc.

31 West 52nd Street
New York, NY 10019-6101
(212) 827-7000
Fax: (212) 827-7248
Web site: www.tdsecurities.com

MBA Recruiting Contact(s):
Maureen C. Dixon
Vice President, Human Resources
Frank Marchelli, Recruiting Coordinator

Company Description

Describe your firm's business and the types of clients served by your finance group(s).

TD Bank Financial Group is a widely held, public corporation whose shares are listed on the Toronto, Montreal, Vancouver, Alberta, Winnipeg, International (London, England), New York, and Tokyo Stock Exchanges. At October 31, 1998, TD ranked as the fourth largest bank in terms of market capitalization.

Formally titled TD Bank Financial Group, but usually referred to as TD Bank or simply TD, the bank was formed in 1955 through the merger of the Bank of Toronto (founded 1855) and the Dominion Bank (established 1869).

In Canada, TD serves individuals, businesses, financial institutions, and governments through a network of over 900 branches from coast to coast. The bank also offers complete trust and fiduciary services in both the personal and business fields.

Internationally, our staff offer a broad range of credit, noncredit, and financial advisory services to businesses, multinational corporations, governments, and correspondent banks through offices in the U.S. and in other financial capitals including Hong Kong, London, Mexico City, Mumbai (India), Santiago (Chile), Singapore, Taipei, Tokyo, and through our subsidiary bank in Australia. We also provide discount brokerage services throughout the globe. Worldwide, the bank employs over 32,000 people.

A major strength of TD is its financial position. TD maintains a position as one of the best capitalized banks in the world, with one of the highest credit ratings of all major North American banks. Financial strength is a major advantage in tough times; customers may be drawn to a bank offering financial stability that also has the capital to invest in service, to pursue new strategies, and to take advantage of opportunities that arise.

Another strength is that TD, unlike its major competitors, has built, rather than bought, its own securities operation and offers integrated corporate and investment banking services. This provides the bank with an edge in its ability to react innovatively to shifting customer needs and changing economic times.

Since its formal establishment in 1980, the U.S.A. Division of TD has successfully developed a solid Corporate Investment Banking business with noted strength in providing financing and advisory services to the media, technology, telecom, energy, health care, forest products, and public finance industries.

In recent years, TD has committed substantial resources to build a securities business in the U.S. Through the formation of TD Securities Inc., we have developed a broad array of products and services in areas where we can competitively add value to our focused industry niches. Since receiving approval to underwrite and deal in corporate debt and equity securities in the United States, we have built a thriving high yield debt business. This has augmented our already strong capabilities in areas such as loan syndication, mergers & acquisitions, and merchant banking.

The Finance MBA's Job Description

Describe the career path and corresponding responsibilities for an MBA at your firm.

Associates at TD Securities are looked upon as vital resources, providing creative input in a variety of disciplines. As such, associates play an integral role in the creation, structure, and completion of a myriad of financial transactions. Day-to-day responsibilities are built upon your continuing support of senior transaction and relationship managers to provide timely and accurate analysis for corporate lending, advisory, treasury, securities products, and/or syndication services.

Associates play an important role in the daily activities of the firm in virtually every arena and consequently must possess the necessary flexibility and dedication to perform efficiently in such an environment.

Associate opportunities in Finance could include placement in one of our specialized industries or product areas including:

Corporate Finance
Energy Finance
Forest Products Finance
High Yield Origination
Media, Technology, Telecom Finance
Merchant Banking
Mergers &Acquisitions
Public Finance
Syndications
Structured Finance

Associate opportunities in Sales and Trading could include placement in:

High Yield Sales &Trading
Institutional Equities Sales &Trading
Structured Finance
Derivative Products
Syndication /Loan Sales
Other Treasury products (FX, Money Markets, and Fixed Income)

Depending upon placement, associates may be asked to:

• Conduct in-depth research for corporate or industry analysis

• Generate detailed financial projections

• Perform investment return analysis

• Foster strong relationships with existing and potential clients

• Be part of a team developing creative financial solutions for clients

The Recruiting Process

Describe your recruiting process and the criteria by which you select candidates. Is prior experience necessary?

To excel as an Associate at TD Securities one must be resourceful, flexible, and demonstrate the ability to work independently. Successful candidates will also possess strong quantitative skills and well developed writing abilities. While senior colleagues provide direction, your path towards promotion and advancement is your own.

TD Securities offers both full-time and summer opportunities to associates and analysts.

Teachers Insurance and Annuity Association-College Retirement Equities Fund (TIAA-CREF)

730 Third Avenue
New York, NY 10017
(800) 842-2733
Web site: www.tiaa-cref.org

MBA Recruiting Contact(s):
Robert J. Burke, Senior Staffing Consultant

Company Description

Describe your firm's business and the types of clients served by your finance group(s).

As the world's largest pension system, with over $250 billion in assets entirely managed internally, TIAA-CREF professionals skillfully invest in virtually every economic sector. TIAA's assets are broadly diversified among private placements, publicly traded bonds, commercial mortgages, and real estate. CREF, the companion corporation, is a registered investment company.

Quality and yield are the bedrock of our investment activities. In fact, TIAA is a top performer in the insurance industry, and its strong balance sheets earn the highest possible ratings from Moody's, Standard & Poor's, Duff & Phelps, and A.M. Best.

TIAA-CREF originated a pension system of portable benefits in 1918 to help ensure the financial security of people employed in education and research. Today, over 2 million professors, research scientists, and other educators turn to TIAA-CREF for expert benefits counseling, affordable insurance protection, and retirement income that cannot be outlived. It also provides high-quality, low-cost mutual funds, and serves as investment manager for college financing programs.

Stable cash flows, innovative strategies, and years of experience make TIAA a leader in direct placement loans to private and public companies, as well as in publicly traded bonds. TIAA also invests in highly structured deals, including private securitized financings, hybrid credit/real estate deals, project financings, and secondary private placements.

The Finance MBA's Job Description

Describe the career path and corresponding responsibilities for an MBA at your firm.

Our steady stream of investment activity is ideal for MBAs who want to put their talent to work immediately, with financings in a broad range of industries. Individual responsibilities are balanced with teamwork at every level, enabling associates to gain broad industry knowledge and market experience in rotations throughout our Securities Division.

Specifically, associates assigned to a private placement team monitor portfolios with investments in about twenty-five companies, valued at about a half-billion dollars. Associates analyze industry trends, make on-site evaluations of potential investments, negotiate new deals, and present recommendations to senior management.

Public market teams evaluate market trends, research bond offerings, develop trading strategies, and present recommendations to senior managers responsible for multibillion-dollar portfolios.

The Recruiting Process

Describe your recruiting process and the criteria by which you select candidates. Is prior experience necessary?

TIAA Investments seeks talented MBAs majoring in finance to join our Securities Division. Superior communications skills and prior credit training and analysis experience at a major financial institution are strongly preferred. Along with quality investing, we emphasize teamwork and a balanced work and personal lifestyle.

A successful screening interview will be followed by an opportunity to meet with Securities directors and associates at our New York City headquarters.

We believe cultural and ethnic diversity is the lifeblood of a successful corporation, and this is reflected in our hiring record, our tradition of promoting from within, and our career development activities.

U.S. Bancorp Piper Jaffray Inc.

222 South Ninth Street
Minneapolis, MN 55402
(612) 342-6000
Web site: www.piperjaffray.com
E-mail: applicant@piperjaffray.com

MBA Recruiting Contact(s):
Rachel Beckman

Company Description

Describe your firm's business and the types of clients served by your finance group(s).

U.S. Bancorp Piper Jaffray Inc.—a full-service investment banking firm headquartered in Minneapolis, MN—is one of the leading investment banks based outside New York City. Established in 1895, it has over 3,200 employees. U.S. Bancorp Piper Jaffray services consist of equity and fixed income capital markets and retail distribution, with 1,500 brokers located in 100 offices across seventeen western states.

U.S. Bancorp Piper Jaffray's capital markets activities encompass corporate finance, equity research, public finance, debt and equity trading, and equity and fixed income sales. The Investment Banking Department consists of 100 professionals who are divided along industry specialties. The Research Department has sixty professionals who, with their Investment Banking peers, lead industry teams. U.S. Bancorp Piper Jaffray has five industry teams—HealthCare, Financial Institutions, Technology, Consumer, and Industrial Growth—as well as functional specialists performing private placements, mergers and acquisitions, venture capital, and valuations. The Investment Banking Department also has offices in Seattle, Chicago, Menlo Park, and San Francisco.

Describe your ownership structure.

U.S. Bancorp Piper Jaffray is owned by U.S. Bancorp, which is listed on the New York Stock Exchange.

How does your approach to finance differ from that of other firms, and what do you consider to be your strengths and distinctive capabilities?

U.S. Bancorp focuses on serving the financial needs of emerging-growth companies. U.S. Bancorp Piper Jaffray is also able to commit its own capital to new ventures. It has made a number of venture capital investments in recent years and intends to increase investment in this area in the future.

U.S. Bancorp Piper Jaffray places strong emphasis on long-term investment banking relationships. The company devotes substantial resources to trading, research coverage, and corporate finance expertise to provide its investment banking clients with the highest levels of service. U.S. Bancorp Piper Jaffray also has one of the industry's lowest turnover rates, which is important in maintaining long-term banking commitments.

The Finance MBA's Job Description

Describe the career path and corresponding responsibilities for an MBA at your firm.

U.S. Bancorp Piper Jaffray emphasizes hiring good people and giving them as much freedom and responsibility as possible—consistent with general corporate objectives—to determine their own focus and goals. The good people rise to the top on their own initiative, and they remain with Piper Jaffray, because no other organization can offer them as much latitude to exercise their initiative. This unstructured atmosphere and emphasis on the individual have made it possible for entrepreneurial people to satisfy many of their goals within the corporate structure.

New associates are hired for industry teams that are compatible with their particular interests and capabilities. Associates are immediately assigned to a wide variety of projects and given as much responsibility as their experience and capabilities permit. A senior officer in the department supervises all client relationships and engagements.

The Recruiting Process

Describe your recruiting process and the criteria by which you select candidates. Is prior experience necessary?

The most successful people in investment banking come to U.S. Bancorp Piper Jaffray with some significant financially related working experience. This experience enables them to contribute effectively to the department at an early stage in their development. Members of the group also must have the confidence, maturity, and personal attributes necessary to develop successful client relationships. In most instances, the current professionals in the department have spent time in financial centers such as New York, or instead preferred the working environment and growth opportunities that a smaller organization can offer and the lifestyle available in our midwestern and western offices.

How many permanent associates and analysts do you hire in a typical year? How many summer interns do you expect to hire? If you have a formal summer program, please describe it. Please be sure to indicate whether the summer program is in place for all offices or just some.

New associates are hired primarily into the Investment Banking Department. Because of the department's size, it is not possible to offer a formal summer training program. U.S. Bancorp Piper Jaffray typically hires five to ten MBA graduates each year.

Wasserstein Perella & Co. Inc.

31 West 52nd Street
New York, NY 10019
(212) 969-2700

MBA Recruiting Contact(s):
Frances A. Lyman, Recruiting Manager

Company Description

Describe your firm's business and the types of clients served by your finance group(s).

Wasserstein Perella Group, Inc. is a leading international investment banking firm active in three related lines of business: (1) advising a global base of clients on matters of corporate strategy, mergers, acquisitions, divestitures and restructurings, and corporate finance; (2) specialized sales, trading, and research of debt and equity securities; and (3) management of investment funds and products that seek superior risk-adjusted returns for investors.

Our firm is dedicated to providing superior client service and building long-term relationships. In pursuit of these goals, Wasserstein Perella has established an international presence through a network of offices in New York, London, Paris, Frankfurt, Tokyo, Chicago, Los Angeles, San Francisco, and Dallas. Our strategic alliance with The Nomura Securities Co., Ltd., the world's largest securities firm, which was formed in 1988, shortly after the firm's founding, gives Wasserstein Perella an unparalleled presence in and access to Japan and the Asian markets. Since its inception, Wasserstein Perella's professional staff has grown to number approximately 500 worldwide.

Wasserstein Perella has participated in many of the largest and most significant mergers and acquisitions in recent history and in some of the most innovative financings. The firm is equally proud of the many small divestitures and other transactions it has managed on behalf of its long-term clients and the numerous occasions when clients have been advised to forego transactions as a result of market or strategic factors. The firm has developed a strong high-yield origination effort targeting financial entrepreneurs and growth companies, and has served as a sounding board for larger clients with respect to various financing alternatives.

Wasserstein Perella's specialized sales, trading, and research activities are carried out through its wholly owned subsidiary, Wasserstein Perella Securities, Inc. ("WPS"). Within WPS, the Grantchester Securities Division is one of the leading dealers of high-yield debt securities. Grantchester traded more than $83 billion of high-yield securities over the last three years and has transacted business with 200 different institutions having varied investment profiles. The WPS Equity Division is a highly focused team that concentrates on the sales, trading, and research of selected equity securities. WPS's Emerging Markets Division provides investor and corporate finance services in the Latin American, Eastern European, African, and Asian markets.

Wasserstein Perella continues to build its asset management capabilities. The firm's focus is on equity and fixed income money management of U.S. securities, selected international products, and an array of higher return, higher risk private investment funds. The cornerstone of this effort to date is the firm's merchant banking fund.

Describe your ownership structure.

Wasserstein Perella is a privately owned corporation. Twenty percent of its equity is held by Nomura Securities, Ltd.

How does your approach to finance differ from that of other firms, and what do you consider to be your strengths and distinctive capabilities?

Wasserstein Perella offers custom-tailored mergers and acquisitions (M&A) and corporate finance solutions to meet clients' unique needs. The firm is known for its ability to solve complex financial and strategic problems. We are also viewed as an objective sounding board for financing decisions, and we are not prejudiced by a need to underwrite securities to cover the overhead of a large underwriting operation.

Discuss changes in your firm's revenues (both domestic and international) and professional staff over the past year; over the past five years.

We have had a gradual diversification of revenues away from domestic M&A toward high-yield and equity sales, trading and research, international M&A, privatizations, and asset management.

The Finance MBA's Job Description

Describe the career path and corresponding responsibilities for an MBA at your firm.

Financial associates at Wasserstein Perella & Co. Inc. are responsible for all aspects of analysis relating to mergers, acquisitions, restructuring, divestitures, and leveraged buyouts. After a relatively short "training" period, associates are expected to be proficient with the fundamental analytical principals of mergers and acquisitions and general corporate finance. Associates will participate in structuring and negotiating M&A transactions and financings and will gain increasing experience and responsibility as they develop expertise in these areas. In addition, associates will play a significant role in the firm's "new business" efforts and ongoing client relationships.

Associates are given responsibilities that are typically one year ahead of those at other investment banks. The typical time period between associate and vice president is three and a half years.

Describe the opportunities for professional mobility between the various departments in your firm.

Wasserstein Perella provides tremendous flexibility between departments and geographic locations.

Discuss the lifestyle aspects of a career with your firm (i.e., average hours per week, amount of travel, flexibility to change offices, corporate culture, etc.).

Lifestyle/culture is characterized as fun and entrepreneurial yet intense. Average hours per week are 60–70. Travel depends on the nature of projects. Associates usually travel 15–25 percent of their time.

The Recruiting Process

Describe your recruiting process and the criteria by which you select candidates. Is prior experience necessary?

We usually conduct two-on-one on-campus interviews, followed by one or two visits to our New York office. Decisions are usually made quickly. We look for smart, energetic self-starters. Grades and previous experience are important factors.

How many permanent associates and analysts do you hire in a typical year? How many summer interns do you expect to hire? If you have a formal summer program, please describe it. Please be sure to indicate whether the summer program is in place for all offices or just some.

Wasserstein Perella typically hires eight to ten associates domestically and one to two internationally. We also hire three to five summer associates.

Weyerhaeuser Company

Tacoma, WA 98477
(206) 924-2367
Web site: www.weyerhaeuser.com

MBA Recruiting Contact(s):
Brian L. Haun, Director
Investment Evaluation Department

Company Description

Describe your firm's business and the types of clients served by your finance group(s).

Weyerhaeuser is an international forest products company whose principal businesses are the growing and harvesting of trees; the manufacture, distribution and sale of forest products, including logs, wood chips, building products, pulp, paper and packaging products; and real estate construction and development. It is also one of North America's largest producers of forest products and a leading recycler of office wastepaper, newspaper, and corrugated boxes. Weyerhaeuser is the world's largest private owner of merchantable softwood timber and the world's largest producer of softwood lumber and market pulp.It is also the top forest products exporter in the U.S. and among the top U.S. exporters overall.We employ approximately 45,000 people in the United States and Canada and have sales greater than $10 billion (Over $1 billion in exports from the U.S.).

Timberlands Division includes:

- Approximately 5.8 million acres (2.4 million hectares) of private timberland owned and leased in the United States (3.8 million in the South, 2.0 million in the Northwest)

- Partner in a venture holding 193,000 acres (approx. 78,100 hectares) in New Zealand

- Weyerhaeuser is a partner in the World Timberfund, holding 62,500 acres (approx. 25,000 hectares) in Australia. It also holds a 97 percent interest in 234,000 acres (94,700 hectares) of private range land being converted to timberland in Uruguay.

- Long-term licensing rights in Canada on about 34 million acres (13.6 million hectares)

The Wood Products Division includes:

- Canadian softwood lumber (produced at 19 locations)

- Southern softwood lumber (produced at 13 locations)

- Western softwood lumber (produced at five locations)

- Hardwood lumber (produced at 12 locations)

- Doors (produced at one location

- Plywood produced at eight locations)

- Oriented strand board (produced at nine locations in the U.S. and Canada)

- Building materials (distributed at 70 customer service centers)

The Pulp, Paper and Packaging Division includes:

- Manufacturing in 23 facilities in the United States and Canada, including pulp, fine paper, containerboard, and bleached paperboard

- Packaging plants operate at 64 locations; plus one linerboard preprint facility; and the Center for Customer Satisfaction, a design and technical center

- Recycled wastepaper collected and processed at 24 facilities

- Weyerhaeuser Real Estate Company engages in commercial development, construction, and sales of single- and multi-family dwellings and business properties in nine states

Corporate Vision. Weyerhaeuser's corporate vision is of a total quality organization gaining competitive advantage by successfully meeting customer needs. The company will leverage its tradition of responsible natural resource stewardship and utilize its unparalleled resource base and highly skilled work force to achieve superior standards of excellence in manufacturing and customer service.

As Weyerhaeuser successfully implements business unit improvement plans, the company expects to see significant growth in earnings from its core businesses. Weyerhaeuser has embarked on a program to achieve and maintain a position as the top competitor in the forest products industry.

How does your approach to finance differ from that of other firms, and what do you consider to be your strengths and distinctive capabilities?

Weyerhaeuser competes both with other broad-line forest products companies (e.g., Georgia Pacific, Champion International, International Paper) and with leaders in specific product segments. Weyerhaeuser has achieved competitive advantage in most of its commodity businesses by building on its traditional strengths:

- Substantial timber resource base in the U.S. and Canada, with recent acquistions in New Zealand and South America.

- Modern, efficient, scale manufacturing facilities with ready access to raw materials and export markets

- Superior technical and research skills

- Overall reputation for quality products, reliable service, outstanding people, and integrity in all business dealings

- Differential advantage in most major export markets

The Finance MBA's Job Description

Describe the career path and corresponding responsibilities for an MBA at your firm.

The Investment Evaluation Department (IED) is the preferred entry point for high-potential MBAs. IED is responsible for providing strategic, financial, and analytical leadership in all acquisition, divestiture, merger, joint venture, and new business evaluations. The group is also responsible for analyzing and forming independent judgments on Weyerhaeuser's major capital investment opportunities. IED is a small group within Weyerhaeuser's finance organization. However, it deals substantially with the company's operating divisions, supporting major strategic and tactical decisions.

The analyst position is the traditional entry point for the department. Analysts typically spend two to three years in IED gaining a broad perspective on Weyerhaeuser's businesses and exposure to senior corporate and operating level managers. The Department's goal is to provide analysts with a good general understanding of Weyerhaeuser businesses as well as the opportunity to get to know many of the company's key managers in preparation for long-term careers in the company. The department project directors and manager provide guidance and

advice as needed. Analysts tend to move into a business unit of their choice, gaining experience in their areas of interest (marketing, finance, operations management, etc.) to lead them into general management positions.

Weyerhaeuser evaluates many proposals to expand or reconfigure its business groups. They include acquisition and joint venture opportunities within existing businesses as well as in new business lines. They may also involve divestment or asset redeployment options aimed at upgrading Weyerhaeuser's existing portfolio of assets. The IED analyst is a key member of the team evaluating an opportunity, with primary responsibility for performing the economic analysis. In many instances analysts help develop the strategic framework for the opportunity. The analyst must also ensure that the presentation of the proposal provides senior management with the key information needed to make the decision. After a decision has been reached, analysts participate in the execution by drafting offering memorandums, working with investment bankers, coordinating buyers' due diligence, advising senior managers during negotiations, and evaluating alternative transaction structures.

Weyerhaeuser competes in highly capital-intensive industries and allocates significant capital resources to its existing businesses. IED brings conceptual and analytical leadership to the capital allocation effort. The analyst is primarily responsible for providing decision makers with independent, thorough, and timely economic analyses of diverse investment proposals. This is accomplished by working closely with business and operating groups, often on site. Some recent projects include the expansion of a joint venture newsprint operation with a Japanese partner, multi-stage modernizations and expansions at two of Weyerhaeuser's largest pulp and paper complexes, and the reconfiguration of our Southern sawmill capacity to better align with available raw material and product markets.

The Recruiting Process

Describe your recruiting process and the criteria by which you select candidates. Is prior experience necessary?

IED is looking for MBAs who want to leverage their superior analytical ability, strong leadership, and interpersonal skills into a long-term general management career at Weyerhaeuser. New analysts should have significant prior work experience, good business judgment, and a sense of perspective. They should also be comfortable working independently in a relatively unstructured environment.

How many permanent associates and analysts do you hire in a typical year? If you have a summer program, please describe it.

IED hires one to three analysts a year, primarily through recruiting at top MBA schools around the United States. There is no summer program.

William Blair & Company

222 West Adams Street
Chicago, IL 60606
Web site: www.wmblair.com

MBA Recruiting Contact(s):
Brian Gannon
Corporate Finance
(312) 364-8114

Bill O'Connell
Debt Finance
(312) 364-8708

David Farina
Research
(312) 364-8918

Robert Newman
Investment Management
(312) 364-8783

Locations of Offices:
Chicago, San Francisco, London, Liechtenstein, and Zurich

Total Number of Professionals (U.S. and worldwide):
454

Company Description

Describe your firm's business and the types of clients served by your finance group(s).

William Blair & Company is a limited liability corporation offering a full range of investment banking and brokerage services to corporations, institutions, municipalities, and private investors across the United States and overseas. William Blair & Company is the largest full-service investment banking firm headquartered in Chicago with nearly 753 employees.

The firm was founded in 1935 to serve small and medium-sized companies and to participate in their growth through equity and debt financings; research, market making, trading, as well as other forms of after-market support; and financial advisory services such as merger and acquisition advice. To that end, the firm's Corporate Finance and Debt Finance Departments have continued to perform originating, structuring, and distrib-

uting securities for middle-market growth companies while also assisting not-for-profit organizations and municipalities with their financing needs. William Blair's Mezzanine Debt Fund, Leveraged Capital Fund, and Venture Capital divisions also focus on providing capital for and making private equity investments in a variety of middle-market growth companies. The firm's Research Department is widely recognized as one of the industry's best in providing research coverage of small to mid-sized growth companies in the United States, following approximately 260 companies and a number of specific industries. Finally, the firm's Investment Management Department currently manages approximately $12 billion for high-net-worth individuals, trusts, foundations, charitable and university endowments, pension and profit-sharing funds, and mutual funds.

Describe your ownership structure.

William Blair & Company is a limited liability corporation (LLC) registered to do business as a member of the New York Stock Exchange. The firm is owned entirely by active principals. William Blair is notable in today's consolidating financial industry for its commitment to remaining an independent firm. As of December 31, 1998, the firm's capital position was stated at $100 million. There are currently 151 principals and nearly 755 employees.

How does your approach to finance differ from that of other firms, and what do you consider to be your strengths and distinctive capabilities?

Throughout the history of William Blair & Company, we have held fast to the objectives upon which the firm was founded: to identify moneymaking ideas for our investing clients and to provide superior execution for our corporate and public issuers. We have accomplished these goals by focusing on identifying high-quality long-term investment opportunities, by providing the highest standards of service, and by being conservative in the way we operate our business and advise our clients. Over the past six decades, we are proud to have helped our clients achieve superior investment returns and attractive financing in both good and bad markets.

Our long-term orientation permeates every aspect of our operations. Our ownership structure provides underlying stability and fosters longevity with the firm. Clients benefit from a continuity of performance and a personal familiarity with their needs that come only from long-standing relationships. Over time, the firm has expanded the scope of its investment banking and brokerage services to ensure our clients' enduring financial growth.

Today, William Blair strives to serve its clients as it has in the past: with prudent judgment, sound advice, and diligent follow-through. We appreciate the confidence our clients have in our abilities. Every day, in all aspects of our business, we work to preserve their trust.

Discuss changes in your firm's revenues (both domestic and international) and professional staff over the past year; over the past five years.

William Blair has enjoyed solid growth in both revenue and professional staff over the past five years. For instance, both 1997 and 1998 were record revenue years for the Corporate Finance Department. While the firm has certainly benefited from the strong equity markets and active merger and acquisition environment in recent years, William Blair prefers to add staff in a controlled manner, avoiding cyclical staff additions and reductions.

William Blair & Company has also expanded its international presence both domestically and internationally by adding offices in San Francisco and Zurich.

The Finance MBA's Job Description

Describe the career path and corresponding responsibilities for an MBA at your firm.

William Blair & Company seeks qualified MBAs who desire to work with mid-sized companies, institutions, municipalities, and investors throughout the country. William Blair & Company recruits these individuals on a continual basis as the firm continues to grow. The firm feels the most effective training program it can offer is immediate exposure to the industry. New associates do not undergo any outside course work but rather are assigned to live projects from the start.

Corporate Finance

Associates in Corporate Finance work in small project teams that typically include a principal, an associate, and an analyst. Associates work with multiple teams on a number of assignments simultaneously, including transactions such as equity offerings, mergers and acquisitions, private placements, as well as other financial advisory projects. From the time they are hired, associates act as generalists, providing them with the flexibility to explore a broad array of industries, clients, and transactions. A decentralized, collegial, and results-oriented management style creates an entrepreneurial atmosphere that both encourages and rewards a high degree of initiative. William Blair expects each MBA that it hires as an associate to become a principal of the firm.

Research

Research analysts typically cover up to fifteen companies in a sector such as health care, retail, technology, finance, and services. New hires select their own area of coverage, although most likely in an area that the MBA had prior work experience. William Blair & Company believes that the best training for a new MBA hire is "on the job" as new hires start researching companies from day one. New hires will have a senior analyst mentor as a guide. Nonetheless, the new hire will be responsible for choosing his or her own investment ideas and executing those ideas. Besides the researching of investment ideas, analysts are often involved in the underwriting process as well as the marketing of the ideas to institutional and retail customers. Roughly half of the analysts in the departments are principals.

Debt Finance

MBAs joining the Debt Finance Department enter as associates with responsibilities that include preparing proposals and marketing materials, assisting in marketing, working with clients on a daily basis, and overseeing details related to the execution of a transaction. Associates work in the fields of corporate debt, financing for not-for-profit institutions, hospitals, and higher education entities, as well as for municipalities. This broad exposure provides a thorough understanding of the fixed income industry, the challenges of working on several financings at once, and the opportunity to be a generalist rather than an expert in only one facet of the industry. The day-to-day operations of the department and its team approach are similar in structure to the Corporate Finance Department.

Investment Management

The Investment Management Department at William Blair is composed of 34 investment professionals. The bulk of these are portfolio managers, about half of whom have research backgrounds and follow a number of stocks, in addition to their account responsibilities. The balance are full-time analysts. The research function in investment management is designed to complement and supplement the William Blair research product. This is done by following companies that have the following attributes: (1) they meet the William Blair criteria for high-quality growth companies; (2) they are desirable for the construction of well-diversified portfolios, and; (3) for reasons having to do with either size or industry affiliation, they are not followed by the William Blair Research department. A new MBA would typically start out as an analyst and be responsible for developing a coverage list of stocks for the department to invest in, over an initial period of at least four to five years. Over the long term, both analytical and portfolio management career tracks are available, with both potentially leading to an invitation to become a principal in the firm. Currently, 25 members of the department are principals in the firm.

Describe the opportunities for professional mobility between the various departments in your firm.

Associates are hired to work within a specific department, although there is open communication between all departments of the firm. The firm addresses the needs of individuals who desire to change their focus and switch departments on an individual basis and after taking into consideration the needs of the firm.

Describe the lifestyle aspects of a career with your firm (i.e., average hours per week, amount of travel, flexibility to change offices, corporate culture, etc.).

A career at William Blair is exciting and rewarding and requires a significant commitment of time and energy. One's average hours and travel schedule will vary depending upon market conditions as well as the number and types of projects on which one is working. People who work at William Blair, however, generally seem to enjoy the lifestyle offered by a career with the firm and fostered by its location in Chicago. In addition, the comparatively small size of the firm relative to Wall Street standards tends to encourage close relationships among co-workers, while the firm's long-term commitment to its employees and the broad partnership is representative of the firm's inclusive, not exclusive, culture.

The Recruiting Process

Describe your recruiting process and the criteria by which you select candidates. Is prior experience necessary?

William Blair's recruiting process varies across departments. While Corporate Finance and Research participate in on-campus interviewing, Debt Finance and Investment Management welcome on-site interviewing through correspondence opportunities. William Blair & Company adheres to school policies in its recruiting practices.

William Blair & Company hopes to attract highly motivated, quality individuals with strong quantitative, communicative, and interpersonal skills. In addition to demonstrating these skills, prior work experience, academic performance, and community service activities are considered in an applicant's evaluation.

How many permanent associates and analysts do you hire in a typical year? How many summer interns do you expect to hire? If you have a formal summer program, please describe it. Please be sure to indicate whether the summer program is in place for all offices or just some.

Hiring is based on the needs of each department. Typically, recruiting goals are set in the fall of the coming recruiting season; however, given the size and nature of the firm and our recruiting process, interviewing occurs on a continuous basis throughout the year. Summer associates are rare across divisions; however, opportunities sometimes present themselves depending on the staffing needs of each department.

The World Bank
The Young Professionals Program

1818 H Street, NW
Washington, DC 20433
(202) 473-0312
Web site: www.worldbank.org

MBA Recruiting Contact(s):
Young Professionals Program Administrator
Fax: (202) 522-3741
E-mail: Young Professionals Program@worldbank.org

Company Description

Describe your firm's business and the types of clients served by your finance group(s).

The World Bank, which consists of the International Bank for Reconstruction and Development (IBRD) and the International Development Association (IDA), promotes economic and social progress in developing nations by helping raise productivity so people may lead better and fuller lives. This is also the aim of the International Finance Corporation (IFC), which works closely with private investors from around the world in promoting commercial enterprises in developing countries. The principal objective of the Multilateral Investment Guarantee Agency (MIGA) is to encourage the flow of investments for productive purposes among member countries and in particular to developing member countries, thus supplementing the activities of the IBRD, IDA, and IFC.

The IBRD, IDA, IFC, and MIGA (collectively known as the World Bank Group) have three interrelated functions: to lend funds; to provide advice, consulting services, and investment promotion; and to serve as a catalyst to stimulate investments by others. The four institutions are closely associated, with IDA, IFC, and MIGA being affiliates of the IBRD. The same president serves all four institutions. The IBRD and IDA (which are jointly referred to as "the Bank") share the same operational staff, while the staff of IFC and MIGA is, for the most part, separate from that of the Bank.

The IBRD, IDA, and IFC differ in the types of financing that they provide for member developing countries. The IBRD makes loans at interest rates that reflect the Bank's cost of borrowing, while IDA provides concessionary financing for the poorest developing countries. Unlike the IBRD and IDA, IFC loans are not government-guaranteed. Rather, the corporation makes loans to private-sector companies at commercial interest rates. The IFC also takes equity positions in companies. MIGA, on the other hand, provides guarantees for non-commercial risks and also policy and advisory services to encourage the flow of capital to developing countries and to assist these countries in creating an attractive investment climate.

Describe your ownership structure.

The IBRD, established in 1945, is the oldest and largest of the institutions. It was conceived at the United Nations Monetary and Financial Conference held in Bretton Woods, New Hampshire (U.S.A.) in July 1944. The IFC was established in 1956, and IDA in 1960. MIGA began its operations in 1988.

The IBRD, IDA, IFC, and MIGA are owned by their member governments and controlled by their board of directors. To date, 180 countries have joined the IBRD. Membership in IDA is open to all members of the IBRD, and most countries have joined. The IFC has 172 member countries. As of July 1997, MIGA had 141 members.

Most of the funds lent by the IBRD come from its borrowing in the world's capital markets. It also receives funds from the capital subscriptions of member countries, repayments on past loans, and sales of loans to other investors. Funding for IDA comes almost entirely from grants provided by its more affluent member countries and from contributions by the IBRD from its net income. The IFC obtains funds from its member governments and from borrowing, mainly from international financial markets. MIGA is financially and legally independent and obtains its funds from its member governments.

The Job Description

Describe the career path and corresponding responsibilities for an MBA at your firm. Describe the opportunities for professional mobility between the various departments in your firm. Discuss the lifestyle aspects of a career with your firm.

There is no typical career path for a Young Professional. Young Professionals move across sectors and regions over the course of their careers. Their two rotational assignments in the program and first regular assignment often expose them to two or more Bank regions within the World Bank Group.

Former Young Professionals work throughout the organization in a variety of staff and managerial positions. They usually start out as financial analysts/economists or investment officers.

Financial analysts and sector economists help identify, appraise, and work with clients in the implementation of projects. Many Young Professionals find themselves working on the appraisal and supervision of projects for, say, a country's financial sector development.

Investment officers in the finance complex manage specific portfolios, conduct risk analysis, experiment with innovative products, and monitor the returns on investments. They also coordinate the work of investment teams and develop investment strategies and support systems.

Operational staff travel three or four times a year to the countries they work on, with such missions generally lasting about three weeks.

The Recruiting Process

Describe your recruiting process and the criteria by which you select candidates. Is prior experience necessary?

The Young Professionals Program (YPP) was established in 1963 as a means of recruiting outstanding recent university graduates. Since then, over 1,000 young professionals (YPs) from over 100 different countries have joined the World Bank Group. The majority of all YPs recruited are still with the organization.

The YPP offers an exciting beginning to a career in the World Bank Group for people under 32 years of age as of January of the selection year, who have strong qualifications in finance, economics, or a related field. We encourage qualified candidates from all member countries to apply. As you consider whether or not to apply, please note the following information.

To apply to the program, candidates must have a master's degree (or equivalent) in finance, economics, or a technical field used in the group's operations, plus a minimum of two years of relevant work experience. The technical fields of particular interest to the Bank Group are education, public health, social sciences, urban planning, and civil engineering.

Fluency in English is required of candidates to the YPP. It is also beneficial that candidates have a speaking proficiency in one or more of the Bank's other most commonly used languages (i.e., Arabic, Chinese, French, Portuguese, and Spanish). Increasingly, proficiency in one or more languages of Eastern Europe and Central Asia is also being sought in YP candidates.

The YPP does not recruit individuals whose primary graduate-level training and work experience are in disciplines such as law, computer science, accounting, marketing, linguistics, etc. Candidates with specializations in those areas should contact the Staffing Division directly.

We will begin reviewing applications for our upcoming selection (March of next year) in July. Should you be selected to proceed to the second phase of the screening process, you will be required to complete a more detailed application package. An application will be available on our Web site (www.worldbank.org/html/extdr/ypp/default.htm) as of June 1, 1998. Any application received after the final deadline will be held for review for the next selection.

How many permanent associates and analysts do you hire in a typical year? How many summer interns do you expect to hire? If you have a formal summer program, please describe it. Please be sure to indicate whether the summer program is in place for all offices or just some.

Competition for the YPP is high. In our last selection, about 45 YPs were selected from a pool of over 6,500 applicants from around the world. Therefore, many candidates whose qualifications exceed the minimum requirements of the program cannot be selected. In fact, in recent selections, successful candidates have generally exceeded the requirements for education and work experience. The average age for selected YPs has been 29. Those YPs with master's-level degrees (in finance, economics, or a technical field) had an average of five years of work experience in areas relevant to the operations of the World Bank Group. Most have gained familiarity with the issues facing developing countries, through work experience, focused study, or extended periods living and traveling in one or more developing countries.

Summer Employment Program

The World Bank's Summer Employment Program, open to all students who are nationals of the Bank's member countries, attracts a large number of highly qualified candidates. The SEP hires approximately 150 summer interns each year. Candidates must have at least a bachelor's degree and be full-time, degree-seeking graduate students in both spring and fall semesters. The program generally requires experience in business concentrations, such as economics, finance, accounting, and statistics. Computer skills, relevant work experience, and familiarity with one or more languages other than English would be useful. Needs also occur in other disciplines, such as agriculture, environment, information systems, and the social sciences. The Bank pays a monthly salary to all summer assistants and provides a travel allowance to contribute to travel expenses, where applicable. The Bank does not offer unpaid or volunteer positions. All summer positions are located in Washington, D.C. The SEP Office is open from December through June of each year. Applications must be received by the last working day in January. Interested candidates may call (202) 473-0309, or send their inquiries to the attention of: The Summer Employment Program, The World Bank, 1818 H Street, NW, Washington, DC 20433. Our Web site is: www.worldbank.org/html/extdr/employ.htm.

Glossary of Finance Terms

Excerpted from Doing Deals: Investment Banks at Work *by Robert G. Eccles and Dwight B. Crane (Boston: Harvard Business School Press, 1988). The following terms and definitions are intended to explain terms used in* Doing Deals *and do not necessarily cover all possible meanings of the terms.*

Arbitrage: occurs when there is an opportunity to buy one security and sell another security and make a riskless profit. An arbitrage opportunity exists when two securities are mispriced relative to each other, so that it is possible to buy one and sell the other and make a risk-free profit. In the investment banking context, the term *arbitrage* is often used to refer to an activity when an acquisition is announced at a higher price than the current stock price of the target firm. The risk arbitrage department of an investment bank then decides whether to buy the stock to take advantage of the higher offer price.

Asset-Backed Securities: a security backed by a pool of assets, such as automobile loans. The cash flow from the pool of assets is used to make interest and principal payments on the securities.

Asset Valuations: usually refers to the valuation of assets in a merger and acquisition transaction. An investment bank is asked to estimate the value of the various parts of the firm that might be acquired.

Block Trading: trading of a large quantity of securities. The New York Stock Exchange considers a block trade to be equal to ten thousand or more shares.

Bond: see **Debt.**

Bought Deal: in securities underwriting, a firm commitment to purchase an entire issue outright from the issuing company. In recent years this term has been used to mean a firm commitment by one or a small number of investment banking firms.

Boutique: a small, specialized securities firm that deals with a limited clientele and offers a limited product line . . . [e.g.,] with advisory services for issuers.

Bridge Loan: a short-term loan made by an investment bank to facilitate a transaction. It is made in anticipation of a security issue that would repay the loan.

Call Date: the date on which issuers have the right to call in or redeem outstanding bonds before their scheduled maturity.

Capital Markets Desk: a group of investment bankers who typically sit on the trading floor. They provide a direct link between issuing customers and the market.

Collaterized Mortgage Obligation (CMO): a security backed by mortgage bonds. The cash flows from the mortgage bonds are typically separated into different portions (e.g., they can be separated into short-, intermediate-, and long-term portions of the mortgages). Each class is paid a fixed rate of interest at regular intervals.

Co-Manager: works with a lead manager and often a group of other co-managers to manage a security underwriting.

Commercial Paper: a short-term debt with maturities ranging from 2 to 270 days, issued by corporations and other short-term borrowers.

Common Stock: a security representing ownership in a public corporation. Owners are entitled to vote on the selection of directors and other corporate matters. They typically receive dividends on their holdings, but corporations are not required to pay dividends. In the event that a corporation is liquidated, the claims of creditors and preferred stockholders take precedence over the claims of those who own common stock.

Convertible Bond: a bond that can be exchanged for a specified number of shares of common stock.

Credit Rating: typically refers to bond and commercial paper ratings assigned by Standard & Poor's, Moody's, or other credit-rating agencies.

Debt: a security that indicates a legal obligation to a borrower to repay principal and interest on specified dates. It is a general name for bonds, notes, mortgages, and other forms of credit obligations.

Distribution: the sale of a new security issue to investors.

Divestiture: the sale of a corporate asset such as a division.

Due Diligence: a process investment banks undertake to assure that information provided in a security offering is accurate.

Earnings per Share (EPS): the net income of a corporation divided by the number of shares outstanding.

Equity: represents ownership in a public corporation as evidenced by holding of common stock or preferred stock.

Eurobond: bond denominated in U.S. dollars or other currencies and sold to investors outside the country whose currency is used (e.g., a U.S. corporation could issue U.S. dollar-denominated securities to European investors).

Fixed-Income Security: a security that pays a fixed rate of return, such as a fixed rate of interest on a corporate bond.

Floating-Rate Debt: a security with interest payments that vary or "float" in response to prevailing interest rates, such as U.S. Treasuries.

Full-Service Firm: an investment bank that offers a wide range of financial services. The term is also used to refer to securities firms that have both extensive retail brokerage and investment banking services for large institutions.

Hedge: an investment strategy used to reduce risk. It typically involves the purchase or sale of contracts designed to offset the change in value of another security.

Hostile Takeover: an acquisition that takes place against the wishes of the management and board of directors of the target company.

Initial Public Offering (IPO): a corporation's first offering of common stock to the public.

Institutional Investor: an organization that holds and trades large volumes of securities such as pension funds, life insurance companies, and mutual funds.

International Bond: a bond issued outside the home country of the borrowing entity. International bonds can be subdivided into Eurobonds and foreign bonds. Foreign bonds are bonds sold primarily in the country of the currency of the issue.

Investment-Grade Bond: typically regarded as a bond with a credit rating of A or better.

Junk Bond: see **Noninvestment-Grade Bonds.**

Lead Manager: works with a group of co-managers to form a syndicate to underwrite a security issue. A lead manager normally "runs the books" (manages the underwriting and determines distribution allocation) and is usually the investment bank that originated the deal.

League Table Rankings: published in various trade magazines that rank security underwriters by the volume of securities underwritten.

Lease: a contract granting use of real estate, equipment, or other fixed assets for a specified period of time in exchange for a series of payments.

Leveraged Buyout (LBO): the purchase of a company, or part of a company, using borrowed funds. The target company's assets frequently serve as security for the loans taken out by the acquiring firm. These loans are then repaid out of the acquired company's cash flow.

Make a Market: trading a security in order to provide liquidity and market prices to investors.

Master Limited Partnership: a limited partnership compromises a general partner, who manages a project and limited partners, who invest money but have limited liability. Frequently, limited partnerships are found in real estate and in oil and gas. A master limited partnership is a limited partnership that is publicly traded to give the investors liquidity.

Merchant Banking: in the context of U.S. investment banking, *merchant banking* refers to activities in which the firm commits its own capital to a transaction, as it does with bridge loans or when it makes equity investments in a company.

Mergers and Acquisitions (M&A): a general term that refers to various combinations of companies. A merger occurs when two or more companies combine; an acquisition occurs when one company takes over a controlling interest in another. M&A groups in investment banks work on these transactions, and they also advise on other kinds of related transactions, such as divestitures and repurchase of significant amounts of corporate stock.

Money-Market Paper: a short-term instrument such as commercial paper that is purchased by corporations and institutions that hold short-term liquid investment portfolios.

Money-Market Preferred Stock: a preferred stock instrument that has been structured to appeal to short-term investors such as investors that purchase regular money-market paper. The preferred stock is repriced every forty-nine days so that it trades like an instrument with a forty-nine-day maturity. From the point of view of the buyer, the advantage of preferred stock is that corporate holders of preferred and other stock only pay income tax on 15% of the dividend.

Mortgage-Backed Security: a security backed by a pool of mortgages. The cash flow from the pool of mortgages is used to make interest and principal payments on the security.

Noninvestment-Grade Bonds: technically, bonds with credit ratings of less than A. They are typically issued by companies without a long track record of sales and earnings or by companies that have experienced difficulty and have questionable credit strength. These securities are often used as a means to finance takeovers.

Origination: obtaining a mandate from an issuer to manage the underwriting and distribution of a new security issue.

Preferred Stock: a class of security that lies somewhere between bonds and common stock. Like interest on debt, dividends are paid on preferred stock at a specified rate, and holders of preferred stock take precedence over holders of common stock in the payment of dividends and liquidation of assets. Creditors, however, are ahead of preferred stockholders in the event of liquidation, and the company does not have a legal obligation to pay preferred stock dividends. Most preferred stock is cumulative, so that if the dividends are not paid for any reason, they accumulate and must be paid before dividends are paid to common stockholders.

Preliminary Prospectus: the first document released by an underwriter describing a new issue to prospective investors. It offers financial details about the issue but does not contain all of the information that will appear in the final prospectus. Portions of the cover page of the preliminary prospectus are printed in red ink, so it is popularly called a red herring.

Primary Market: the first time a security is sold to investors.

Private Placement: securities that are directly placed with an institutional investor, such as an insurance company, rather than sold through a public issue. Private placements do not have to be registered with the Securities and Exchange Commission, so these placements can occur more rapidly and with less information made available to the public.

Recapitalization: a change in a corporation's capital structure such as when the corporation exchanges bonds for outstanding stock. Some companies have been recapitalized in this fashion to make them less attractive targets for takeover.

Refinancing: when outstanding bonds are retired by using proceeds from the issuance of new securities. Refinancings are undertaken to reduce the interest rate or to otherwise improve the terms of the outstanding debt.

Restrictive Covenants: terms in a debt agreement that are designed to protect the creditor's interests. Covenants normally cover such matters as minimum amounts of working capital, maximum debt-equity ratios, and limits on dividend payments.

Retail Distribution: the capability of a securities firm to distribute securities to individual investors through retail brokers.

Secondary Trading: trading of securities that have already been issued in the primary marketplace. Thus, proceeds of secondary-market sales accrue to selling dealers and investors, not to the companies that originally issued the securities.

Securities and Exchange Commission (SEC): the federal agency created by the Securities Exchange Act of 1934 to administer that act and the Securities Act of 1933. The SEC is made up of five commissioners, appointed by the president. The statutes they administer are designed to promote full public disclosure and protect the investing public against malpractice in the securities markets. All issues of securities in the United States must be registered with the SEC.

Shelf Registration (Rule 415): a rule adopted by the SEC in 1982 that allows a corporation to preregister a public offering of securities. That is, they can preregister for up to two years prior to a public offering of securities. Once the security has been registered it is "on the shelf" and the company can go to market with the security as conditions become favorable.

Special Bracket Firm: an investment banking firm that leads the bulk of securities underwritten in the United States. The six special bracket firms [in 1987] are First Boston; Goldman, Sachs; Merrill Lynch; Morgan Stanley; Salomon Brothers; and Shearson Lehman Brothers.

Swap: has two meanings in the context of the securities markets. First, *swap* refers to the act of swapping from one type of security to another, such as an investor who swaps out of bonds into equities. Second, in a more recent use of the word, *swap* refers to debt obligations that are swapped between two borrowers (e.g., a borrower with floating-rate debt may swap its interest payment obligations with a borrower of fixed-rate debt; thus, the floating-rate debt issuer converts its debt into a fixed rate obligation).

Syndicate: a group of investment banks that agree to purchase a new issue of securities from an issuer for resale to the investment public. These investment banks agree to underwrite the securities. That is, they guarantee to purchase the securities. This group of banking firms is normally part of the selling group that distributes the security to the ultimate investors.

Syndicate Desk: coordinates the underwriting function of an investment bank. It helps price the security, works with the other members of the syndicate, and determines the allocation between retail and institutional investors.

Tax-Exempt Bond: a bond whose interest is exempt from taxation by federal, state, or local authorities. It is frequently called a municipal bond even though it may have been issued by a state government or agency or by an entity that is not a municipality. General obligation bonds are backed by the full faith and credit of the issuing entity. These bonds may be underwritten by commercial banks as well as by investment banks. Revenue bonds are backed by the anticipated revenues of the issuing authority. Under present legislation, commercial banks may not underwrite revenue bonds.

Tender Offer: an offer to buy shares of a corporation for cash or securities, or both, often with the objective of taking control of a target company. The Securities and Exchange Commission requires a corporate investor accumulating 5% or more of a target company to disclose the investment.

Thrift Institution: the major forms of thrift institutions are savings and loans and savings banks. These and other organizations receive consumer savings deposits and invest most of their assets in residential mortgages.

Tombstone: an advertisement placed in newspapers and magazines by investment bankers to announce an offering of securities. It gives basic details about the issue and lists the underwriting group members in a manner that indicates the relative size of their participation.

Underwrite: securities firms underwrite a securities issue by assuming the risk of buying the issue and then reselling the securities to the public either directly or through dealers.

U.S. Treasuries: securities issued by the federal government to borrow money.

Wirehouse: a national or international brokerage firm that has a large retail network of branch offices.

Finance Career Resources

Carol J. Elsen
Corporate Reports/Business Information Librarian
Baker Library
Harvard Business School

For those MBAs expanding their job search to companies not included in this book, the following guide provides additional job search resources. Directories, books, journals, and Web sites are arranged into the following sections according to the various stages of the career planning process. The printed or electronic resources are available at many college and university libraries.

Career Planning includes resources that feature career advice as well as salary and relocation information.

Targeting Companies identifies Web sites that allow searching for companies by industry, geography, and/or size.

Researching Companies: Profiles lists company directories by category. Most of these directories also have geographic and other indices for targeting companies:

- General

- Hedge Funds

- Investment Banking and Securities

- M&A and Buyouts

- Money Management

- Private Equity and Venture Capital

Researching Companies & Industries: Journals and News lists journals and Web sites for finding news and information on companies and industries.

Researching Companies & Industries: Statistics lists Web sites that include league tables and other statistics on companies and industries.

Networking Tools focuses on business and trade association sites that provide contact names.

Identifying Job Opportunities includes banks of job postings that can be searched by industry, function, keyword, and/or geographic location.

Career Planning

Baker Library Industry Guides
[http://www.library.hbs.edu/industry/]
Baker Library has guides for *Investment Banking/Investment Management* and *Finance & Venture Capital* that point to key Web and printed sources of information related to these industries.

Careers in Finance
[http://www.careers-in-finance.com/]
Find overviews, salary information, top firms, job market outlooks, and job listings for investment banking, corporate finance, financial planning, money management, and more.

Careers.wsj.com
[http://careers.wsj.com/]
The *Wall Street Journal* has put together a well organized site that is easy to use and includes a job bank, salary surveys, relocation information and excellent career planning articles on a variety of topics.

Vault.com Career Guide to Investment Banking
[http://www.vault.com/]

Get an insider's view on the players and all aspects of the game. Vault.com membership is free.

Vault.com Guide to Finance Interviews
[http://www.vault.com/]

From industry overviews and lingo to negotiating to brainteasers, this guide will get you ready to interview. Vault.com membership is free.

WetFeet.com
[http://wetfeet.com/]
Get the inside scoop on companies, industries, job-hunting strategies, résumés, diversity, networking, career management, and interviewing from the Wet Feet experts. Printed guides on companies and industries (including venture capital, investment banking, and mutual funds) are also available for a fee.

Targeting Companies

Brokers and Brokerage Firms
[http://www.moneypages.com/syndicate/finance/broker.html]
The syndicate's list of links to dozens of investment banks.

Hoover's Online
[http://www.hoovers.com/]
Search the Hoover's database of brief company profiles. From the company profile, link to financial statements, news, and quotes for the selected company.

IPO Express
[http://www.edgar-online.com/ipoexpress/]
Find news, pricing and other information on the latest initial public offerings. Search IPOs by underwriter, industry, date of filing, personal names, etc.

FreeEDGAR
[http://www.freeedgar.com/]
EDGAROnline's free service allows full text searching of companies' SEC filings from 1994 on. Also search by filing type and date.

Preselected Lists of Companies
[http://www.library.hbs.edu/compind/lists.htm#Preselected]
Find links to ranked lists of companies from the Baker Library Home Page.

Researching Companies: Profiles–General

America's Corporate Finance Directory
New Providence, NJ: National Register Publishing Company.
This directory focuses on U.S. public and private companies with revenue income or pension assets over $100,000,000. Large subsidiaries of foreign companies are also included. Indexes include financial responsibility, company, SIC code, geographic, private companies, and an integrated company index. Annual companion to the *Corporate Finance Sourcebook.*

CorporateInformation
[http://www.corporateinformation.com/]
Search this site by company name to find company profiles from dozens of Web sites.

Financial Yellow Book
New York: Leadership Directories.
More than 800 public and private U.S. financial institutions and 31,000 executives and board members are covered in this directory. Profiles for each company include name, address, e-mail address, Web site, officers, subsidiaries, divisions, affiliates, and board of directors. Indexes by type of organization, geography, and personal name. Semi-annual.

Major Financial Institutions of Europe
London: Graham & Whiteside.
Covers Austria, Belgium, Cyprus, Denmark, Finland, France, Germany, Greece, Ireland, Israel, Italy, Liechtenstein, Luxembourg, the Netherlands, Norway, Portugal, Spain, Sweden, Switzerland, and the United Kingdom. Listings include directors, board members, principal activities, principal shareholders, number of employees, parent companies, and subsidiaries. Alphabetical index to all companies. Annual.

Researching Companies: Profiles–Hedge Funds

MAR/Hedge Performance & Evaluation Directory
New York: Managed Account Reports.
This directory provides information on risk, return, benchmark comparisons, fees, and investment strategies for 1,200 hedge funds and fund of funds. Rankings by assets and by style (event-driven managers, global emerging managers, market neutral managers, etc.) are included. Quarterly.

Researching Companies: Profiles–Investment

Banking and Securities

Corporate Finance Sourcebook
New Providence, NJ: National Register Publishing Company.
This directory is a comprehensive guide to capital investment sources and financial services including cash managers, U.S. and international venture capital firms, lenders, lessors, commercial and investment banks and bankers, intermediaries, corporate real estate services, merchant banking, business insurance brokers, securities analysts, and CPAs. Over 3,400 firms are covered. Annual companion to *America's Corporate Finance Directory.*

Securities Industry Yearbook
New York: Securities Industry Association.
Ranking of 700 Securities Industry Association members by capital, number of offices, employees, and registered representatives. Includes industry trends and statistics. Annual.

Standard & Poor's Security Dealers of North America
New York: Standard & Poor's Corporation.
Brokers, distributors, dealers, and underwriters are listed geographically and alphabetically. Data for security dealers include officers, exchange and association membership, type of business, employer's industry number, and number of employees. Sections for foreign offices and representatives, new addresses, and discontinued firms are included—as are North American and major worldwide exchanges and associations. Semi-annual.

Researching Companies: Profiles–M&A and Buyouts

Directory of Buyout Financing Sources
New York: Securities Data Publishing.
Profiles more than 900 worldwide firms that provide debt and equity financing for buyouts. Indexes include industry preferences, international activities, and geographic listings (by state). Annual companion to the *Directory of M&A Intermediaries.*

Directory of M&A Intermediaries
New York: Securities Data Publishing.
Contains detailed profiles of over 800 investment banks, business brokers, law firms, and other intermediaries throughout the world. It contains articles and statistics on mergers and acquisitions and leveraged buyouts. Annual companion to the *Directory of Buyout Financing Sources.*

Researching Companies: Profiles–Money

Management

Money Market Directory of Pension Funds and Their Investment Managers
Charlottesville, VA: Money Market Directories.
This directory covers 46,000 organizations managing $6.4 trillion in assets. There are sections for funds and investment managers, indexes by geography, as well as rankings by assets and by tax-exempt funds under management. Investment managers are listed by type of activity (e.g., global custodians, international investment services, 401K/defined contribution service providers, investment manager consultants, etc.). Annual.

Nelson's Directory of Investment Managers
Port Chester, NY: Nelson Publications.
A comprehensive view of 2,300 investment management firms. Indexes featured in this directory are by geography, total assets managed, investment managers by organiza-

tion, type of investment, specialties, and products offered. This directory also includes a special index of minority- and women-owned investment firms. Annual.

Nelson's World's Best Money Managers
Port Chester, NY: Nelson Publications.
Rankings in this survey of institutional money managers include the top ten, twenty, forty managers in all areas of financial management, including U.S. and international equity, growth, small cap, large cap, fixed income, etc. Ratings are based on results of the Performance Presentation Standards of the Association for Investment Management and Research. Quarterly.

Researching Companies: Profiles–Private Equity and Venture Capital

British Venture Capital Association Directory
London: British Venture Capital Association.
Company profiles list address, telephone and fax numbers, contact names, funds managed, investment preferences, overseas offices, current portfolio size, and type of organization. Annual.

Directory of Alternative Investment Programs
Wellesley, MA: Asset Alternatives, Inc.
The *Directory of Alternative Investment Programs* provides hard to find information on 500 of the largest U.S. pension funds (public and corporate), endowments, foundations, banks, finance, and insurance companies. In the CD-ROM version, the indexing allows easy searching by investor information, type of program, portfolio, and commitments (funds invested in, type of funds, commitment amount, total fund size). Also includes information on the funds in which each organization invests. Annual.

Directory of Private Equity Investors
New York: Securities Data Publishing.
This directory provides profiles of 700 capital sources in the field of private equity. There are articles on private equity and detailed profiles of the larger investors. There are several sections of short directory listings for investment advisors, public pension plans, corporate pension plans, endowments and foundations, insurance companies, and financial corporations. Includes indexes by company name, personnel, location (U.S. state), investment interest, preferred investment size, and assets under management. Annual.

EVCA Yearbook
London: Ernst & Young; European Venture Capital Association.

This is a comprehensive survey of the European private equity and venture capital industry. Statistics on European private equity are listed overall, and by country. There is also a directory of the members of the European Venture Capital Association, listed by country. Annual.

Galante's Venture Capital & Private Equity Directory
Wellesley, MA: Asset Alternatives.
This directory covers a wide variety of organizations including venture capital, M&A, LBO, and merchant banking firms, corporate pension funds, small business investment companies (SBICs) and associations. Company entries include Web site, investment pace and policies, and a description of the firm's focus. The CD-ROM version is searchable by firm name; geographic location; type of firm; size (capital managed, number of employees); activity level (actively seeking, will consider, not seeking); investment or buyout size; means of compensation; funding stage preferences (R&D, seed, bridge, LBO, etc.); and geographic preferences. Annual.

Guide to Venture Capital in Asia
Hong Kong: AVCJ Holdings Limited.
Sections include a history and prospective of venture capital in seventeen countries in the Asia Pacific region, details of the industry by country, and profiles of 900 worldwide venture capital firms operating in Asia, Europe, Israel, and the U.S. Company name, location, fund, and name indexes are included. There is a geographical index as well as a listing of venture capital associations in Asia. Charts and graphs. Annual.

Pratt's Guide to Venture Capital Sources
New York: Securities Data Publishing.
Profiles of U.S. venture capital firms are listed by state. Pratt's also includes a section of foreign firms. Indexes by company, personal name, industry preference, and stage preference. This guide includes articles on the background of venture capital, how to raise venture capital, and sources of financing and business development. Statistics on the venture capital industry are also included. Annual.

The Venture Capital Report Guide to Venture Capital in the UK & Europe
London: Financial Times Management.
Introductory sections include detailed information on preparing business plans and personal experience of entrepreneurs. Profiles of U.K. venture capital firms are arranged by country and include firm history, sources of funds, fees, decision-making process, key management, and profiles of investments. There are indexes of investees, people, and investors. Annual.

Researching Companies & Industries: Journals and News

The Asian Venture Capital Journal
Hong Kong: AVCJ. Monthly.
Also on the Web at: http://www.asenet.com/

Barron's
Chicopee, MA: Dow Jones. Weekly.

Buyouts
New York: Securities Data Publishing.
Twenty-five issues/year.

Corporate News on the Net
[http://www.businesswire.com/]
Current news for Business Wire member companies.

CNNfn: the financial network
[http://www.cnnfn.com/]
Cable News Network Financial News has daily news articles and briefs on business, finance, and the economy.

European Venture Capital Journal
New York: Securities Data Publishing. Bimonthly.
Also on the Web at: http://evcj.nvst.com/pEVCHome.asp

Financial Times
New York: F.T. Publications. Daily.
Also on the Web at: http://www.FT.com/

Futures Magazine
Chicago: Futures Magazine.
Fifteen issues/year.
Also on the Web at: http://www.futuresmag.com/

The IPO Reporter
New York: Securities Data Publishing.
Weekly.

Institutional Investor
New York: Institutional Investor.
Monthly.
Also on the Web at: http://www.iimagazine.com/

Investment Dealers' Digest
New York: IDD.
Weekly.

Investor's Business Daily
Los Angeles: Investor's Business Daily.

Daily.
Also on the Web at: http://www.investors.com/

Mergers & Acquisitions
New York: Securities Data Publishing.
Bimonthly.

NASBIC News
Washington: National Association of Small Business
Investment Companies.
Bimonthly.
Sample issue on the Web at: http://www.nasbic.org/
pubs.html#NEWS1

Pensions & Investments
Chicago: Crain Communication.
Biweekly.
Also on the Web at: http://www.pionline.com/

PR Newswire
[http://www.prnewswire.com/]

PR Newswire offers the latest press releases on companies, industries, and executives. Releases are from participating PR Newswire members.

Private Equity Analyst
Wellesley, MA: Asset Alternatives.
Monthly.
Sample issue on the Web at: http://www.assetalt.com/
products/news/peasamp.htm

Private Equity Week
New York: Securities Data Publishing.
Weekly.

RCM Financial Group LLC
[http://www.rcmfinancial.com/fin_news.htm]
There are numerous links to financial and business news
sites, including audio news, U.S. regional news, and international news. Also included are several search options
from within the site.

Red Herring
San Francisco: Flipside Communications.
Monthly. Also on the Web at: http://www.herring.com/

Risk
London: Risk Magazine.
Monthly.
Tables of contents available on the Web at: http://
www.riskpublications.com/risk/index.htm

Start-Up
Belgium: European Seed Capital Fund Network.
Quarterly.

Upside
San Franciso: Upside Publishing.
Monthly.
Also on the Web at: http://www.upsidetoday.com/

Venture Capital Journal
New York: Securities Data Publishing.
Monthly.
Also on the Web at: http://vcj.NVST.com/
pVCJHome.asp

Wall Street Journal Interactive Edition
[http://interactive.wsj.com/home.html]
Up-to-date coverage of the top stories in business and
finance. News and information from *Barron's, Wall Street
Journal, Asian Wall Street Journal* and *Wall Street Journal Europe*. Also includes information on investing,
taxes, college financing, retirement planning, and other
personal finance topics. Available by subscription, free
during a trial period.

Researching Companies & Industries: Statistics

Finding Investment Banks' Recent Activities
[http:// www.netresource.com/wsn/]
Baker Library's site for finding league tables.

Investment Management/Investment Banking-Rankings
[http://www.library.hbs.edu/industry/investment-
directories.htm#rankings]
The Rankings section of this Baker Library guide highlights sources of rankings for firms in many different
financial industries.

Wall Street Net
[http:// www.netresource.com/wsn/]
Wall Street Net offers up-to-date information on corporate debt and equity financing. Includes sections on featured financings, done deals, deals in registration, international data, mergers and acquisitions, league tables,
banks, accounting firms, and stock exchanges. Much of
the information on deals is searchable by investment
bank, instrument type, industry category, and company
name.

Networking Tools

Association for Investment Management and Research
[http://www.aimr.com/]
The certifying organization for Chartered Financial Analysts, the Association for Investment Management and
Research is an international, nonprofit organization of investment professionals and educators with 30,000 mem-

bers. Information about and publications of the association are included.

The American Risk and Insurance Association
[http://www.aria.org/jri.htm]
The Web site for this association covers articles on risk and insurance theory and issues. Abstracts from 1986 to the present are searchable by keyword.

Financial Executives Institute
[http://www.fei.org/]
FEI is an organization of 14,000 CFOs, controllers, treasurers, and finance VPs for U.S. and Canadian companies. Information is provided on association conferences, technical issues, publications, career services, and legislative/regulatory issues.

National Association of Real Estate Investment Trusts
[http://www.nareit.com/]
This site provides information on the performance of the REIT industry as well as articles on the industry and information on conferences and activities of the association.

National Association of Securities Dealers.
[http://www.nasd.com/]
NASD is the largest securities industry self-regulatory organization in the United States. The Web site has sections on individual investor services, public policy, academic research, market data and research, and services.

Securities Industry Association
[http://www.sia.com/]
SIA is a trade association for North American securities firms. There is a list of members with links to their home pages, articles, and issue briefs.

Security Traders Association
[http://www.securitytraders.org/]
Trade association for North American and European security traders. Web site lists local affiliates with contact names, e-mail addresses and telephone numbers.

Identifying Job Opportunities

Bloomberg Financial Markets
[http://www.bloomberg.com/fun/jobs.html]
Bloomberg's Web site provides searchable finance job listings as well as general career planning information.

Careers.wsj.com
[http://careers.wsj.com/]

The *Wall Street Journal* has put together a well organized site that is easy to use and includes a job bank, salary surveys, relocation information and excellent career planning articles on a variety of topics.

Financial Job Network
[http://www.fjn.com/]
Search financial jobs by function, product/industry, country, state, or title.

Internet.com
[http://jobs.internet.com/]
Search Internet industry jobs by metropolitan area, job type, salary range, and keywords. Lots of MBA jobs listed.

Jobs in the Money
[http://www.jobsinthemoney.com/]
Search thousands of finance jobs by keyword, job function, state, or country.

CareerShop
[http://www.careershop.com/]
This "meta" job search site searches dozens of job banks at once. Select specific sites to search by job category, city, state, and keyword.

Mailing List

This is a mailing list of the firms profiled in this book. Entries are arranged alphabetically by firm and contain the name of the MBA recruiting contact, firm, address, and phone number. Some entries contain alternate contacts. Please refer to the company profile to see if another contact would be more appropriate for you. Before sending letters to the firms on the list, always call to verify the address and the name of the recruiting contact.

Barbara H. Boyle
Managing Director—Investment Banking
A.G. Edwards & Sons, Inc.
One North Jefferson
St. Louis, MO 63103
(314) 955-3000
Web site: www.agedwards.com
E-mail: boylebh@agedwards.com

Mariclare Scott
AMVESCAP, PLC
1315 Peachtree Street, N.E.
Atlanta, GA 30309
(404) 724-4254
Fax: (404) 898-1884

Rachel Goldgrob
Banco Pactual S.A.
Av. Rep. do Chile, 230/29° andar
Rio de Janeiro-RJ, 20.031-170
Brazil
55 21 272-1300
Fax: 55 21 533-1661

Tazmin Walker
Manager, Recruitment—Europe/Asia
Barclays Capital
5 North Colonnade
Canary Wharf
London, E14 4BB
United Kingdom
Web site: www.barcap.com

Lisa Tomlin-Houston
Manager, Recruitment—Americas
Barclays Capital
222 Broadway
New York, NY 10038
USA

Bear, Stearns & Co. Inc.
245 Park Avenue
New York, NY 10167
Investment Banking:
Melissa Salerno
MBA Recruiting Manager
(212) 272-9203
Fax: (212) 272-3052
Debt and Equity Markets:
Amy Williams
MBA Recruiting Manager
(212) 272-3586

Jeff Watchorn
Emma Loewen
BMO Nesbitt Burns Inc.
1 First Canadian Place
4th Floor, P.O. Box 150
Toronto, Ontario M5X 1H3
Canada
(416) 359-4001

Justin Kulo
Recruiting Manager
Broadview Int'l. LLC
One Bridge Plaza
Fort Lee, NJ 07024
(201) 346-9000
Fax: (201) 346-9191
Web site: www.broadview.com

Brandi Tamo
Recruiting Administrator
Chase H&Q
One Bush Street
San Francisco CA 94104
(800) 227-3958
Fax: (415) 439-3016
Web site: www.chasehq.com

Suzy Taherian, Manager
Finance MBA Development Program
Chevron Corporation
575 Market Street
Suite 3438
San Francisco, CA 94105
(415) 894-2752
Web site: www.chevron.com

Credit Suisse First Boston
Eleven Madison Avenue
New York, NY 10010
(212) 325-4444
Web site: www.csfb.com
Office of Global Recruiting:
Lori Todd, Assistant Vice President
Kelly Davis, Assistant Vice President
Investment Banking/Private Equity:
Jennifer Bruch, Vice President
Equity:
Sheila Cull, Vice President
Fixed Income:
Joanne Giardinelli, Assistant Vice President
Europe:
Sophie Walker, Assistant Vice President,
Investment Banking:
Michelle DeSena, Equity/Fixed Income

Lisa Brezonik
Human Resources Manager
Dain Rauscher Wessels
60 South Sixth Street
Minneapolis, MN 55402
(612) 371-2711
Fax: (612) 371-2763
Web site: www.dainrauscher.com
E-mail: jobs@dainrauscher.com

J. Morton Davis, Chairman
D.H. Blair Investment Banking Corp.
44 Wall Street
New York, NY 10005
(212) 495-4000
Web site: www.dhblair.com

Donaldson, Lufkin & Jenrette
277 Park Avenue
New York, NY 10172
(212) 892-3000
Web site: www.dlj.com
Investment Banking:
Elizabeth Derby, Senior Vice President
(212) 892-7217
Investment Services Group, Fixed Income and Equities:
Gladys Chen, Vice President
(212) 892-3904
Fax: (212) 892-2265

Susan D. Livingston
Ewing Monroe Bemiss & Co.
Riverfront Plaza, West Tower
901 East Byrd Street, Suite 1650
Richmond, VA 23219
(804) 780-1916
Fax: (804) 780-1901

Claudius E. "Bud" Watts IV
First Union Securities, Inc.
101 South Tryon Street, 40th Floor
Charlotte, NC 28280
(704) 348-1051
Fax: (704) 348-1099

FMC College Relations
FMC Corporation
200 East Randolph Drive
Chicago, IL 60601
(312) 861-6000
Fax: (312) 861-5913
Web site: www.fmc.com

Kathleen Gallagher
Ford Motor Company
World Headquarters Building
11th Floor—East Wing
The American Road
Dearborn, MI 48121
(313) 323-0850
Web site: www.ford.com/recruiting

Niharika Taskar
General Motors Corporation
GM Building
767 Fifth Avenue
New York, NY 10153
(212) 418-6100
Web site: www.gm.com

Goldman Sachs & Co.
85 Broad Street
New York, NY 10004
(212) 902-1000
Web site: www.gs.com
Equities:
Tamara Eden, Associate
Fixed Income, Currency and Commodities:
Wendy Doyle, Associate
Global Investment Research:
Anne Marie O'Reilly, Associate
Investment Banking:
Penny Petrow, Associate

Investment Management (Asset Management
Candidates):
Christina Schmittner, Associate
Investment Management (Wealth Management
Candidates):
Sarah McNamara, Vice President
Merchant Banking:
Elizabeth Burban, Vice President

Giles Tucker
E-mail: gtucker@harriswilliams.com
Harris Williams & Co.
707 East Main Street, 19th Floor
Richmond, VA 23219
(804) 648-0072
Fax: (804) 648-0073
One Montgomery Street, Suite 2250
San Francisco, CA 94104
(415) 288-4260
Fax: (415) 288-4269

Employment Response Center
Hewlett-Packard Company
Employment Response Center
3000 Hanover Street/ms: 20APP
Palo Alto, CA 94304-1181
(415) 852-8473
Web sites: www.hp.com or www.jobs.hp.com

IBM Staffing Services
IBM Corporation
3808 Six Forks Road
Raleigh, NC 27609
(800) 964-4473
Web site: www.ibm.com

Terri Reinhart
Recruiting Coordinator, Investment Banking
ING Baring Furman Selz LLC
55 East 52nd Street
35th Floor
New York, NY 10055
(212) 808-2190
Fax: (212) 808-2189
Web site: www.furmanselz.com

J.P. Morgan & Co. Incorporated
60 Wall Street
New York, NY 10260
Web site: www.jpmorgan.com
Investment Banking:
Alison Trumbower, Associate
Markets (Sales, Trading & Research):
Gladys Chen, Associate
Private Client Group and
Investment Management:
Michelle Bucaria (nee Wright), Vice President

Lehman Brothers
Three World Financial Center
New York, NY 10285
(212) 526-7000
Web site: www.lehman.com
Global Debt and Capital Markets:
Joseph Valenti
(212) 526-2555
Sales, Trading & Research:
Kristin Williams
(212) 526-4843

Andrea C. Beldecos
Director & Manager
Corporate & Institutional Client Group Recruiting
Merrill Lynch & Co., Inc.
World Financial Center
250 Vesey Street
New York, NY 10281-1331
(212) 449-4374
Web site: www.ml.com

Morgan Stanley Dean Witter
1585 Broadway, 16th Floor
New York, NY 10036
(212) 761-4000
Fax: (212) 761-0290
Web site: www.msdw.com/career/recruiting
North America Recruiting Contacts:
Attn: *Division of Interest*
Firmwide Recruiting:
Katie Leonard
Investment Banking Recruiting:
Patricia Palumbo, Vice President
Fixed Income Sales, Trading and Research Recruiting:
Jennifer Edwards, Recruiting Manager
Institutional Equity, Equity Research, Equity Financing
Services:
Erica Weiner

Private Wealth Management:
Courtney Phillips
Institutional Investment Management, Private Equity,
Capital Partners:
Maria Hurley
Morgan Stanley Dean Witter
European Recruiting Contact(s):
25 Cabot Square, Canary Wharf
London, E14 4QA, England
Firmwide Recruiting:
Rebecca Neale
Investment Banking:
Charlotte Thatcher
Equity Sales & Trading:
Donna Gardner
Fixed Income Sales, Trading & Research:
Frances Bailey
Private Wealth Management:
Sarah Scott
Southeast Asia Recruiting Contact:
Morgan Stanley Dean Witter Asia Ltd.
Recruiting Manager, Human Resources
30th Floor, 3 Exchange Square
Hong Kong
Japan Recruiting Contact:
MSDW Japan, Ltd.
Recruiting Manager, Human Resources
Yebisu Garden Place Tower
20-3, Ebisu 4 Chome
Shibuyu-Ku, Tokyo 150, Japan

Peter Jelley
Mergers and Acquisitions
National Bank Financial Inc.
The Exchange Tower
2 First Canadian Place
Suite 3200, Box 21
Toronto, Ontario M5X 1J9
Canada
(416) 869-3707
Web site: www.nbfinancial.com

Stephen L. Shapiro
Vice President
NM Rothschild & Sons Canada Limited
1 First Canadian Place
Suite 3800
P.O. Box 77
Toronto, Ontario M5X 1B1
Canada
(416) 369-9600
Fax: (416) 864-1261

Human Resources Department
Nomura Securities International, Inc.
2 World Financial Center
Building B
New York, NY 10281
Web site: www.nomurany.com

PaineWebber Incorporated
1285 Avenue of the Americas
New York, NY 10019
(212) 713-2000
Web site: www.painewebber.com
Recruiting Web site: www.painewebber.com/on-campus
Investment Banking:
Ashlee Gandy
(212) 713-3406
Fax: (212) 713-9719
E-mail: ashlee_gandy@painewebber.com
Public Finance:
Stephanie Gammone
(212) 713-4657
Fax: (212) 713-6051
E-mail: sgammone@painewebber.com
Real Estate Investment Banking:
Karen Larsen
(212) 713-8745
Fax: (212) 713-7947
E-mail: klarsen@painewebber.com

Diane M. Coffey
Managing Director
Peter J. Solomon Company
767 Fifth Avenue, 26th Floor
New York, NY 10153
(212) 508-1600
Web site: www.pjsolomon.com

Dave Meyrowitz
Assistant to the Chairman
Raymond James Financial, Inc.
880 Carrillon Parkway
St. Perersburg, FL 33716
Web site: www.rjf.com

Jim Fasano
Vice President
RBC Dominion Securities Inc.
P.O. Box 50
Royal Bank Plaza, South Tower
Toronto, Ontario
M5J 2W7
Canada
(416) 842-7588
Fax: (416) 842-7555
Web site: www.rbcds.com

Pam Smith, Assistant
The Robinson-Humphrey Company, LLC
Atlanta Financial Center
3333 Peachtree Road, NE
Atlanta, GA 30326
(404) 266-6919

Salomon Smith Barney
388 Greenwich St.
New York, NY 10013
(212) 816-6000
Investment Banking Recruiting:
Recruiting Manager
Sales and Trading Recruiting:
Susan H. Glendon, Vice President
(212) 723-9541

Matthew R. Simmons
President
Simmons & Company International
700 Louisiana, Suite 5000
Houston, Texas 77002
(713) 236-9999
Fax: (713) 223-7800

Patricia B. Davis
Vice President
Stonebridge Associates, LLC
Ten Post Office Square
Suite 1330
Boston, MA 02109
(617) 357-1770
Fax: (617) 357-4933

Maureen C. Dixon
Vice President, Human Resources
TD Securities Inc.
31 West 52nd Street
New York, NY 10019-6101
(212) 827-7000
Fax: (212) 827-7248
Web site: www.tdsecurities.com

Robert J. Burke
Senior Staffing Consultant
**Teachers Insurance and
Annuity Association-College
Retirement Equities Fund
(TIAA-CREF)**
730 Third Avenue
New York, NY 10017
(800) 842-2733
Web site: www.tiaa-cref.org

Rachel Beckman
U.S. Bancorp Piper Jaffray Inc.
222 South Ninth Street
Minneapolis, MN 55402
(612) 342-6000
Web site: www.piperjaffray.com
E-mail: applicant@piperjaffray.com

Frances A. Lyman
Recruiting Manager
Wasserstein Perella & Co. Inc.
31 West 52nd Street
New York, NY 10019
(212) 969-2700

Brian L. Haun, Director
Investment Evaluation Department
Weyerhaeuser Company
Tacoma, WA 98477
(206) 924-2367
Web site: www.weyerhaeuser.com

William Blair & Company
222 West Adams Street
Chicago, IL 60606
Web site: www.wmblair.com
Corporate Finance:
Brian Gannon
(312) 364-8114
Debt Finance:
Bill O'Connell
(312) 364-8708
Research:
David Farina
(312) 364-8918
Investment Management:
Robert Newman
(312) 364-8783

Young Professionals Program Administrator
The World Bank
1818 H Street, NW
Washington, DC 20433
(202) 473-0312
Fax: (202) 522-3741
E-mail: youngprofessionalsprogram@worldbank.org
Web site: www.worldbank.org

Tools for Leadership . . .

Tools for Scholarship . . .

Harvard Business Review

For over 75 years, one publication has been defined as indispensable for those who aspire to succeed in business . . . the same publication that was voted the most influential magazine in the United States in a 1992 survey of over 1,700 opinion leaders. The *Harvard Business Review*.

HBR is synonymous with excellence in business education. Subscribers are exposed to groundbreaking work and new management strategies in articles authored by leading executives in companies from around the world. It's not a view from the ivory tower . . . it's a view from the boardroom, the corner office, the production line. From the real world of business.

Every issue of *HBR* has articles that show you how real-life managers are motivating and leading people; how executives in business today are developing the financial tools to allow their companies to grow; how managers are using new technologies to approach marketing in ways that were impossible just a few years ago; how organizations are coping with the ever changing business environment of a global economy.

Harvard Business Review is the magazine your competitors will be reading in a few years. Shouldn't you start reading it now?

SPECIAL OFFER FOR STUDENTS OF BUSINESS

Over 200,000 executives in companies around the world pay over $95 a year for access to the invaluable information found in every bimonthly issue of *HBR*. As a student you are entitled to a very special price of $48 for a one-year, six-issue subscription.

To subscribe at this special rate, please send your name and address, along with a copy of your valid student I.D. from an accredited college or university, to:

HARVARD BUSINESS REVIEW
Subscription Services
P. O. Box 52623
Boulder, CO 80322-2623

Payment must accompany the order. Please enclose a check, or your VISA, MasterCard, or American Express card number and expiration date, with your order. This offer is valid for subscriptions addressed within the United States only.